SCENES FROM EURIPIDES'
IPHIGENIA IN AULIS
AND
IPHIGENIA IN TAURIS

PAGE OF A MANUSCRIPT OF 'IPHIGENIA IN TAURIS'.

This is the last page of the fourteenth-century vellum manuscript in the Laurentian Library at Florence. The lines are written in pairs across both columns, not down each column in the usual way. Lines 441–453 in this book start at l. 2 in the second column and end at l. 9 in the same column. Line 450 (l. 8 in the first column) ought to have *Aθ.* (for Athena) prefixed, and the next line has *Aπο.* (for Apollo) prefixed by mistake. The last line of the MS. contains the titles of both the Iphigenia plays.

EURIPIDES

SCENES FROM IPHIGENIA IN AULIS
&
IPHIGINIA IN TAURIS

Edited with Introduction,
Notes and Vocabulary by

E.C. KENNEDY

Bristol Classical Press

This impression 2003
This edition published in 1981 by
Bristol Classical Press
an imprint of
Gerald Duckworth & Co. Ltd.
61 Frith Street, London W1D 3JL
Tel: 020 7434 4242
Fax: 020 7434 4420
inquiries@duckworth-publishers.co.uk
www.ducknet.co.uk

First published in 1954 by Macmillan & Co. Ltd.

A catalogue record for this book is available
from the British Library

ISBN 0 906515 97 1

Cover illustration: woman tearing her hair in mourning, from
an Attic red-figure funeral vase (loutrophoros) by the
Kleophrades Painter, ca. 480 BC; Louvre, Paris.
[Drawing by Jean Bees]

PREFACE

ONLY three or four Greek plays are available with vocabulary and notes suitable for beginners, and most of these were produced over 50 years ago when pupils had read far more Greek than they have today at the same age. I have therefore edited two extracts of about 450 lines each from the most interesting parts of the *Iphigenia* plays, which I hope will enlarge the range of reading matter available in the middle forms of schools. The notes are full enough to make the text intelligible to boys and girls whose knowledge of Greek is not yet very great, and I have not hesitated to explain quite elementary points of syntax or even grammar, e.g. when an aorist imperative occurs I have sometimes mentioned it so that readers should not spend time puzzling over what may still be an unfamiliar part of a verb. None of the choruses is included, but the analysis contains brief summaries of the choral odes as well as of the spoken passages ; a general view of the whole of each play is thus given, and the selections are intended to be an introduction to Greek tragedy. Each play is self-contained and can be read independently of the other.

I have consulted the following editions of the plays : *Iphigenia in Aulis* : F. A. Paley (Bell, 1880), C. E. S. Headlam (Cambridge, 1889) and E. B. England (Macmillan, 1892) ; *Iphigenia in Tauris* : Paley, as before, England (Macmillan, 1886), and M. Platnauer

(Oxford, 1938), of which the last named has been especially valuable. The text is Gilbert Murray's Oxford Classical Text, by kind permission of the publishers, with omissions and alterations noted in an appendix given on pages 100–101 ; the alterations of course have good authority and were made only because they give a reading more intelligible to beginners.   In *Iphigenia in Aulis* I have included only what was, by common consent of scholars, written by Euripides himself.   Other books consulted include G. Murray's *Euripides and his Age*, M. A. Haigh's *Tragic Drama of the Greeks* and *Attic Theatre*, and A. W. Pickard-Cambridge's *Dithyramb, Tragedy and Comedy, Theatre of Dionysus in Athens*, and *Dramatic Festivals of Athens*.

E. C. KENNEDY

MALVERN, *November* 1953

CONTENTS

LIST OF ILLUSTRATIONS,
MAPS AND PLANS

INTRODUCTION

THE LEGEND OF IPHIGENIA

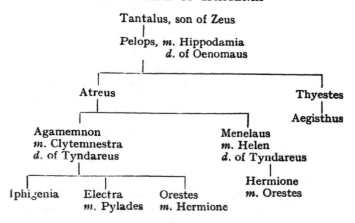

Tantalus, son of Zeus
|
Pelops, *m.* Hippodamia
d. of Oenomaus

Atreus — Thyestes
|
Aegisthus

Agamemnon
m. Clytemnestra
d. of Tyndareus

Menelaus
m. Helen
d. of Tyndareus

Iphigenia   Electra   Orestes
m. Pylades   *m.* Hermione

Hermione
m. Orestes

The descendants of Tantalus were under a curse, which originated because he tried to test the wisdom of the gods by serving up the flesh of his son Pelops to them at a banquet. Only Demeter, who was mourning for the loss of her daughter, failed to recognize the human flesh and ate one shoulder, which was replaced by an ivory one when Pelops was restored to life. Tantalus was punished in Hades for his impiety by having to stand in a lake whose water always receded from his lips when he tried to drink it, while bunches of grapes hanging close to his mouth always eluded him when he tried to eat them.

Pelops grew up and wanted to marry Hippodamia, daughter of Oenomaus, king of Elis, who used to make all her suitors compete against him in a chariot race ; he promised to give his daughter to the one who defeated him, but those who lost the race were killed. Pelops won unfairly, for he bribed Myrtilus, the charioteer of Oenomaus, to remove the linch-pins of his master's chariot, so that Oenomaus was thrown out and killed. But Pelops refused to pay the promised reward and flung Myrtilus into the sea ; Myrtilus' dying words were a terrible curse on the whole family of Pelops. Another version of the story, mentioned in *Iphigenia in Tauris* 264, is that Pelops killed Oenomaus with his spear. Angered at the death of his son Myrtilus, Hermes gave the house of Pelops a lamb with a golden fleece (no connection with the Golden Fleece brought back by Jason and the Argonauts), the possession of which carried the kingship with it ; he did this to cause strife between members of the family.

The sons of Pelops, Atreus and Thyestes, killed their half-brother and fled to Mycenae, of which Atreus became king. Thyestes fell in love with Atreus' wife and with her help robbed him of the golden lamb, hoping thus to obtain the kingship, but Atreus punished him by serving up his own children to him at a feast and then banished him. Thyestes cursed his brother, and when his son Aegisthus, who was brought up by his uncle Atreus, was sent by him to kill his own father, the father and son recognized each other, whereupon Aegisthus killed Atreus instead.

Atreus' sons were Agamemnon and Menelaus. Agamemnon, king of Mycenae, married Clytemnestra,

daughter of Tyndareus, and Menelaus, now king of
Sparta, married her sister Helen ; but Helen's elopement with Paris, son of King Priam of Troy, who was
promised ' the fairest woman in Greece ' as a reward if
he gave the prize in a beauty-contest among three
goddesses to Aphrodite, caused the Trojan war,
because all Helen's unsuccessful suitors had been bound
by an oath to join in getting her back if anyone stole
her away from her husband. They therefore assembled
at Aulis in Boeotia with an army and a fleet collected
from all over Greece, under the leadership of Agamemnon, to go on an expedition to Troy to recover Helen.
At Aulis they were held back by contrary winds sent by
Artemis, who could be appeased, according to the seer
Calchas, only if Agamemnon sacrificed his daughter
Iphigenia in payment of a vow made many years
before ; other reasons for the anger of the goddess are
given in different versions of the story. The king sent
for his daughter on the pretext of having arranged to
marry her to Achilles, and in spite of passionate protests
by her mother Clytemnestra and Iphigenia's own
appeals for mercy, which later changed to a noble
resolve to die bravely for the good of Greece, she was
led to the altar to die. In his ' Dream of Fair Women '
Tennyson describes a meeting with Helen and Iphigenia. Helen appears first.

    At length I saw a lady within call,
      Stiller than chisell'd marble, standing there ;
    A daughter of the gods, divinely tall,
      And most divinely fair.

Her loveliness with shame and with surprise
   Froze my swift speech : she turning on my face
The star-like sorrows of immortal eyes,
   Spoke slowly in her place.

' I had great beauty : ask not thou my name :
   No one can be more wise than destiny.
Many drew swords and died. Where'er I came
   I brought calamity.'

' No marvel, sovereign lady : in fair field
   Myself for such a face had boldly died,'
I answer'd free ; and turning I appeal'd
   To one that stood beside.

But she, with sick and scornful look averse,
   To her full height her stately stature draws ;
' My youth,' she said, ' was blasted with a curse :
   This woman was the cause.

' I was cut off from hope in that sad place,
   Which men call'd Aulis in those iron years :
My father held his hand upon his face ;
   I, blinded with my tears,

' Still strove to speak : my voice was thick with sighs
   As in a dream. Dimly I could descry
The stern black-bearded kings with wolfish eyes,
   Waiting to see me die.

' The high masts flicker'd as they lay afloat ;
   The crowds, the temples, waver'd, and the shore ;
The bright death quiver'd at the victim's throat ;
   Touch'd ; and I knew no more.'

Whereto the other with a downward brow :
' I would the white cold heavy-plunging foam,
Whirled by the wind, had roll'd me deep below,
Then when I left my home.'

But in our version of the story Artemis relented and
at the last moment substituted a deer which was
sacrificed on the altar instead of Iphigenia, whom the
goddess carried off to be her priestess in the land of the
Tauri (the Crimea), where it was her duty to prepare
for sacrifice any Greeks who came to the country.

After the fall of Troy ten years later, Agamemnon
returned home to Mycenae, where Clytemnestra, who
had never forgiven him for being willing to sacrifice
Iphigenia, had fallen in love with his cousin Aegisthus.
Together they plotted his death and killed him as soon
as he arrived.   Agamemnon's brave daughter Electra
conveyed her young brother Orestes to a place of safety,
and when he grew up he returned home and avenged
his father by killing his mother and Aegisthus.

For this he was relentlessly pursued by the avenging
Furies, even after he was acquitted of matricide at the
court of the Areopagus at Athens.   Apollo promised
him relief from the madness with which they attacked
him if he brought back an image of Artemis from the
Tauric land.   In company with his faithful friend
Pylades, who had married his sister Electra, he went
there, but was seized and was about to be dedicated to
the altar by Iphigenia when the identity of brother and
sister was revealed at the last moment.   All three
managed to escape with the image of the goddess and
came safely home to Greece.

Such is the legend of Iphigenia. But Euripides ingeniously combined with it two other features. Among the prehistoric Greeks there had been human sacrifices offered to a goddess called Artemis Tauropolos, also known as Hecate and Iphigenia, whose worship continued in certain parts of Attica but without the sacrifice of human victims. Human blood was also offered to a virgin goddess in the land of the Tauri, with whom the Greeks identified their own Artemis Tauropolos. At the end of *Iphigenia in Tauris* Euripides introduces Athena, who tells Orestes to institute the worship of this goddess at Halae and Brauron in Attica, but without human sacrifices ; Iphigenia is to be her priestess at Brauron, where she will die and be buried. Thus the three separate strands are woven into a connected and credible whole.

THE ORIGIN AND DEVELOPMENT OF TRAGEDY

The name Tragedy, τραγῳδία, is said to have meant ' goat-singing '. The old explanation is that men dressed as goat-like satyrs took part in a choral song in honour of Dionysus, called a dithyramb, and the leader became the actor of tragedy. But there are various arguments against accepting this view, and a modern theory is that the name implied singing in competition for the prize of a goat or round a sacrificial goat, and that experiments in lyrics dealing with serious or ' tragic ' themes were made in the Peloponnese early in the sixth century B.C. and became associated with the worship of Dionysus, especially at Sicyon. It is generally accepted that in about 534 B.C. Thespis broke fresh ground by producing at Athens a performance in which the lyric odes sung by a Chorus were interspersed with speeches delivered by an actor (ὑποκριτής or 'answerer', because he replied to the questions of the Chorus) in the form of verse called iambic trimeters or senarii. With this primitive drama was probably blended the Peloponnesian lyric 'tragedy', and from the fusion of the two elements arose the Greek tragic plays of the fifth century.

Whatever the origin of tragedy, it is certain that the performance of plays was part of a religious ceremony at the festival of Dionysus. They were produced at Athens, the great centre of tragedy, and indeed of all literature in the fifth century, at the two Dionysiac festivals, the Lenaea in January and the Great or City Dionysia in the spring ; it is with the Great Dionysia that the performance of plays is particularly associated, and the festival was attended by visitors from all parts of Greece. The altar of the god stood in the centre of the ὀρχήστρα, the circular space in front of the stage in which the Chorus sang and danced, and the festival included a procession in which his statue was carried in a chariot.

To the single actor introduced by Thespis a second was added by the poet Aeschylus (525–456), who is regarded as the second founder of tragedy ; he reduced the part taken by the Chorus and made real dialogue, the representation of character, and dramatic action possible. Sophocles (496–406) introduced a third actor and stage scenery, both of which were used by Aeschylus in his later plays, and he increased the number of the Chorus from 12 to 15. He was a great artist, the most

xvi EURIPIDES, IPHIGENIA

polished of the three tragedians whose work has survived, and his addition of a third actor added variety to the dialogue and to the working out of the plot.

A tragedy at Athens was usually produced only once. The dramatic performances at the Great Dionysia were competitions among the three poets whose plays were selected from a much larger entry by a magistrate called the *archon*. He then appointed from among the richer citizens three men whose duties as *chorēgi* were to train the Chorus and produce the play, at their own expense, for the poet to whom each was allotted. Each dramatist exhibited four plays, a ' tetralogy ', at the festival, one after the other on the same day ; three were tragedies, a ' trilogy ', which might be successive phases of the same legend or independent plays, and the fourth was a ' satyric ' drama, a grotesque and semi-comic version of an ancient legend with a chorus of ' satyrs ', attendants on Dionysus with human bodies and the ears and tails of horses. Only one satyric play survives, the *Cyclops* of Euripides. There was also a contest among three[1] comic poets, who produced one comedy each.

The total number of plays exhibited at the Great Dionysia was thus fifteen, nine tragedies, three satyric dramas, and three comedies, written by six different poets. The prizes were awarded by judges who were drawn by lot from a preliminary list, and the votes of only five, again drawn by lot, of the ten judges eventually counted. Aeschylus won thirteen victories, each

[1] The number was three during the Peloponnesian War, 431–404, when the *Iphigenia* plays were produced ; in normal years it was five.

representing four plays, so that fifty-two of his total number of ninety plays received the first prize. Sophocles won eighteen times, with seventy-two plays out of his total of about one hundred and thirty. Euripides won only five times, with twenty plays out of a total of about ninety ; but he had the misfortune to compete with Sophocles on many occasions. That the Athenian judges were sometimes fallible is shown by the fact that Sophocles' *Oedipus Rex*, one of the greatest tragedies of all time, was defeated by the work of an inferior poet, and Euripides' *Medea*, another great play, obtained only third prize when it was performed. But Euripides has been victorious in the competition for survival, for whereas only seven each of the plays of Aeschylus and Sophocles have come down to us, seventeen or eighteen of Euripides' plays can be read today. In the case of some of these, however, it was accident rather than their own merit that caused them to survive, for not all of his extant plays are in the highest class.

The three actors who among them played all the parts except that taken by the leader of the Chorus were called the *protagonistes, deuteragonistes* and *tritagonistes* respectively. The protagonist took the leading parts, so far as they could be combined, and the other two the rest in order of importance. From the time of Thespis actors had worn masks with convential features, each appropriate to his part, a lofty head-dress, brightly-coloured flowing robes, and soft shoes coming half-way up the calf. Both male and female characters were played by men, who must have been highly trained in voice production to make themselves heard in the vast open-air theatre. Apart from the actual voice, all acting had to be done by gestures because the face was hidden by the mask, and in any case facial expressions would not have been seen by most of the audience so far away from the stage.

An integral part of a tragedy, as we have already seen, was the Chorus of twelve, later fifteen, performers under their leader called a *coryphaeus*. The Chorus had originally the largest part of the play to perform, but it was gradually reduced in importance as far as the plot was concerned. In Aeschylus it still had a major function in the development of the action, whereas in Sophocles it played no actual part in the plot but was closely concerned with one of the leading characters. In Euripides the Chorus was still less important in the drama itself, and its presence was sometimes even an embarrassment ; for example, in *Iphigenia in Aulis* the Chorus was aware of the king's intention to sacrifice his daughter but never warned either her or her mother of the impending blow. But in all three dramatists the Chorus sang odes of great poetic beauty, which even in Euripides had some bearing on the legend of the tragedy which was being unfolded on the stage. The Chorus usually consisted of old men of the district, or women, and wore ordinary Greek dress with masks. They remained in the *orchēstra* throughout the performance, and sang and danced to the music of the flute. The leader of the Chorus often took part in the dialogue with the characters. No choric odes are included in the extracts from the plays given in this book because they are usually too difficult for beginners and contain unfamiliar ' Doric ' forms of words.

THE GREEK THEATRE

The Theatre of Dionysus at Athens, in which all the great plays of the fifth century B.C. were performed, was situated on the south-eastern slope of the hill on which the Acropolis rose. First came the circular open space in which the Chorus sang and danced, called the ὀρχήστρα, about 66 feet in diameter, with an altar of Dionysus in the middle. The stage lay to the south-east of the *orchēstra*, probably on the same level, and was about 66 feet long and 12 to 15 feet deep, with the wooden stage-buildings, two storeys high, called the σκηνή, behind it. The name, from which ' scene ' is derived, originally meant the tent or booth in which the actors changed their costumes, and was afterwards applied both to the stage and to the stage-buildings. The structure was painted to represent a house or temple and had three doors and side wings, projecting towards the auditorium. To the north-west lay the auditorium, dug out of the slope of the hill and banked up in the shape of an irregular horse-shoe, with wooden seats arranged in tiers and divided into blocks by radiating gangways.

The present remains of the theatre date from the middle of the fourth century B.C., when the auditorium was rebuilt in stone. Alterations were made in Roman times, and the stage was brought forward so that the *orchēstra* is not now a complete circle. The size of the stone auditorium, which is probably about the same as that of the old wooden one, is nearly 290 feet from side to side and a little more from stage to back. Most of the seats have disappeared, but it is thought that the theatre could hold about 17,000 people.

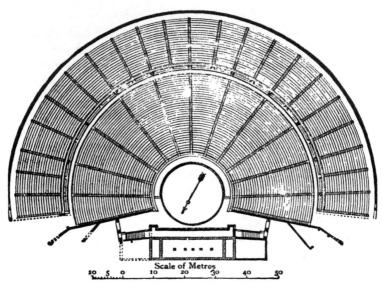

Scale of Metros

GROUND PLAN OF THE THEATRE AT EPIDAURUS.

The Greek theatre in the best state of preservation
today is the one at Epidaurus in the northern Peloponnese, of which the ground plan is given on this page.
                        This is a stone theatre,
built in the fourth century B.C., which could probably
hold about the same number of spectators as the
Athenian theatre. It is much more regular in plan than
the Theatre of Dionysus, being a perfect semi-circle
with an extra block of seats on each side. Its dimen-
sions are about 350 feet from side to side, and 225 from
stage to back. The *orchēstra* is about 65 feet in diameter, and the stage 75 feet long and 15 feet deep. The

spaces between the stage and the nearest seats of the auditorium were called *parodoi* and were used both for the audience to enter the theatre and for the Chorus to reach the *orchēstra*. Apart from the fact that the seats and stage-buildings at Epidaurus are stone, whereas those in the fifth-century Athenian theatre were wood, the photograph gives quite a good idea of what the theatre in which these plays of Euripides were first performed was like. A contrivance like a crane, called a μηχανή, was used to bring a god or goddess into view above the stage to speak an epilogue or round off a play with divine intervention, like Athena in *Iphigenia in Tauris* and perhaps Artemis in the original ending of *Iphigenia in Aulis*. Such a deity was called a *deus* (or *dea*) *ex machina*. There was no curtain, and everything was open to the sky.

Admission to the Athenian theatre was originally free, but to prevent long queues waiting to get into the best seats, an admission fee of two obols was charged for seats which were reserved in advance ; the obol was a tiny silver coin, one-sixth of a drachma, worth about 1½d., but with a much higher purchasing power. Later in the fifth century this fee was paid by the state out of the ' theoric fund '. People of both sexes and all ages went to the theatre. On the first day of the festival there was a solemn procession in which the statue of Dionysus was carried to the theatre, and competitions in ' dithyrambic ' songs in honour of the gods were held. The next three days were given up to the performance of plays. The dramatic contests began soon after dawn and the five plays performed each day followed one another almost without a break, so that spectators brought their food with them and picnicked during the less interesting scenes. The weather is usually fine in Attica at the end of March, and the theatre must have been a brilliant sight with the huge audience in its brightly coloured clothes watching the actors and Chorus playing their parts on the stage and in the *orchēstra*. But it must have been very uncomfortable to sit tightly packed for so many hours on hard wooden benches without backs ; many of the spectators therefore brought cushions to sit on. Athenians were a critical audience, applauding scenes that appealed to them and hissing off the stage plays and actors who did not reach the required standard.

A tragedy began with a prologue. This was written in iambic verse, like nearly all the other scenes spoken by the actors, which were called ' epeisodia '. The English word ' episode ' is derived from this, because in the earliest tragedies the choric part was the more important and the actors' parts were merely ' episodes ', but the comparative importance of the spoken and sung portions became reversed. The choral odes were called ' stasima ', except the first, which accompanied the entrance of the Chorus to the *orchēstra* and was called the ' parodos '. The last part of the play, the portion that came after the final ' stasimon ', was called the ' exodos '. There were also choric songs and lyrical passages divided between Chorus and actors and lyrics sung by actors alone. None of the choric or lyrical passages are included in this book and the ' epeisodia ' have usually been greatly reduced in length.

EURIPIDES

Little is known of the life of Euripides, who was born in 485 or 480 B.C. and died in 406. His parents were probably well-to-do, and he soon showed a tendency towards poetry and philosophy ; he became the friend of the leading philosophers in Athens. He was of a studious disposition and held practically no public office, spending much of his time in retirement at Salamis. His life and character were pure and upright, and not even the hostility of the comic poets attempted to besmirch them. Some time before his death he withdrew from Athens to the court of Archelaus, king of Macedon, where he wrote his last two plays and died at the age of about 78.

As a poet, Euripides shows a marked contrast with Aeschylus and Sophocles. He uses the same language, the same form and the same legends as his predecessors, but his treatment of plot and character is often very different, being realistic and unconventional, and he has been accused of being an agnostic and a rationalist in matters of religion. He introduced to the Greek stage two features of great importance in the development of the drama, romantic love between man and woman and the representation of his characters, not as heroic or idealized types, but as real live people with the strength and weakness of human beings ' as they really are ', not ' as they ought to be ', to use Sophocles' criticism of Euripides as recorded by Aristotle. He also gave some of his plots an exciting, almost melodramatic, turn, and his women in particular are drawn with a masterly hand.

The plays of Euripides enjoyed great popularity among the Greeks, not so much during his lifetime, when they were regarded with suspicion by the older generation, though younger people admired them greatly, as in the century that followed his death, and they have had a deep influence on later Greek and Roman literature. The contemporary poet Aristophanes satirizes him unsparingly and often unfairly in his comedies, and the philosopher Aristotle has some adverse criticism of him, but calls him ' the most moving ' of poets. It is said that after their defeat in Sicily in 413 many Athenians obtained food and drink during their flight by singing lyrics of Euripides, and others who had been captured and sold into slavery were set free because they could recite and teach their owners passages from his plays hitherto unknown to them.

It has already been mentioned that the choral odes of Euripides have little connection with the plot and are often mere interludes, though they usually deal with some aspect of the legend with which the play is concerned and are expressed in artistic and beautiful language. His prologues have been criticized as being mere narratives giving a summary of the story up to the point where the play begins and sometimes too ' genealogical ' in their opening lines—like those in the two *Iphigenia* plays—and he often used a *deus* (or *dea*) *ex machina* to speak a kind of epilogue and round off the story. On the whole it would perhaps be true to say that though Euripides lacks the heroic manner of Aeschylus and the supreme art of Sophocles he is a dramatist who grips the attention of spectator or reader by the originality of his plots, the psychology and insight of his character-studies and the beauty of his language. Of his 17 or 18 plays, the most famous are *Medea*, the story of the jealousy and revenge of a woman wronged by her husband ; *Alcestis*, a tragi-comedy in which a wife is willing to die for her husband and comes back from the grave ; *Hippolytus*, the story of the unwilling and tragic love of a woman for her step-son ; and the *Bacchae*, almost his last work, the story of the triumph of the god Dionysus over un-believers.

The exact date of production of the two *Iphigenia* plays is unknown. Although the chronology of the legend of *Iphigenia in Aulis* naturally precedes that of *Iphigenia in Tauris*, yet *Iphigenia in Tauris* was written first and was produced in 414–412 B.C. Nothing is known about the other plays in the trilogy nor what reception it got on the stage. *Iphigenia in Aulis* was written in the last years of the poet's life, perhaps at the court of Archelaus of Macedon, and was produced after his death in 406 by his son the younger Euripides, together with the *Bacchae* and the lost *Alcmaeon in Corinth* ; it was probably this trilogy that won the prize awarded to Euripides posthumously.

Iphigenia in Aulis was left unfinished at the poet's death and contains additions by other hands, some probably by his son, others by later ' editors ', and the final scene, as we now have it, by a much later and ignorant imitator ; none of these passages is included in the present selection. The play, as originally written by Euripides, though incomplete, is beautiful, moving, and full of interest, and contains some brilliant characterizations. Agamemnon is ambitious but weak and irresolute and continually changes his mind, first under pressure from his brother Menelaus, then through genuine love for his daughter, and then again from fear of the anger of the army which demands her sacrifice. Menelaus is a selfish bully, who at first is willing to send his niece to her death in his eagerness to recover his treacherous wife. He later repents and urges Agamemnon not to slay the maiden, but it is too late, for the soldiers insist on her sacrifice and Agamemnon has at last made up his mind to stick to his original purpose.

Clytemnestra is a devoted mother who is cruelly treated by her husband, on whom she is later destined to take a terrible revenge for the loss of her daugher. Achilles is noble and courageous, ready to give his life to save the girl whom he pities for her unhappy lot and then admires for her courage. Iphigenia herself at first pleads for life with all the despair of a girl doomed to die through no fault of her own, and then resolves to meet death with heroic fortitude for the sake of her country. The scene in which she talks innocently to her father about her impending departure from him, which he knows is to be her death, is full of pathos and ' tragic irony '.

Iphigenia in Tauris has one of the best and most exciting plots in Greek tragedy, and in fact is not a ' tragedy ' at all in the modern sense of the word, because there is a happy ending in which everybody is satisfied. The sister who is about to prepare for sacrifice her own long-lost brother unawares, the long suspense when it seems that nothing can save him, the revealing of their identity in the nick of time, the joy at their mutual recognition, the plans for escape foiled at the last minute—all this makes a play, almost a ' thriller ', of the greatest interest. The characters, too, are excellently drawn, especially that of Iphigenia herself, who longs for home and yet cannot forget the dreadful scene at Aulis years before ; she hates the Greeks from whom she received no mercy and in whose sacrifice she is ready to play her part and yet she wishes to send a letter begging her brother to take her home to Argos. Orestes and Pylades are romantic heroes who with noble self-sacrifice are eager each to give his life for his friend. Thoas is not a figure who arouses much interest, and we feel that a man who is ready to sacrifice all Greeks who come to his country just because they are foreigners deserves to be deceived. The appearance of Athena at the end of the play was necessary so that Euripides could combine the three elements of the legend—the old Greek human sacrifices, the worship of the Tauric goddess and the story of Iphigenia—into one connected story ; the play could easily have ended with the escape of the Greek party without divine intervention.

Finally, a note on the titles of the two plays. In Greek they were called Ἰφιγένεια ἡ ἐν Αὐλίδι and Ἰφιγένεια ἡ ἐν Ταύροις, meaning ' Iphigenia in (or " at ") Aulis ' and ' Iphigenia among the Taurians '. These were Latinized into *Iphigenia in Aulide* and *Iphigenia in Tauris*, but the plays are now commonly and conveniently, though illogically, called *Iphigenia in Aulis* and *Iphigenia in Tauris*, one being an English and the other a Latin title.

The Iambic Metre

Most of the spoken parts of a Greek tragedy were written in 'iambic trimeters' or 'iambic senarii', usually called for short 'iambics'. In its simplest form the line consisted of six 'feet', each foot being an 'iambus', a short syllable followed by a long one, like

$$\breve{\ } \ \bar{\ } \mid \breve{\ } \ \bar{\ } \mid \bar{\ } \parallel \bar{\ } \mid \breve{\ } \ \bar{\ } \mid \breve{\ } \ \mid \breve{\ } \ \bar{\ }$$
δόμων | πίτνον|τα ‖ πᾶν δ' | ἐρείψ|ιμον | στέγος.

The last syllable in the line can be either long or short.

But speeches consisting of lines all exactly like this would be very monotonous to hear, so for the sake of variety 'spondees', two long syllables, were allowed in the first, the third, and the fifth foot, like

$$\bar{\ } \ \bar{\ } \mid \breve{\ } \ \bar{\ } \mid \bar{\ } \parallel \bar{\ } \mid \breve{\ } \ \bar{\ } \mid \bar{\ } \ \bar{\ } \mid \breve{\ } \ \bar{\ }$$
παῖδ' οὖν | ἐν οἴκ|οις ‖ σὴ | Κλυται|μήστρα | δάμαρ.

This line contains three spondees, but one or two are equally possible.

In addition to this, on the assumption that one long syllable is metrically equal to two shorts, the long syllable of the iambus and spondee could be 'resolved' into two short syllables, thus producing a 'tribrach', ∪∪∪, an 'anapaest', ∪∪–, and a 'dactyl', –∪∪. A tribrach was allowed in any of the first four feet, like

$$\bar{\ } \ \bar{\ } \mid \breve{\ } \ \bar{\ } \mid \breve{\ } \ \bar{\ } \mid \breve{\ } \ \bar{\ } \parallel \breve{\ } \ \breve{\ } \ \breve{\ } \mid \bar{\ } \ \bar{\ } \mid \breve{\ } \ \bar{\ }$$
Ἕλλην|ικὸν | συνή|γαγ' ‖ Ἀγα|μέμνων | ἄναξ,

a dactyl in the first or third foot, like

$$\bar{\ } \ \breve{\ } \ \breve{\ } \mid \breve{\ } \ \bar{\ } \mid \bar{\ } \parallel \bar{\ } \mid \breve{\ } \ \bar{\ } \mid \breve{\ } \ \bar{\ } \mid \breve{\ } \ \bar{\ }$$
Ἀρτέμι|δι κλει | ναῖς ‖ ἐν | πτυχαῖσ|ιν Αὐ|λίδος,

and an anapaest in the first foot only, like

$$\breve{\ } \ \breve{\ } \ \bar{\ } \mid \breve{\ } \ \bar{\ } \mid \bar{\ } \parallel \bar{\ } \mid \breve{\ } \ \bar{\ } \mid \bar{\ } \ \bar{\ } \mid \breve{\ } \ \bar{\ }$$
βασιλεῦ|σιν εἴ|πῃ ‖ κᾆ|τα ληφ|θῶμεν | βίᾳ.

Anapaests are allowed for proper names, if they could

not otherwise appear in the line at all, in any foot except the last.

Every line must have a ' caesura ', or break between words, in the third or the fourth foot or in both, which is marked in the examples given above by a double line. The complete scheme for iambics is

```
ᴗ-   |ᴗ-  |ᴗ‖-  |ᴗ‖-  |ᴗ-  |ᴗᴗ
--        -|-     -|-        --
ᴗᴗᴗ  |ᴗᴗᴗ |ᴗ‖ᴗᴗ |ᴗ‖ᴗᴗ |ᴗᴗᴗ
-ᴗᴗ        -‖ᴗᴗ
ᴗᴗ-
```

Aeschylus and Sophocles were sparing in their use of ' resolved ' feet. Sophocles has 4 per cent in the earliest of his plays and 11 per cent in the latest. But Euripides in the course of his career allowed himself far more ' resolved ' feet. In his earliest plays he has only 5 per cent, but in *Iphigenia in Tauris*, about the eleventh of his surviving plays, he has 25 per cent and in *Iphigenia in Aulis*, one of his last, he has as many as 41 per cent.

Another form of metre, which appears in *Iphigenia in Aulis* lines 70–112, 238–279 and 343–376, was the ' trochaic tetrameter ', usually called ' trochaics '. This originally consisted of seven ' trochees ', -ᴗ, and one final syllable which could be either short or long, so that the line was similar to an iambic verse with the addition of -ᴗ- at the beginning. Spondees and ' resolved ' feet were allowed in trochaics in much the same way as in iambics. The metres of the choric odes, none of which appear in this book, are too complicated to explain shortly.

SCANSION

The scansion of iambics is comparatively easy. First count up the number of syllables in the line. If there are twelve, each foot must be an iambus or a spondee ; if thirteen or fourteen, there will be one or two resolved feet. The following general. rules for the quantity of syllables will be useful :

(i) η, ω, diphthongs, contracted syllables, and vowels with a circumflex accent are always long.

(ii) ε and ο are short but become long when followed by ζ, ξ, ψ, or two consonants, either in the same word or in two different words. To this rule there is an important exception.

(iii) A short vowel can either remain short or be lengthened when it is followed by a ' mute ' (β, δ, θ, π, κ, τ, φ, χ) and a ' liquid ' (λ, μ, ν, ρ) in the same word. Thus the α of πατρός can be either long or short, but the ο must be lengthened if the next word begins with a consonant.

(iv) Final α of the first declension singular is usually long when preceded by a vowel or ρ, and short when preceded by a consonant (except ρ). Neuter plural α is short. ᾳ is always long. Final ι and final υ are usually short.

(v) θεά and θεός are sometimes scanned as one long syllable instead of as two syllables of which the first is short. This is pointed out in the notes whenever it occurs in these two plays.

Mark the syllables which you know to be short or long according to the rules given above and you will probably have little difficulty in finding the length of the remaining syllables. Don't forget to mark the ' caesura ' in the third or fourth foot with a wavy line.

ΙΦΙΓΕΝΕΙΑ Η ΕΝ ΑΥΛΙΔΙ
IPHIGENIA IN AULIS

ΤΑ ΤΟΥ ΔΡΑΜΑΤΟΣ ΠΡΟΣΩΠΑ
CHARACTERS OF THE PLAY

ΑΓΑΜΕΜΝΩΝ, Agamemnon, leader of the Greek host against Troy.

ΠΡΕΣΒΥΤΗΣ, an old man, a slave of Clytemnestra.

ΜΕΝΕΛΑΟΣ, Menelaus, brother of Agamemnon and husband of Helen.

ΚΛΥΤΑΙΜΗΣΤΡΑ, Clytemnestra, wife of Agamemnon.

ΙΦΙΓΕΝΕΙΑ, Iphigenia, daughter of Agamemnon and Clytemnestra.

ΑΧΙΛΛΕΥΣ, Achilles, son of Peleus and Thetis, a Greek leader.

The scene is the Greek camp at Aulis, in front of Agamemnon's tent.

The play was first produced at the Great or City Dionysia at Athens a year or two after 406 B.C.

IPHIGENIA IN AULIS

Lines 1–55. Agamemnon enters and speaks the Prologue. He tells the story of the wooing of Helen and how she chose Menelaus from among many suitors, whom her father had bound by an oath to help get her back if anyone stole her away. When she eloped with Paris to Troy, all Greece banded together to recover her and chose Agamemnon as leader. The host assembled at Aulis was prevented from sailing to Troy by contrary winds which the seer Calchas said were sent by Artemis until Agamemnon should sacrifice his daughter Iphigenia to her. At first he refused, but Menelaus persuaded him to write a letter bidding his wife send the maiden to Aulis to marry Achilles.

ΑΓΑΜΕΜΝΩΝ

Ἐγένοντο Λήδᾳ Θεστιάδι τρεῖς παρθένοι,
Φοίβη Κλυταιμήστρα τ᾽, ἐμὴ ξυνάορος,
Ἑλένη τε· ταύτης οἱ τὰ πρῶτ᾽ ὠλβισμένοι
μνηστῆρες ἦλθον Ἑλλάδος νεανίαι.
δειναὶ δ᾽ ἀπειλαὶ καὶ κατ᾽ ἀλλήλων φόνος   5
ξυνίσταθ᾽, ὅστις μὴ λάβοι τὴν παρθένον.
τὸ πρᾶγμα δ᾽ ἀπόρως εἶχε Τυνδάρεῳ πατρί,
δοῦναί τε μὴ δοῦναί τε, τῆς τύχης ὅπως
ἅψαιτ᾽ ἄριστα. καί νιν εἰσῆλθεν τάδε·
ὅρκους συνάψαι δεξιάς τε συμβαλεῖν   10
μνηστῆρας ἀλλήλοισι καὶ δι᾽ ἐμπύρων
σπονδὰς καθεῖναι κἀπαράσασθαι τάδε·
ὅτου γυνὴ γένοιτο Τυνδαρὶς κόρη,
τούτῳ ξυναμυνεῖν, εἴ τις ἐκ δόμων λαβὼν
οἴχοιτο τόν τ᾽ ἔχοντ᾽ ἀπωθοίη λέχους,   15
κἀπιστρατεύσειν καὶ κατασκάψειν πόλιν
Ἕλλην᾽ ὁμοίως βάρβαρόν θ᾽ ὅπλων μέτα.

1

ἐπεὶ δ' ἐπιστώθησαν—εὖ δέ πως γέρων
ὑπῆλθεν αὐτοὺς Τυνδάρεως πυκνῇ φρενί—
δίδωσ' ἑλέσθαι θυγατρὶ μνηστήρων ἕνα,   20
ὅτου πνοαὶ φέροιεν Ἀφροδίτης φίλαι.
ἣ δ' εἵλεθ', ὅς σφε μήποτ' ὤφελεν λαβεῖν,
Μενέλαον. ἐλθὼν δ' ἐκ Φρυγῶν ὁ τὰς θεὰς
κρίνας ὅδ', ὡς ὁ μῦθος Ἀργείων ἔχει,
Λακεδαίμον', ἀνθηρὸς μὲν εἱμάτων στολῇ   25
χρυσῷ δὲ λαμπρός, βαρβάρῳ χλιδήματι,
ἐρῶν ἐρῶσαν ᾤχετ' ἐξαναρπάσας
Ἑλένην πρὸς Ἴδης βούσταθμ', ἔκδημον λαβὼν
Μενέλαον. ὃ δὲ καθ' Ἑλλάδ' οἰστρήσας δρόμῳ
ὅρκους παλαιοὺς Τυνδάρεω μαρτύρεται,   30
ὡς χρὴ βοηθεῖν τοῖσιν ἠδικημένοις.
    τοὐντεῦθεν οὖν Ἕλληνες ᾄξαντες δορί,
τεύχη λαβόντες στενόπορ' Αὐλίδος βάθρα
ἥκουσι τῆσδε, ναυσὶν ἀσπίσιν θ' ὁμοῦ
ἵπποις τε πολλοῖς ἅρμασίν τ' ἠσκημένοι.   35
κἀμὲ στρατηγεῖν πᾶσι Μενέλεω χάριν
εἵλοντο, σύγγονόν γε. τἀξίωμα δὲ
ἄλλος τις ὤφελ' ἀντ' ἐμοῦ λαβεῖν τόδε.
ἠθροισμένου δὲ καὶ ξυνεστῶτος στρατοῦ
ἥμεσθ' ἀπλοίᾳ χρώμενοι κατ' Αὐλίδα.   40
Κάλχας δ' ὁ μάντις ἀπορίᾳ κεχρημένοις
ἀνεῖλεν Ἰφιγένειαν ἣν ἔσπειρ' ἐγὼ
Ἀρτέμιδι θῦσαι τῇ τόδ' οἰκούσῃ πέδον,
καὶ πλοῦν τ' ἔσεσθαι καὶ κατασκαφὰς Φρυγῶν.
    κλύων δ' ἐγὼ ταῦτ', ὀρθίῳ κηρύγματι   45
Ταλθύβιον εἶπον πάντ' ἀφιέναι στρατόν,
ὡς οὔποτ' ἂν τλὰς θυγατέρα κτανεῖν ἐμήν.
οὗ δή μ' ἀδελφὸς πάντα προσφέρων λόγον
ἔπεισε τλῆναι δεινά. κἀν δέλτου πτυχαῖς

γράψας ἔπεμψα πρὸς δάμαρτα τὴν ἐμὴν 50
πέμπειν Ἀχιλλεῖ θυγατέρ᾽ ὡς γαμουμένην,
τό τ᾽ ἀξίωμα τἀνδρὸς ἐκγαυρούμενος,
συμπλεῖν τ᾽ Ἀχαιοῖς οὕνεκ᾽ οὐ θέλοι λέγων,
εἰ μὴ παρ᾽ ἡμῶν εἶσιν ἐς Φθίαν λέχος·
πειθὼ γὰρ εἶχον τήνδε πρὸς δάμαρτ᾽ ἐμήν. 55

*Agamemnon cannot bear to sacrifice his daughter and gives a
faithful old servant another letter to take to Clytemnestra,
telling her not to send Iphigenia to Aulis after all. The
Chorus of women of Chalcis in Euboea sings an ode saying
that they have come over to the mainland to see the fleet and
army at Aulis. Lines 56–112. Menelaus snatches the letter away from the
old man, and the noise of the quarrel causes Agamemnon to
come out of the tent. During an angry altercation he finds
that Menelaus has opened and read the letter. (Menelaus
accuses him of intriguing to get supreme command of the host
and of being willing at first to sacrifice his daughter to enable
the fleet to sail ; this part of the speech is omitted.) Agamemnon retorts that Menelaus wants the expedition to set out only
so that he can recover Helen ; let him, then, lead it himself,
but he must not expect his brother to sacrifice Iphigenia to
further such selfish ends.*

ΠΡΕΣΒΥΤΗΣ

    Μενέλαε, τολμᾷς δείν᾽, ἅ σ᾽ οὐ τολμᾶν χρεών.

ΜΕΝΕΛΑΟΣ

    ἄπελθε· λίαν δεσπόταισι πιστὸς εἶ.

Πρ. καλόν γέ μοι τοὔνειδος ἐξωνείδισας.

Με. κλαίοις ἄν, εἰ πράσσοις ἃ μὴ πράσσειν σε δεῖ.

Πρ. οὐ χρῆν σε λῦσαι δέλτον, ἣν ἐγὼ ᾽φερον. 60

Με. οὐδέ γε φέρειν σὲ πᾶσιν Ἕλλησιν κακά.

Πρ. ἄλλοις ἁμιλλῶ ταῦτ᾽· ἄφες δὲ τήνδ᾽ ἐμοί.

Με. οὐκ ἂν μεθείμην. Πρ. οὐδ᾽ ἔγωγ᾽ ἀφήσομαι.

Με. σκήπτρῳ τάχ᾽ ἆρα σὸν καθαιμάξω κάρα.

Πρ. ἀλλ᾽ εὐκλεές τοι δεσποτῶν θνήσκειν ὕπερ.   65

Με. μέθες· μακροὺς δὲ δοῦλος ὢν λέγεις λόγους.

Πρ. ὦ δέσποτ᾽, ἀδικούμεσθα. σὰς δ᾽ ἐπιστολὰς
    ἐξαρπάσας ὅδ᾽ ἐκ χερῶν ἐμῶν βίᾳ,
    Ἀγάμεμνον, οὐδὲν τῇ δίκῃ χρῆσθαι θέλει.

Αγ. ἔα·
    τίς ποτ᾽ ἐν πύλαισι θόρυβος καὶ λόγων ἀκοσμία;   70

Με. οὑμὸς οὐχ ὁ τοῦδε μῦθος κυριώτερος λέγειν.

Αγ. σὺ δὲ τί τῷδ᾽ ἐς ἔριν ἀφῖξαι, Μενέλεως, βίᾳ τ᾽ ἄγεις;

Με. βλέψον εἰς ἡμᾶς, ἵν᾽ ἀρχὰς τῶν λόγων ταύτας λάβω.

Αγ. μῶν τρέσας οὐκ ἀνακαλύψω βλέφαρον, Ἀτρέως γεγώς;

Με. τήνδ᾽ ὁρᾷς δέλτον, κακίστων γραμμάτων ὑπηρέτιν;   75

Αγ. εἰσορῶ· καὶ πρῶτα ταύτην σῶν ἀπάλλαξον χερῶν.

Με. οὔ, πρὶν ἂν δείξω γε Δαναοῖς πᾶσι τἀγγεγραμμένα.

Αγ. ἦ γὰρ οἶσθ᾽ ἃ μή σε καιρὸς εἰδέναι σήμαντρ᾽ ἀνείς;

Με. ὥστε σ᾽ ἀλγῦναί γ᾽, ἀνοίξας ἃ σὺ κάκ᾽ εἰργάσω λάθρᾳ.

Αγ. ποῦ δὲ κἄλαβές νιν; ὦ θεοί, σῆς ἀναισχύντου φρενός.   80

Με. προσδοκῶν σὴν παῖδ᾽ ἀπ᾽ Ἄργους, εἰ στράτευμ᾽
    ἀφίξεται.

Αγ. τί δέ σε τἀμὰ δεῖ φυλάσσειν; οὐκ ἀναισχύντου τόδε;

Με. ὅτι τὸ βούλεσθαί μ᾽ ἔκνιζε· σὸς δὲ δοῦλος οὐκ ἔφυν.

Αγ. οὐχὶ δεινά; τὸν ἐμὸν οἰκεῖν οἶκον οὐκ ἐάσομαι;

Με. πλάγια γὰρ φρονεῖς, τὰ μὲν νῦν, τὰ δὲ πάλαι, τὰ δ᾽
    αὐτίκα.   85

Αγ. εὖ κεκόμψευσαι πονηρά· γλῶσσ᾽ ἐπίφθονον σοφή.

Με. νοῦς δέ γ᾽ οὐ βέβαιος ἄδικον κτῆμα κοὐ σαφὲς φίλοις.

Αγ. βούλομαί σ᾽ εἰπεῖν κακῶς αὖ, βραχέα, μὴ λίαν ἄνω
    βλέφαρα πρὸς τἀναιδὲς ἀγαγών, ἀλλὰ σωφρονεστέρως,
    ὡς ἀδελφὸν ὄντ᾽· ἀνὴρ γὰρ χρηστὸς αἰδεῖσθαι φιλεῖ.   90
    εἰπέ μοι, τί δεινὰ φυσᾷς αἱματηρὸν ὄμμ᾽ ἔχων;

τίς ἀδικεῖ σε; τοῦ κέχρησαι; χρηστὰ λέκτρ' ἐρᾷς λαβεῖν;
οὐκ ἔχοιμ' ἄν σοι παρασχεῖν· ὧν γὰρ ἐκτήσω, κακῶς
ἦρχες. εἶτ' ἐγὼ δίκην δῶ σῶν κακῶν, ὁ μὴ σφαλείς;
οὐ δάκνει σε τὸ φιλότιμον τοὐμόν, ἀλλ' ἐν ἀγκάλαις   95
εὐπρεπῆ γυναῖκα χρῄζεις, τὸ λελογισμένον παρεὶς
καὶ τὸ καλόν, ἔχειν. πονηροῦ φωτὸς ἡδοναὶ κακαί.
εἰ δ' ἐγώ, γνοὺς πρόσθεν οὐκ εὖ, μετετέθην εὐβουλίᾳ,
μαίνομαι; σὺ μᾶλλον, ὅστις ἀπολέσας κακὸν λέχος
ἀναλαβεῖν θέλεις, θεοῦ σοι τὴν τύχην διδόντος εὖ.   100
ὤμοσαν τὸν Τυνδάρειον ὅρκον οἱ κακόφρονες
φιλόγαμοι μνηστῆρες—ἡ δέ γ' Ἐλπίς, οἶμαι μέν, θεός,
κἀξέπραξεν αὐτὸ μᾶλλον ἢ σὺ καὶ τὸ σὸν σθένος—
οὓς λαβὼν στράτευ'· ἕτοιμοι δ' εἰσὶ μωρίᾳ φρενῶν.
οὐ γὰρ ἀσύνετον τὸ θεῖον, ἀλλ' ἔχει συνιέναι   105
τοὺς κακῶς παγέντας ὅρκους καὶ κατηναγκασμένους.
τἀμὰ δ' οὐκ ἀποκτενῶ 'γὼ τέκνα· κοὐ τὸ σὸν μὲν εὖ
παρὰ δίκην ἔσται κακίστης εὔνιδος τιμωρίᾳ,
ἐμὲ δὲ συντήξουσι νύκτες ἡμέραι τε δακρύοις,
ἄνομα δρῶντα κοὐ δίκαια παῖδας οὓς ἐγεινάμην.   110
ταῦτά σοι βραχέα λέλεκται καὶ σαφῆ καὶ ῥᾴδια·
εἰ δὲ μὴ βούλῃ φρονεῖν εὖ, τἄμ' ἐγὼ θήσω καλῶς.   112

*The brothers continue to exchange angry words, and a messenger
reports that Clytemnestra and Iphigenia are approaching.
Agamemnon gives way to despair at the thought of breaking
the terrible news to them, for he seems now determined again
to sacrifice his daughter.*

*Lines 113–154. Menelaus repents of his cruel demands
and urges Agamemnon to disregard the words of Calchas and
send Iphigenia away in secret.*

Με. Πέλοπα κατόμνυμ', ὃς πατὴρ τοὐμοῦ πατρὸς
τοῦ σοῦ τ' ἐκλήθη, τὸν τεκόντα τ' Ἀτρέα,

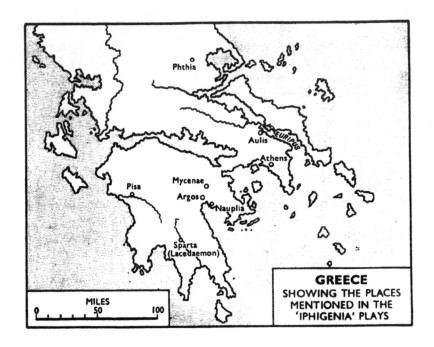

GREECE
SHOWING THE PLACES
MENTIONED IN THE
'IPHIGENIA' PLAYS

MILES
0 50 100

ἦ μὴν ἐρεῖν σοι τἀπὸ καρδίας σαφῶς   115
καὶ μὴ 'πίτηδες μηδέν, ἀλλ' ὅσον φρονῶ.
   ἐγώ σ' ἀπ' ὅσσων ἐκβαλόντ' ἰδὼν δάκρυ
ᾤκτιρα, καὐτὸς ἀνταφῆκά σοι πάλιν
καὶ τῶν παλαιῶν ἐξαφίσταμαι λόγων,
οὐκ ἐς σὲ δεινός· εἰμὶ δ' οὗπερ εἶ σὺ νῦν·   120
καί σοι παραινῶ μήτ' ἀποκτείνειν τέκνον
μήτ' ἀνθελέσθαι τοὐμόν. οὐ γὰρ ἔνδικον
σὲ μὲν στενάζειν, τἀμὰ δ' ἡδέως ἔχειν,
θνήσκειν τε τοὺς σούς, τοὺς δ' ἐμοὺς ὁρᾶν φάος.
   τί βούλομαι γάρ; οὐ γάμους ἐξαιρέτους   125
ἄλλους λάβοιμ' ἄν, εἰ γάμων ἱμείρομαι;

6

ἀλλ' ἀπολέσας ἀδελφόν, ὅν μ' ἥκιστα χρῆν,
Ἑλένην ἕλωμαι, τὸ κακὸν ἀντὶ τἀγαθοῦ;
ἄφρων νέος τ' ἦ, πρὶν τὰ πράγματ' ἐγγύθεν ·
σκοπῶν ἐσεῖδον οἷον ἦν κτείνειν τέκνα.   130
ἄλλως τέ μ' ἔλεος τῆς ταλαιπώρου κόρης
ἐσῆλθε, συγγένειαν ἐννοουμένῳ,
ἦ τῶν ἐμῶν ἕκατι θύεσθαι γάμων
μέλλει. τί δ' Ἑλένης παρθένῳ τῇ σῇ μέτα;
ἴτω στρατεία διαλυθεῖσ' ἐξ Αὐλίδος,   135
σὺ δ' ὄμμα παῦσαι δακρύοις τέγγων τὸ σόν,
ἀδελφέ, κἀμὲ παρακαλῶν ἐς δάκρυα.
εἰ δέ τι κόρης σῆς θεσφάτων μέτεστι σοί,
μὴ 'μοὶ μετέστω· σοὶ νέμω τοὐμὸν μέρος.
ἀλλ' ἐς μεταβολὰς ἦλθον ἀπὸ δεινῶν λόγων;   140
εἰκὸς πέπονθα· τὸν ὁμόθεν πεφυκότα
στέργων μετέπεσον. ἀνδρὸς οὐ κακοῦ τροποὶ
τοιοίδε, χρῆσθαι τοῖσι βελτίστοις ἀεί.
Αγ. αἰνῶ σε, Μενέλα', ὅτι παρὰ γνώμην ἐμὴν
ὑπέθηκας ὀρθῶς τοὺς λόγους σου τ' ἀξίως.   145
ἀλλ' ἥκομεν γὰρ εἰς ἀναγκαίας τύχας,
θυγατρὸς αἱματηρὸν ἐκπρᾶξαι φόνον.
Με. πῶς; τίς δ' ἀναγκάσει σε τήν γε σὴν κτανεῖν;
Αγ. ἅπας Ἀχαιῶν σύλλογος στρατεύματος.
Με. οὔκ, ἤν νιν εἰς Ἄργος γ' ἀποστείλῃς πάλιν.   150
Αγ. λάθοιμι τοῦτ' ἄν. ἀλλ' ἐκεῖν' οὐ λήσομεν.
Με. τὸ ποῖον; οὔτοι χρὴ λίαν ταρβεῖν ὄχλον.
Αγ. Κάλχας ἐρεῖ μαντεύματ' Ἀργείων στρατῷ.
Με. οὔκ, ἤν θάνῃ γε πρόσθε· τοῦτο δ' εὐμαρές.

*Agamemnon fears that Odysseus will rouse the army against him
if he does not sacrifice his daughter and asks Menelaus not to
reveal the truth to Clytemnestra until it is too late. The
Chorus recalls the Judgment of Paris, which caused this*

8   IPHIGENIA IN AULIS

*expedition against Troy, and greets Clytemnestra, who
arrives in a chariot with Iphigenia and her infant brother
Orestes.
Lines 155–201. Iphigenia greets her father, and a conversation follows which is full of ' tragic irony ', for Agamemnon and the audience know that she must die, while she
thinks that she is leaving him to embark on a happy marriage.
Clytemnestra too is deceived.*

ΙΦΙΓΕΝΕΙΑ

ὦ πάτερ, ἐσεῖδόν σ' ἀσμένη πολλῷ χρόνῳ.   155

Αγ. καὶ γὰρ πατὴρ σέ· τόδ' ἴσον ὑπὲρ ἀμφοῖν λέγεις.

Ιφ. χαῖρ'· εὖ δέ μ' ἀγαγὼν πρός σ' ἐποίησας, πάτερ.

Αγ. οὐκ οἶδ' ὅπως φῶ τοῦτο καὶ μὴ φῶ, τέκνον.

Ιφ. ἔα·
    ὡς οὐ βλέπεις ἔκηλον ἄσμενός μ' ἰδών.

Αγ. πόλλ' ἀνδρὶ βασιλεῖ καὶ στρατηλάτῃ μέλει.   160

Ιφ. παρ' ἐμοὶ γενοῦ νῦν, μὴ 'πὶ φροντίδας τρέπου.

Αγ. ἀλλ' εἰμὶ παρὰ σοὶ νῦν ἅπας κοὐκ ἄλλοθι.

Ιφ. μέθες νυν ὀφρὺν ὄμμα τ' ἔκτεινον φίλον.

Αγ. ἰδού, γέγηθά σ' ὡς γέγηθ' ὁρῶν, τέκνον.

Ιφ. κἄπειτα λείβεις δάκρυ' ἀπ' ὀμμάτων σέθεν;   165

Αγ. μακρὰ γὰρ ἡμῖν ἡ 'πιοῦσ' ἀπουσία.

Ιφ. μέν', ὦ πάτερ, κατ' οἶκον ἐπὶ τέκνοις σέθεν.

Αγ. θέλω μέν, ὃ θέλω δ' οὐκ ἔχων ἀλγύνομαι.

Ιφ. ὄλοιντο λόγχαι καὶ τὰ Μενέλεω κακά.

Αγ. ἄλλους ὀλεῖ πρόσθ' ἀμὲ διολέσαντ' ἔχει.   170

Ιφ. ὡς πολὺν ἀπῆσθα χρόνον ἐν Αὐλίδος μυχοῖς.

Αγ. καὶ νῦν γέ μ' ἴσχει δή τι μὴ στέλλειν στρατόν.

Ιφ. ποῦ τοὺς Φρύγας λέγουσιν ᾠκίσθαι, πάτερ;

Αγ. οὗ μήποτ' οἰκεῖν ὤφελ' ὁ Πριάμου Πάρις.

Ιφ. μακρὰν ἀπαίρεις, ὦ πάτερ, λιπὼν ἐμέ.   175

Αγ. εἰς ταὐτὸν αὖθις, ὦ θύγατερ, ἥξεις πατρί.

Ιφ. φεῦ·
εἴθ' ἦν καλόν μοι σοί τ' ἄγειν σύμπλουν ἐμέ.
Αγ. ἔτ' ἔστι καὶ σοὶ πλοῦς, ἵν' ἀμμνήσῃ πατρός.
Ιφ. σὺν μητρὶ πλεύσασ' ἢ μόνη πορεύσομαι;
Αγ. μόνη, μονωθεῖσ' ἀπὸ πατρὸς καὶ μητέρος. 180
Ιφ. οὔ πού μ' ἐς ἄλλα δώματ' οἰκίζεις, πάτερ;
Αγ. ἔασον· οὐ χρὴ τοιάδ' εἰδέναι κόρας.
Ιφ. σπεῦδ' ἐκ Φρυγῶν μοι, θέμενος εὖ τἀκεῖ, πάτερ.
Αγ. θῦσαί με θυσίαν πρῶτα δεῖ τιν' ἐνθάδε.
Ιφ. ἀλλὰ ξὺν ἱεροῖς χρὴ τό γ' εὐσεβὲς σκοπεῖν. 185
Αγ. εἴσῃ σύ· χερνίβων γὰρ ἑστήξῃ πέλας.
Ιφ. στήσομεν ἄρ' ἀμφὶ βωμόν, ὦ πάτερ, χορούς;
Αγ. ζηλῶ σὲ μᾶλλον ἢ 'μὲ τοῦ μηδὲν φρονεῖν.
χώρει δὲ μελάθρων ἐντός—ὀφθῆναι κόραις
πικρόν—φίλημα δοῦσα δεξιάν τέ μοι, 190
μέλλουσα δαρὸν πατρὸς ἀποικήσειν χρόνον.
ὦ στέρνα καὶ παρῇδες, ὦ ξανθαὶ κόμαι,
ὡς ἄχθος ὑμῖν ἐγένεθ' ἡ Φρυγῶν πόλις
Ἑλένη τε.—παύω τοὺς λόγους· ταχεῖα γὰρ
νοτὶς διώκει μ' ὀμμάτων ψαύσαντά σου. 195
ἴθ' ἐς μέλαθρα. [Exit Iphigenia.
σὲ δὲ παραιτοῦμαι τάδε,
Λήδας γένεθλον, εἰ κατῳκτίσθην ἄγαν,
μέλλων Ἀχιλλεῖ θυγατέρ' ἐκδώσειν ἐμήν.
ἀποστολαὶ γὰρ μακάριαι μέν, ἀλλ' ὅμως
δάκνουσι τοὺς τεκόντας, ὅταν ἄλλοις δόμοις 200
παῖδας παραδιδῷ πολλὰ μοχθήσας πατήρ.

After Iphigenia leaves the stage her parents discuss her supposed marriage to Achilles. Clytemnestra insists on staying to prepare her daughter for the ceremony, though Agamemnon tries to persuade her to return home so that she should not be present at the sacrifice. The king and queen then withdraw

*into the royal tent, and the Chorus sings an ode foretelling
the destruction of Troy and the woes in store for the Trojan
women, all of which are caused by Helen. Achilles enters
and asks for Agamemnon, to whom he intends to complain
of the long delay at Aulis.*

*Lines 202–279. Clytemnestra enters, and a conversation
at cross-purposes follows between her and Achilles about his
coming marriage to Iphigenia, of which he has heard nothing.
Both are puzzled and angry at the deception, when the old
servant, after making sure that they are alone, reveals the
whole story of Agamemnon's determination to sacrifice his
daughter.*

ΚΛΥΤΑΙΜΗΣΤΡΑ

    ὦ παῖ θεᾶς Νηρῇδος, ἔνδοθεν λόγων
    τῶν σῶν ἀκούσασ' ἐξέβην πρὸ δωμάτων.

ΑΧΙΛΛΕΥΣ

    ὦ πότνι' αἰδώς, τήνδε τίνα λεύσσω ποτὲ
    γυναῖκα, μορφὴν εὐπρεπῆ κεκτημένην;   205

Κλ. οὐ θαῦμά σ' ἡμᾶς ἀγνοεῖν, οἷς μὴ πάρος
    προσῆκες· αἰνῶ δ' ὅτι σέβεις τὸ σωφρονεῖν.

Αχ. τίς δ' εἶ; τί δ' ἦλθες Δαναϊδῶν ἐς σύλλογον,
    γυνὴ πρὸς ἄνδρας ἀσπίσιν πεφραγμένους;

Κλ. Λήδας μέν εἰμι παῖς, Κλυταιμήστρα δέ μοι   210
    ὄνομα, πόσις δέ μοὐστὶν Ἀγαμέμνων ἄναξ.

Αχ. καλῶς ἔλεξας ἐν βραχεῖ τὰ καίρια.
    αἰσχρὸν δέ μοι γυναικὶ συμβάλλειν λόγους.

Κλ. μεῖνον—τί φεύγεις;—δεξιάν τ' ἐμῇ χερὶ
    σύναψον, ἀρχὴν μακαρίαν νυμφευμάτων.   215

Αχ. τί φῄς; ἐγώ σοι δεξιάν; αἰδοίμεθ' ἂν
    Ἀγαμέμνον', εἰ ψαύοιμεν ὧν μή μοι θέμις.

Κλ. θέμις μάλιστα, τὴν ἐμὴν ἐπεὶ γαμεῖς
    παῖδ', ὦ θεᾶς παῖ ποντίας Νηρῇδος.

Αχ. ποίους γάμους φῄς; ἀφασία μ' ἔχει, γύναι·   220

εἰ μή τι παρανοοῦσα καινουργεῖς λόγον.

Κλ. πᾶσιν τόδ' ἐμπέφυκεν, αἰδεῖσθαι φίλους
καινοὺς ὁρῶσι καὶ γάμου μεμνημένοις.

Αχ. οὐπώποτ' ἐμνήστευσα παῖδα σήν, γύναι,
οὐδ' ἐξ Ἀτρειδῶν ἦλθέ μοι λόγος γάμων.   225

Κλ. τί δῆτ' ἂν εἴη; σὺ πάλιν αὖ λόγους ἐμοὺς
θαύμαζ'· ἐμοὶ γὰρ θαύματ' ἐστὶ τὰ παρὰ σοῦ.

Αχ. εἴκαζε· κοινόν ἐστιν εἰκάζειν τάδε·
ἄμφω γὰρ οὐ ψευδόμεθα τοῖς λόγοις ἴσως.

Κλ. ἀλλ' ἢ πέπονθα δεινά; μνηστεύω γάμους   230
οὐκ ὄντας, ὡς εἴξασιν· αἰδοῦμαι τάδε.

Αχ. ἴσως ἐκερτόμησε κἀμὲ καὶ σέ τις.

Photo: Anderson

ACHILLES AND AJAX PLAYING DICE.

From a sixth-century B.C. Greek vase in the Vatican Museum,
signed by Exekias. For a description of this painting see page 21.

ἀλλ' ἀμελίᾳ δὸς αὐτὰ καὶ φαύλως φέρε.

ΚΛ. χαῖρ'· οὐ γὰρ ὀρθοῖς ὄμμασίν σ' ἔτ' εἰσορῶ,
  ψευδὴς γενομένη καὶ παθοῦσ' ἀνάξια.   235

ΑΧ. καὶ σοὶ τόδ' ἐστὶν ἐξ ἐμοῦ· πόσιν δὲ σὸν
  στείχω ματεύσων τῶνδε δωμάτων ἔσω.

ΠΡ. ὦ ξέν', Αἰακοῦ γένεθλον, μεῖνον· ὦ, σέ τοι λέγω,
  τὸν θεᾶς γεγῶτα παῖδα, καὶ σέ, τὴν Λήδας κόρην.

ΑΧ. τίς ὁ καλῶν πύλας παροίξας; ὡς τεταρβηκὼς καλεῖ. 240

ΠΡ. δοῦλος, οὐχ ἁβρύνομαι τῷδ'· ἡ τύχη γὰρ οὐκ ἐᾷ.

ΑΧ. τίνος; ἐμὸς μὲν οὐχί· χωρὶς τἀμὰ κἀγαμέμνονος.

ΠΡ. τῆσδε τῆς πάροιθεν οἴκων, Τυνδάρεω δόντος πατρός.

ΑΧ. ἕσταμεν· φράζ', εἴ τι χρήζεις, ὧν μ' ἐπέσχες οὕνεκα.

ΠΡ. ἦ μόνω παρόντε δῆτα ταῖσδ' ἐφέστατον πύλαις; 245

ΑΧ. ὡς μόνοιν λέγοις ἄν, ἔξω δ' ἐλθὲ βασιλείων δόμων.

ΚΛ. δεξιᾶς ἕκατι μὴ μέλλ', εἴ τί μοι χρήζεις λέγειν.

ΠΡ. οἶσθα δῆτ' ἔμ', ὅστις ὢν σοὶ καὶ τέκνοις εὔνους ἔφυν;

ΚΛ. οἶδά σ' ὄντ' ἐγὼ παλαιὸν δωμάτων ἐμῶν λάτριν.

ΠΡ. χὤτι μ' ἐν ταῖς σαῖσι φερναῖς ἔλαβεν Ἀγαμέμνων
  ἄναξ;   250

ΚΛ. ἦλθες εἰς Ἄργος μεθ' ἡμῶν κἀμὸς ἦσθ' ἀεί ποτε.

ΠΡ. ὧδ' ἔχει. καὶ σοὶ μὲν εὔνους εἰμί, σῷ δ' ἧσσον πόσει.

ΚΛ. ἐκκάλυπτε νῦν ποθ' ἡμῖν οὕστινας λέγεις λόγους.

ΠΡ. παῖδα σὴν πατὴρ ὁ φύσας αὐτόχειρ μέλλει κτενεῖν.

ΚΛ. πῶς; ἀπέπτυσ', ὦ γεραιέ, μῦθον· οὐ γὰρ εὖ φρονεῖς.

ΠΡ. φασγάνῳ λευκὴν φονεύων τῆς ταλαιπώρου δέρην. 256

ΚΛ. ὦ τάλαιν' ἐγώ. μεμηνὼς ἆρα τυγχάνει πόσις;

ΠΡ. ἀρτίφρων, πλὴν ἐς σὲ καὶ σὴν παῖδα· τοῦτο δ' οὐ
  φρονεῖ.

ΚΛ. ἐκ τίνος λόγου; τίς αὐτὸν οὐπάγων ἀλαστόρων; 259

ΠΡ. θέσφαθ', ὥς γέ φησι Κάλχας, ἵνα πορεύηται στρατός.

ΚΛ. ποῖ; τάλαιν' ἐγώ, τάλαινα δ' ἦν πατὴρ μέλλει κτενεῖν.

Πρ. Δαρδάνου πρὸς δώμαθ', Ἑλένην Μενέλεως ὅπως λάβῃ.
Κλ. εἰς ἄρ' Ἰφιγένειαν Ἑλένης νόστος ἦν πεπρωμένος;
Πρ. πάντ' ἔχεις· Ἀρτέμιδι θύσειν παῖδα σὴν μέλλει πατήρ.
Κλ. ὁ δὲ γάμος τίν' εἶχε πρόφασιν, ᾧ μ' ἐκόμισεν ἐκ δόμων;
Πρ. ἵν' ἀγάγοις χαίρουσ' Ἀχιλλεῖ παῖδα νυμφεύσουσα
   σήν. 266
Κλ. ὦ θύγατερ, ἥκεις ἐπ' ὀλέθρῳ, καὶ σὺ καὶ μήτηρ σέθεν.
Πρ. οἰκτρὰ πάσχετον δύ' οὖσαι· δεινὰ δ' Ἀγαμέμνων ἔτλη.
Κλ. οἴχομαι τάλαινα, δάκρυον τ' ὄμματ' οὐκέτι στέγει.
Πρ. εἴπερ ἀλγεινὸν τὸ τέκνων στερόμενον, δακρυρρόει. 270
Κλ. σὺ δὲ τάδ', ὦ γέρον, πόθεν φῂς εἰδέναι πεπυσμένος;
Πρ. δέλτον ᾠχόμην φέρων σοι πρὸς τὰ πρὶν γεγραμμένα.
Κλ. οὐκ ἐῶν ἢ ξυγκελεύων παῖδ' ἄγειν θανουμένην;
Πρ. μὴ μὲν οὖν ἄγειν· φρονῶν γὰρ ἔτυχε σὸς πόσις τότ' εὖ.
Κλ. κᾆτα πῶς φέρων γε δέλτον οὐκ ἐμοὶ δίδως λαβεῖν;
Πρ. Μενέλεως ἀφείλεθ' ἡμᾶς, ὃς κακῶν τῶνδ' αἴτιος. 276
Κλ. ὦ τέκνον Νηρῇδος, ὦ παῖ Πηλέως, κλύεις τάδε;
Αχ. ἔκλυον οὖσαν ἀθλίαν σε, τὸ δ' ἐμὸν οὐ φαύλως φέρω.
Κλ. παῖδά μου κατακτενοῦσι σοῖς δολώσαντες γάμοις. 279

Clytemnestra appeals for help to Achilles, who chivalrously
promises to defend Iphigenia with his own life, if an attempt
to turn Agamemnon from his purpose fails; he then leaves
the stage. The Chorus sings an ode about the marriage of
Peleus and Thetis, Achilles' parents. Clytemnestra informs
Agamemnon, in the presence of Iphigenia, that she knows of
his cruel scheme. He attempts to deny it, but in vain, and
Clytemnestra asks how he can bear to deprive his faithful wife
of her beloved daughter for the sake of a woman like Helen.
   Lines 280–342. Iphigenia makes a pitiful appeal for
mercy to the father who loves her so much. Why should she
die because Helen has eloped with Paris? She begs Agamemnon in the name of her infant brother Orestes not to send
her to her death, but he replies sadly that he must do it for the
sake of Greece and its future safety.

Ιφ. εἰ μὲν τὸν Ὀρφέως εἶχον, ὦ πάτερ, λόγον,   280
πείθειν ἐπᾴδουσ᾽, ὥσθ᾽ ὁμαρτεῖν μοι πέτρας,
κηλεῖν τε τοῖς λόγοισιν οὓς ἐβουλόμην,
ἐνταῦθ᾽ ἂν ἦλθον· νῦν δέ, τἀπ᾽ ἐμοῦ σοφά,
δάκρυα παρέξω· ταῦτα γὰρ δυναίμεθ᾽ ἄν.
ἱκετηρίαν δὲ γόνασιν ἐξάπτω σέθεν   285
τὸ σῶμα τοὐμόν, ὅπερ ἔτικτεν ἥδε σοι,
μή μ᾽ ἀπολέσῃς ἄωρον· ἡδὺ γὰρ τὸ φῶς
βλέπειν· τὰ δ᾽ ὑπὸ γῆς μή μ᾽ ἰδεῖν ἀναγκάσῃς.
πρώτη σ᾽ ἐκάλεσα πατέρα καὶ σὺ παῖδ᾽ ἐμέ·
πρώτη δὲ γόνασι σοῖσι σῶμα δοῦσ᾽ ἐμὸν   290
φίλας χάριτας ἔδωκα κἀντεδεξάμην.
λόγος δ᾽ ὁ μὲν σὸς ἦν ὅδ᾽· Ἆρά σ᾽, ὦ τέκνον,
εὐδαίμον᾽ ἀνδρὸς ἐν δόμοισιν ὄψομαι,
ζῶσάν τε καὶ θάλλουσαν ἀξίως ἐμοῦ;
οὑμὸς δ᾽ ὅδ᾽ ἦν αὖ περὶ σὸν ἐξαρτωμένης   295
γένειον, οὗ νῦν ἀντιλάζυμαι χερί·
Τί δ᾽ ἆρ᾽ ἐγὼ σέ; πρέσβυν ἆρ᾽ ἐσδέξομαι
ἐμῶν φίλαισιν ὑποδοχαῖς δόμων, πάτερ,
πόνων τιθηνοὺς ἀποδιδοῦσά σοι τροφάς;
τούτων ἐγὼ μὲν τῶν λόγων μνήμην ἔχω,   300
σὺ δ᾽ ἐπιλέλησαι, καί μ᾽ ἀποκτεῖναι θέλεις.
μή, πρός σε Πέλοπος καὶ πρὸς Ἀτρέως πατρὸς
καὶ τῆσδε μητρός, ἣ πρὶν ὠδίνουσ᾽ ἐμὲ
νῦν δευτέραν ὠδῖνα τήνδε λαμβάνει.
τί μοι μέτεστι τῶν Ἀλεξάνδρου γάμων   305
Ἑλένης τε; πόθεν ἦλθ᾽ ἐπ᾽ ὀλέθρῳ τὠμῷ, πάτερ;
βλέψον πρὸς ἡμᾶς, ὄμμα δὸς φίλημά τε,
ἵν᾽ ἀλλὰ τοῦτο κατθανοῦσ᾽ ἔχω σέθεν
μνημεῖον, ἢν μὴ τοῖς ἐμοῖς πεισθῇς λόγοις.
ἀδελφέ, μικρὸς μὲν σύ γ᾽ ἐπίκουρος φίλοις,   310
ὅμως δὲ συνδάκρυσον, ἱκέτευσον πατρὸς

τὴν σὴν ἀδελφὴν μὴ θανεῖν· αἴσθημά τοι
κἂν νηπίοις γε τῶν κακῶν ἐγγίγνεται.
ἰδοὺ σιωπῶν λίσσεταί σ᾽ ὅδ᾽, ὦ πάτερ.
ἀλλ᾽ αἴδεσαί με καὶ κατοίκτιρον βίου.   315
ναί, πρὸς γενείου σ᾽ ἀντόμεσθα δύο φίλω·
ὃ μὲν νεοσσός ἐστιν, ἣ δ᾽ ηὐξημένη.
ἐν συντεμοῦσα πάντα νικήσω λόγον·
τὸ φῶς τόδ᾽ ἀνθρώποισιν ἥδιστον βλέπειν,
τὰ νέρθε δ᾽ οὐδέν· μαίνεται δ᾽ ὃς εὔχεται   320
θανεῖν. κακῶς ζῆν κρεῖσσον ἢ καλῶς θανεῖν.
Αγ. ἐγὼ τά τ᾽ οἰκτρὰ συνετός εἰμι καὶ τὰ μή,
φιλῶ τ᾽ ἐμαυτοῦ τέκνα· μαινοίμην γὰρ ἄν.
δεινῶς δ᾽ ἔχει μοι ταῦτα τολμῆσαι, γύναι,
δεινῶς δὲ καὶ μή· τοῦτο γὰρ πρᾶξαί με δεῖ.   325
ὁρᾶθ᾽ ὅσον στράτευμα ναύφρακτον τόδε,
χαλκέων θ᾽ ὅπλων ἄνακτες Ἑλλήνων ὅσοι,
οἷς νόστος οὐκ ἔστ᾽ Ἰλίου πύργους ἔπι,
εἰ μή σε θύσω, μάντις ὡς Κάλχας λέγει,
οὐδ᾽ ἔστι Τροίας ἐξελεῖν κλεινὸν βάθρον.   330
μέμηνε δ᾽ Ἀφροδίτη τις Ἑλλήνων στρατῷ
πλεῖν ὡς τάχιστα βαρβάρων ἐπὶ χθόνα,
παῦσαί τε λέκτρων ἁρπαγὰς Ἑλληνικῶν·
οἳ τὰς ἐν Ἄργει παρθένους κτενοῦσί μου
ὑμᾶς τε κἀμέ, θέσφατ᾽ εἰ λύσω θεᾶς.   335
οὐ Μενέλεώς με καταδεδούλωται, τέκνον,
οὐδ᾽ ἐπὶ τὸ κείνου βουλόμενον ἐλήλυθα,
ἀλλ᾽ Ἑλλάς, ᾗ δεῖ, κἂν θέλω κἂν μὴ θέλω,
θῦσαί σε· τούτου δ᾽ ἥσσονες καθέσταμεν.
ἐλευθέραν γὰρ δεῖ νιν ὅσον ἐν σοί, τέκνον,   340
κἀμοὶ γενέσθαι, μηδὲ βαρβάρων ὕπο
Ἕλληνας ὄντας λέκτρα συλᾶσθαι βίᾳ.

16   IPHIGENIA IN AULIS

Iphigenia sings an ode lamenting the cruelty of her fate, and wishes that the Judgment of Paris, the cause of her present plight, had never taken place. Achilles now enters and sees Iphigenia for the first time. He says that the army, led by Odysseus, demands her sacrifice, but that he will defend her, even though his own troops threaten to kill him if he tries to save her life.

Lines 343–438. Iphigenia's mood has now changed to one of heroic fortitude. She thanks Achilles for his offer of help, but says that Greece requires her sacrifice, which she is willing to give. The Greeks must not fight each other for her sake, and her memorial will be the Greek victory over the barbarians. Achilles admires her courage, and would be proud to marry her ; he will be near the altar if she changes her mind and wishes to live. Iphigenia bids farewell to her mother ; she tells her not to mourn her death or raise a mound in her memory, nor even to be angry with Agamemnon, who is slaying her against his will in order to save Greece. She is now ready to walk to the altar.

Ιφ.   μῆτερ, εἰσακούσατε
τῶν ἐμῶν λόγων· μάτην γάρ σ᾽ εἰσορῶ θυμουμένην
σῷ πόσει. τὰ δ᾽ ἀδύναθ᾽ ἡμῖν καρτερεῖν οὐ ῥᾴδιον.
τὸν μὲν οὖν ξένον δίκαιον αἰνέσαι προθυμίας·   346
ἀλλὰ καὶ σὲ τοῦθ᾽ ὁρᾶν χρή, μὴ διαβληθῇ στρατῷ,
καὶ πλέον πράξωμεν οὐδέν, ὅδε δὲ συμφορᾶς τύχῃ.
οἷα δ᾽ εἰσῆλθέν μ᾽, ἄκουσον, μῆτερ, ἐννοουμένην·
κατθανεῖν μέν μοι δέδοκται· τοῦτο δ᾽ αὐτὸ βούλομαι 350
εὐκλεῶς πρᾶξαι, παρεῖσά γ᾽ ἐκποδὼν τὸ δυσγενές.
δεῦρο δὴ σκέψαι μεθ᾽ ἡμῶν, μῆτερ, ὡς καλῶς λέγω·
εἰς ἔμ᾽ Ἑλλὰς ἡ μεγίστη πᾶσα νῦν ἀποβλέπει,
κἂν ἐμοὶ πορθμός τε ναῶν καὶ Φρυγῶν κατασκαφαὶ
τάς τε μελλούσας γυναῖκας, ἤν τι δρῶσι βάρβαροι,
μηκέθ᾽ ἁρπάζειν ἐᾶν τούσδ᾽ ὀλβίας ἐξ Ἑλλάδος,   356
τὸν Ἑλένης τείσαντας ὄλεθρον, ἣν ἀνήρπασεν Πάρις.

ταῦτα πάντα κατθανοῦσα ῥύσομαι, καί μου κλέος,
'Ελλάδ' ὡς ἠλευθέρωσα, μακάριον γενήσεται.
καὶ γὰρ οὐδέ τοί τι λίαν ἐμὲ φιλοψυχεῖν χρεών· 360
πᾶσι γάρ μ' Ἕλλησι κοινὸν ἔτεκες, οὐχὶ σοὶ μόνῃ.
ἀλλὰ μυρίοι μὲν ἄνδρες ἀσπίσιν πεφραγμένοι,
μυρίοι δ' ἐρέτμ' ἔχοντες, πατρίδος ἠδικημένης,
δρᾶν τι τολμήσουσιν ἐχθροὺς χὔπὲρ 'Ελλάδος θανεῖν,
ἡ δ' ἐμὴ ψυχὴ μί' οὖσα πάντα κωλύσει τάδε; 365
τί τὸ δίκαιον τοῦτό γ'; ἆρ' ἔχοιμ' ἂν ἀντειπεῖν ἔπος;
κἀπ' ἐκεῖν' ἔλθωμεν· οὐ δεῖ τόνδε διὰ μάχης μολεῖν
πᾶσιν 'Αργείοις γυναικὸς εἵνεκ' οὐδὲ κατθανεῖν.
εἷς γ' ἀνὴρ κρείσσων γυναικῶν μυρίων ὁρᾶν φάος.
εἰ βεβούληται δὲ σῶμα τοὐμὸν Ἄρτεμις λαβεῖν, 370
ἐμποδὼν γενήσομαι 'γὼ θνητὸς οὖσα τῇ θεῷ;
ἀλλ' ἀμήχανον· δίδωμι σῶμα τοὐμὸν 'Ελλάδι.
θύετ', ἐκπορθεῖτε Τροίαν. ταῦτα γὰρ μνημεῖά μου
διὰ μακροῦ, καὶ παῖδες οὗτοι καὶ γάμοι καὶ δόξ' ἐμή.
βαρβάρων δ' Ἕλληνας ἄρχειν εἰκός, ἀλλ' οὐ βαρ-
βάρους, 375
μῆτερ, 'Ελλήνων· τὸ μὲν γὰρ δοῦλον, οἱ δ' ἐλεύθεροι.
Αχ. 'Αγαμέμνονος παῖ, μακάριόν μέ τις θεῶν
ἔμελλε θήσειν, εἰ τύχοιμι σῶν γάμων.
ζηλῶ δὲ σοῦ μὲν 'Ελλάδ', 'Ελλάδος δὲ σέ.
εὖ γὰρ τόδ' εἶπας ἀξίως τε πατρίδος. 380
μᾶλλον δὲ λέκτρων σῶν πόθος μ' ἐσέρχεται
ἐς τὴν φύσιν βλέψαντα· γενναία γὰρ εἶ.
ὅρα δ'· ἐγὼ γὰρ βούλομαί σ' εὐεργετεῖν
λαβεῖν τ' ἐς οἴκους· ἄχθομαί τ', ἴστω Θέτις,
εἰ μή σε σώσω Δαναΐδαισι διὰ μάχης 385
ἐλθών. ἄθρησον· ὁ θάνατος δεινὸν κακόν.
Ιφ. ἡ Τυνδαρὶς παῖς διὰ τὸ σῶμ' ἀρκεῖ μάχας
ἀνδρῶν τιθεῖσα καὶ φόνους· σὺ δ', ὦ ξένε,

18 IPHIGENIA IN AULIS

μὴ θνῆσκε δι᾽ ἐμὲ μηδ᾽ ἀποκτείνῃς τινά,
ἔα δὲ σῶσαί μ᾽ Ἑλλάδ᾽, ἢν δυνώμεθα.   390
Αχ. ὦ λῆμ᾽ ἄριστον, οὐκ ἔχω πρὸς τοῦτ᾽ ἔτι
λέγειν, ἐπεί σοι τάδε δοκεῖ· γενναῖα γὰρ
φρονεῖς· τί γὰρ τἀληθὲς οὐκ εἴποι τις ἄν;
ὅμως δ᾽, ἴσως γὰρ κἂν μεταγνοίης τάδε,
ἐλθὼν τάδ᾽ ὅπλα θήσομαι βωμοῦ πέλας,   395
ὡς οὐκ ἐάσων σ᾽ ἀλλὰ κωλύσων θανεῖν.
χρήσῃ δὲ καὶ σὺ τοῖς ἐμοῖς λόγοις τάχα,
ὅταν πέλας σῆς φάσγανον δέρης ἴδῃς.
Ιφ. μῆτερ, τί σιγῇ δακρύοις τέγγεις κόρας;
Κλ. ἔχω τάλαινα πρόφασιν ὥστ᾽ ἀλγεῖν φρένα.   400
Ιφ. παῦσαι· ᾽μὲ μὴ κάκιζε· τάδε δέ μοι πιθοῦ.
Κλ. λέγ᾽· ὡς παρ᾽ ἡμῶν οὐδὲν ἀδικήσῃ, τέκνον.
Ιφ. μήτ᾽ οὖν γε τὸν σὸν πλόκαμον ἐκτέμῃς τριχός.
Κλ. τί δὴ τόδ᾽ εἶπας, τέκνον; ἀπολέσασά σε;
Ιφ. οὐ σύ γε· σέσωσμαι, κατ᾽ ἐμὲ δ᾽ εὐκλεὴς ἔσῃ.   405
Κλ. πῶς εἶπας; οὐ πενθεῖν με σὴν ψυχὴν χρεών;
Ιφ. ἥκιστ᾽, ἐπεί μοι τύμβος οὐ χωσθήσεται.
Κλ. τί δαί; τὸ θνῄσκειν, οὐ τάφος, νομίζεται.
Ιφ. βωμὸς θεᾶς μοι μνῆμα τῆς Διὸς κόρης.
Κλ. ἀλλ᾽, ὦ τέκνον, σοὶ πείσομαι· λέγεις γὰρ εὖ.   410
Ιφ. ὡς εὐτυχοῦσά γ᾽ Ἑλλάδος τ᾽ εὐεργέτις.
Κλ. τί δὴ κασιγνήταισιν ἀγγελῶ σέθεν;
Ιφ. μηδ᾽ ἀμφὶ κείναις μέλανας ἐξάψῃ πέπλους.
Κλ. εἴπω δὲ παρὰ σοῦ φίλον ἔπος τι παρθένοις;
Ιφ. χαίρειν γ᾽. Ὀρέστην τ᾽ ἔκτρεφ᾽ ἄνδρα τόνδε μοι.   415
Κλ. προσέλκυσαί νιν ὕστατον θεωμένη.
Ιφ. ὦ φίλτατ᾽, ἐπεκούρησας ὅσον εἶχες φίλοις.
Κλ. ἔσθ᾽ ὅ τι κατ᾽ Ἄργος δρῶσά σοι χάριν φέρω;
Ιφ. πατέρα τὸν ἀμὸν μὴ στύγει, πόσιν γε σόν.
Κλ. δεινοὺς ἀγῶνας διὰ σὲ δεῖ κεῖνον δραμεῖν.   420

Ιφ. ἄκων μ᾽ ὑπὲρ γῆς Ἑλλάδος διώλεσεν.

Κλ. δόλῳ δ᾽, ἀγεννῶς Ἀτρέως τ᾽ οὐκ ἀξίως.

Ιφ. τίς μ᾽ εἶσιν ἄξων πρὶν σπαράσσεσθαι κόμης;

Κλ. ἔγωγε μετὰ σοῦ.... Ιφ. μὴ σύ γ᾽· οὐ καλῶς λέγεις.

Κλ. πέπλων ἐχομένη σῶν. Ιφ. ἐμοί, μῆτερ, πιθοῦ· 425
μέν᾽· ὡς ἐμοί τε σοί τε κάλλιον τόδε.
πατρὸς δ᾽ ὀπαδῶν τῶνδέ τίς με πεμπέτω
Ἀρτέμιδος ἐς λειμῶν᾽, ὅπου σφαγήσομαι.

Κλ. ὦ τέκνον, οἴχῃ; Ιφ. καὶ πάλιν γ᾽ οὐ μὴ μόλω.

Κλ. λιποῦσα μητέρα; Ιφ. ὡς ὁρᾷς γ᾽, οὐκ ἀξίως. 430

Κλ. σχές, μή με προλίπῃς. Ιφ. οὐκ ἐῶ στάζειν δάκρυ.
ὑμεῖς δ᾽ ἐπευφημήσατ᾽, ὦ νεάνιδες,
παιᾶνα τῇμῇ συμφορᾷ Διὸς κόρην
Ἄρτεμιν· ἴτω δὲ Δαναΐδαις εὐφημία.
κανᾶ δ᾽ ἐναρχέσθω τις, αἰθέσθω δὲ πῦρ 435
προχύταις καθαρσίοισι, καὶ πατὴρ ἐμὸς
ἐνδεξιούσθω βωμόν· ὡς σωτηρίαν
Ἕλλησι δώσουσ᾽ ἔρχομαι νικηφόρον.

Iphigenia raises the processional chant and moves unflinchingly towards the altar while the Chorus sings a last ode in her honour. At this point Euripides' play, as we now have it, ends, left unfinished at his death in 406 B.C., though a few lines survive which seem to show that he intended the play to conclude with the appearance of Artemis as dea ex machina (see Introduction, page xxiv) to console Clytemnestra with the news that she had snatched Iphigenia away from the altar at the last moment and substituted a deer. The younger Euripides, son of the poet, probably wrote another prologue— both prologues survive—and completed the play, which he produced soon after 406, but the ending disappeared at some later date and another scene, in which a messenger describes the preparations for the sacrifice, was substituted ; various other passages were also interpolated at the same time. But the end of the substituted ending was itself lost, and the very poor lines, written by a much later hand, that relate the disappearance of Iphigenia and the sacrifice of a deer in her place, are a second variation that took the place of the original ending of the play.

A NOTE ON 'ACHILLES AND AJAX PLAYING DICE' (page 11)

This is the most famous work of Exekias, c. 535 B.C., the finest Athenian vase-painter of the black-figure period (6th century). The players are sitting on blocks of wood, with a third block between them as a table. Their shields stand behind them, with Ajax's helmet resting on his shield. Their names appear above their heads, *AXIΛΕΟΣ* (᾽Αχιλλέως) and *AIANTOΣ*, in the genitive case, meaning ' (the figure) of Aias '; Achilles' name is written in retrograde characters, i.e. from right to left. The game was a kind of backgammon, combining skill with chance. Dice were thrown, and the cast entitled the player to make a certain move. Achilles has thrown two twos, or a one and a three, and says *TEΣAPA*, ' four ', and will make a move accordingly. Ajax has thrown a one and a two and says *TPIA*, ' three ', (also written backwards). On the left is the signature of the artist, who both made the vase and painted the figures : ᾽Εξηκίας ἐποίησεν, ' Exekias made it ', and to the right are the words ᾽Ονητορίδης καλός, ' Onetorides (is) handsome ' ; he was a friend of Exekias, who thus immortalized his name.

ΙΦΙΓΕΝΕΙΑ Η ΕΝ ΤΑΥΡΟΙΣ
IPHIGENIA IN TAURIS

ΤΑ ΤΟΥ ΔΡΑΜΑΤΟΣ ΠΡΟΣΩΠΑ
CHARACTERS OF THE PLAY

ΙΦΙΓΕΝΕΙΑ,	Iphigenia, daughter of Agamemnon.
ΟΡΕΣΤΗΣ,	Orestes, brother of Iphigenia.
ΠΥΛΑΔΗΣ,	Pylades, friend of Orestes.
ΘΟΑΣ,	Thoas, king of the Taurians.
ΑΓΓΕΛΟΣ,	a messenger, one of the Taurians.
ΑΘΗΝΑ,	Athena, a goddess.

The scene is the front of the temple of Artemis in the land of the Taurians (the Crimea).

The play was first produced at the Great or City Dionysia at Athens about 414–412 B.C.

IPHIGENIA IN TAURIS

Lines 1-57. Iphigenia enters and speaks the Prologue. She describes her ancestry and how her father Agamemnon intended to sacrifice her to Artemis at Aulis in order to obtain good weather for the assembled fleet to sail to Troy, but Artemis substituted a deer on the altar and carried her off to be her priestess in the land of the Taurians, where she has to prepare for sacrifice any Greeks who come to the land. She then relates a dream she has just had, from which she infers that her brother Orestes, who was an infant at the time of her supposed sacrifice, is dead.

ΙΦΙΓΕΝΕΙΑ

Πέλοψ ὁ Ταντάλειος ἐς Πῖσαν μολὼν
θοαῖσιν ἵπποις Οἰνομάου γαμεῖ κόρην,
ἐξ ἧς Ἀτρεὺς ἔβλαστεν· Ἀτρέως δ᾽ ἄπο
Μενέλαος Ἀγαμέμνων τε· τοῦ δ᾽ ἔφυν ἐγώ,
τῆς Τυνδαρείας θυγατρὸς Ἰφιγένεια παῖς,   5
ἣν ἀμφὶ δίναις ἅς θάμ᾽ Εὔριπος πυκναῖς
αὔραις ἑλίσσων κυανέαν ἅλα στρέφει,
ἔσφαξεν Ἑλένης οὕνεχ᾽, ὡς δοκεῖ, πατὴρ
Ἀρτέμιδι κλειναῖς ἐν πτυχαῖσιν Αὐλίδος.
    ἐνταῦθα γὰρ δὴ χιλίων ναῶν στόλον   10
Ἑλληνικὸν συνήγαγ᾽ Ἀγαμέμνων ἄναξ,
τὸν καλλίνικον στέφανον Ἰλίου θέλων
λαβεῖν Ἀχαιοῖς τούς θ᾽ ὑβρισθέντας γάμους
Ἑλένης μετελθεῖν, Μενέλεῳ χάριν φέρων.
δεινῆς δ᾽ ἀπλοίας πνευμάτων τε τυγχάνων,   15
ἐς ἔμπυρ᾽ ἦλθε, καὶ λέγει Κάλχας τάδε·
Ὦ τῆσδ᾽ ἀνάσσων Ἑλλάδος στρατηγίας,
Ἀγάμεμνον, οὐ μὴ ναῦς ἀφορμίσῃ χθονός,

23

πρὶν ἂν κόρην σὴν Ἰφιγένειαν Ἄρτεμις
λάβῃ σφαγεῖσαν· ὅ τι γὰρ ἐνιαυτὸς τέκοι   20
κάλλιστον, ηὔξω φωσφόρῳ θύσειν θεᾷ.
παῖδ᾽ οὖν ἐν οἴκοις σὴ Κλυταιμήστρα δάμαρ
τίκτει—τὸ καλλιστεῖον εἰς ἔμ᾽ ἀναφέρων—
ἦν χρή σε θῦσαι.
                                    καί μ᾽ Ὀδυσσέως τέχναις
μητρὸς παρείλοντ᾽ ἐπὶ γάμοις Ἀχιλλέως.   25
ἐλθοῦσα δ᾽ Αὐλίδ᾽ ἡ τάλαιν᾽ ὑπὲρ πυρᾶς
μεταρσία ληφθεῖσ᾽ ἐκαινόμην ξίφει·
ἀλλ᾽ ἐξέκλεψεν ἔλαφον ἀντιδοῦσά μου
Ἄρτεμις Ἀχαιοῖς, διὰ δὲ λαμπρὸν αἰθέρα
πέμψασά μ᾽ ἐς τήνδ᾽ ᾤκισεν Ταύρων χθόνα,   30
οὗ γῆς ἀνάσσει βαρβάροισι βάρβαρος
Θόας, ὃς ὠκὺν πόδα τιθεὶς ἴσον πτεροῖς
ἐς τοὔνομ᾽ ἦλθε τόδε ποδωκείας χάριν.
ναοῖσι δ᾽ ἐν τοῖσδ᾽ ἱερέαν τίθησί με.
ἃ καινὰ δ᾽ ἥκει νὺξ φέρουσα φάσματα,   35
λέξω πρὸς αἰθέρ᾽, εἴ τι δὴ τόδ᾽ ἔστ᾽ ἄκος.
ἔδοξ᾽ ἐν ὕπνῳ τῆσδ᾽ ἀπαλλαχθεῖσα γῆς
οἰκεῖν ἐν Ἄργει, παρθένοισι δ᾽ ἐν μέσαις
εὕδειν, χθονὸς δὲ νῶτα σεισθῆναι σάλῳ,
φεύγειν δὲ κἄξω στᾶσα θριγκὸν εἰσιδεῖν   40
δόμων πίτνοντα, πᾶν δ᾽ ἐρείψιμον στέγος
βεβλημένον πρὸς οὖδας ἐξ ἄκρων σταθμῶν.
μόνος λελεῖφθαι στῦλος εἷς ἔδοξέ μοι
δόμων πατρῴων, ἐκ δ᾽ ἐπικράνων κόμας
ξανθὰς καθεῖναι, φθέγμα δ᾽ ἀνθρώπου λαβεῖν,   45
κἀγὼ τέχνην τήνδ᾽ ἣν ἔχω ξενοκτόνον
τιμῶσ᾽ ὑδραίνειν αὐτὸν ὡς θανούμενον,
κλαίουσα. τοὔναρ δ᾽ ὧδε συμβάλλω τόδε·
τέθνηκ᾽ Ὀρέστης, οὗ κατηρξάμην ἐγώ.

IPHIGENIA IN TAURIS 25

στῦλοι γὰρ οἴκων παῖδές εἰσιν ἄρσενες· 50
θνήσκουσι δ' οὓς ἂν χέρνιβες βάλωσ' ἐμαί.
νῦν οὖν ἀδελφῷ βούλομαι δοῦναι χοὰς
παροῦσ' ἀπόντι—ταῦτα γὰρ δυναίμεθ' ἄν—
σὺν προσπόλοισιν, ἃς ἔδωχ' ἡμῖν ἄναξ
Ἑλληνίδας γυναῖκας. ἀλλ' ἐξ αἰτίας 55
οὔπω τίνος πάρεισιν; εἶμ' ἔσω δόμων
ἐν οἷσι ναίω τῶνδ' ἀνακτόρων θεᾶς.

[Exeunt

Enter Orestes and his friend Pylades. They see the grim relics of
human sacrifice on the altar.
Lines 58-93. Orestes describes how he has been driven in
madness from land to land by the Furies because he killed his
mother Clytemnestra to avenge her murder of his father and
how Apollo bade him fetch an image of Artemis from this
Tauric land. Pylades advises waiting until night, when
they may be able to steal the image from the temple.

ΟΡΕΣΤΗΣ

ὦ Φοῖβε, ποῖ μ' αὖ τήνδ' ἐς ἄρκυν ἤγαγες
χρήσας, ἐπειδὴ πατρὸς αἷμ' ἐτεισάμην,
μητέρα κατακτάς; διαδοχαῖς δ' Ἐρινύων 60
ἠλαυνόμεσθα φυγάδες ἔξεδροι χθονὸς
δρόμους τε πολλοὺς ἐξέπλησα καμπίμους.
ἐλθὼν δέ σ' ἠρώτησα πῶς τροχηλάτου
μανίας ἂν ἔλθοιμ' ἐς τέλος πόνων τ' ἐμῶν,
οὓς ἐξεμόχθουν περιπολῶν καθ' Ἑλλάδα. 65
σὺ δ' εἶπας ἐλθεῖν Ταυρικῆς μ' ὅρους χθονός,
ἔνθ' Ἄρτεμις σὴ σύγγονος βωμοὺς ἔχοι,
λαβεῖν τ' ἄγαλμα θεᾶς, ὅ φασιν ἐνθάδε
ἐς τούσδε ναοὺς οὐρανοῦ πεσεῖν ἄπο·
λαβόντα δ' ἢ τέχναισιν ἢ τύχῃ τινί, 70

THE DEATH OF AEGISTHUS.

From a fifth-century B.C. Attic vase at Vienna. Orestes is stabbing Aegisthus for the second time, while blood pours from both wounds. Beside him is his sister Chrysothemis (*I.T.* 164, n. ; her name is written backwards), looking away, towards Clytemnestra (not shown in this panel), who is trying to come to the rescue ; Orestes will kill his mother next.

κίνδυνον ἐκπλήσαντ᾽, Ἀθηναίων χθονὶ
δοῦναι—τὸ δ᾽ ἐνθένδ᾽ οὐδὲν ἐρρήθη πέρα—
καὶ ταῦτα δράσαντ᾽ ἀμπνοὰς ἕξειν πόνων.
ἥκω δὲ πεισθεὶς σοῖς λόγοισιν ἐνθάδε
ἄγνωστον ἐς γῆν, ἄξενον. σὲ δ᾽ ἱστορῶ, 75
Πυλάδη—σὺ γάρ μοι τοῦδε συλλήπτωρ πόνου—
τί δρῶμεν; ἀμφίβληστρα γὰρ τοίχων ὁρᾷς
ὑψηλά· πότερα δωμάτων προσαμβάσεις
ἐμβησόμεσθα; πῶς ἂν οὖν λάθοιμεν ἄν;
ἢ χαλκότευκτα κλῇθρα λύσαντες μοχλοῖς—

26

ὧν οὐδὲν ἴσμεν; ἢν δ' ἀνοίγοντες πύλας
ληφθῶμεν ἐσβάσεις τε μηχανώμενοι,
θανούμεθ'. ἀλλὰ πρὶν θανεῖν, νεὼς ἔπι
φεύγωμεν, ἧπερ δεῦρ' ἐναυστολήσαμεν.

ΠΥΛΑΔΗΣ

φεύγειν μὲν οὐκ ἀνεκτὸν οὐδ' εἰώθαμεν,   85
τὸν τοῦ θεοῦ δὲ χρησμὸν οὐ κακιστέον·
ναοῦ δ' ἀπαλλαχθέντε κρύψωμεν δέμας
κατ' ἄντρ' ἃ πόντος νοτίδι διακλύζει μέλας—
νεὼς ἄπωθεν, μή τις εἰσιδὼν σκάφος
βασιλεῦσιν εἴπῃ κᾆτα ληφθῶμεν βίᾳ.   90
ὅταν δὲ νυκτὸς ὄμμα λυγαίας μόλῃ,
τολμητέον τοι ξεστὸν ἐκ ναοῦ λαβεῖν
ἄγαλμα πάσας προσφέροντε μηχανάς.   [*Exeunt*

The Chorus of captive Greek maidens, now attendants on Iphigenia, sings a lament for the ruined house of Atreus and for
the hard lot of Greek exiles in the Tauric land. A herdsman
enters to tell Iphigenia that two Greek strangers, one named
Pylades, have reached the land and have been captured after
the other one in a fit of madness attacked some cattle. It
is Iphigenia's duty to consecrate them to the altar for sacrifice. Thinking that her brother is dead and remembering her
own intended slaughter at Aulis for the sake of Helen, she
steels herself to be ruthless. The Chorus sings an ode wondering
who the strangers are and wishing that Helen, the cause of so
many woes, might be slain on the altar here. The captives
are brought on to the stage, where Iphigenia sees her brother
for the first time without knowing who he is.
    Lines 94–171. Iphigenia asks Orestes his name, which he
refuses to give, and enquires about the return of the Greeks
from Troy, and about her own parents, of whose death she
now hears for the first time. She also learns that despite her
dream Orestes is somewhere alive.

Ιφ. πότερος ἄρ' ὑμῶν ἐνθάδ' ὠνομασμένος
Πυλάδης κέκληται; τόδε μαθεῖν πρῶτον θέλω.   95
Ορ. ὅδ', εἴ τι δή σοι τοῦτ' ἐν ἡδονῇ μαθεῖν.
Ιφ. ποίας πολίτης πατρίδος Ἕλληνος γεγώς;
Ορ. τί δ' ἂν μαθοῦσα τόδε πλέον λάβοις, γύναι;
Ιφ. πότερον ἀδελφὼ μητρός ἐστον ἐκ μιᾶς;
Ορ. φιλότητί γ'· ἐσμὲν δ' οὐ κασιγνήτω, γύναι.   100
Ιφ. σοὶ δ' ὄνομα ποῖον ἔθεθ' ὁ γεννήσας πατήρ;
Ορ. τὸ μὲν δίκαιον Δυστυχὴς καλοίμεθ' ἄν.
Ιφ. οὐ τοῦτ' ἐρωτῶ· τοῦτο μὲν δὸς τῇ τύχῃ.
Ορ. ἀνώνυμοι θανόντες οὐ γελώμεθ' ἄν.
Ιφ. τί δὲ φθονεῖς τοῦτ'; ἢ φρονεῖς οὕτω μέγα;   105
Ορ. τὸ σῶμα θύσεις τοὐμόν, οὐχὶ τοὔνομα.
Ιφ. οὐδ' ἂν πόλιν φράσειας ἥτις ἐστί σοι;
Ορ. ζητεῖς γὰρ οὐδὲν κέρδος, ὡς θανουμένῳ.
Ιφ. χάριν δὲ δοῦναι τήνδε κωλύει τί σε;
Ορ. τὸ κλεινὸν Ἄργος πατρίδ' ἐμὴν ἐπεύχομαι.   110
Ιφ. πρὸς θεῶν, ἀληθῶς, ὦ ξέν', εἰ κεῖθεν γεγώς;
Ορ. ἐκ τῶν Μυκηνῶν γ', αἵ ποτ' ἦσαν ὄλβιαι.
Ιφ. φυγὰς δ' ἀπῆρας πατρίδος, ἢ ποίᾳ τύχῃ;
Ορ. φεύγω τρόπον γε δή τιν' οὐχ ἑκὼν ἑκών.
Ιφ. καὶ μὴν ποθεινός γ' ἦλθες ἐξ Ἄργους μολών.   115
Ορ. οὔκουν ἐμαυτῷ γ'· εἰ δὲ σοί, σὺ τοῦτ' ἔρα.
Ιφ. ἆρ' ἄν τί μοι φράσειας ὧν ἐγὼ θέλω;
Ορ. ὡς ἐν παρέργῳ τῆς ἐμῆς δυσπραξίας.
Ιφ. Τροίαν ἴσως οἶσθ', ἧς ἀπανταχοῦ λόγος.
Ορ. ὡς μήποτ' ὤφελόν γε μηδ' ἰδὼν ὄναρ.   120
Ιφ. φασίν νιν οὐκέτ' οὖσαν οἴχεσθαι δορί.
Ορ. ἔστιν γὰρ οὕτως οὐδ' ἄκραντ' ἠκούσατε.
Ιφ. Ἑλένη δ' ἀφῖκται δῶμα Μενέλεω πάλιν;
Ορ. ἥκει, κακῶς γ' ἐλθοῦσα τῶν ἐμῶν τινι.
Ιφ. καὶ ποῦ 'στι; κἀμοὶ γάρ τι προυφείλει κακόν.   125

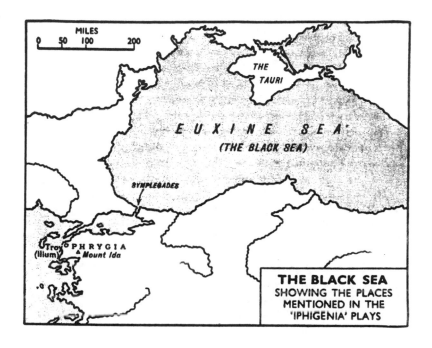

THE BLACK SEA
SHOWING THE PLACES
MENTIONED IN THE
'IPHIGENIA' PLAYS

Ορ. Σπάρτῃ ξυνοικεῖ τῷ πάρος ξυνευνέτῃ.
Ιφ. ὦ μῖσος εἰς "Ελληνας, οὐκ ἐμοὶ μόνῃ.
Ορ. ἀπέλαυσα κἀγὼ δή τι τῶν κείνης γάμων.
Ιφ. νόστος δ᾽ Ἀχαιῶν ἐγένεθ᾽, ὡς κηρύσσεται;
Ορ. ὡς πάνθ᾽ ἅπαξ με συλλαβοῦσ᾽ ἀνιστορεῖς.   130
Ιφ. πρὶν γὰρ θανεῖν σε, τοῦδ᾽ ἐπαυρέσθαι θέλω.
Ορ. ἔλεγχ᾽, ἐπειδὴ τοῦδ᾽ ἐρᾷς· λέξω δ᾽ ἐγώ.
Ιφ. Κάλχας τις ἦλθε μάντις ἐκ Τροίας πάλιν;
Ορ. ὄλωλεν, ὡς ἦν ἐν Μυκηναίοις λόγος.
Ιφ. ὦ πότνι᾽, ὡς εὖ.—τί γὰρ ὁ Λαέρτου γόνος;   135
Ορ. οὔπω νενόστηκ᾽ οἶκον, ἔστι δ᾽, ὡς λόγος.

29

Ιφ. ὅλοιτο, νόστου μήποτ' ἐς πάτραν τυχών.

Ορ. μηδὲν κατεύχου· πάντα τἀκείνου νοσεῖ.

Ιφ. Θέτιδος δ' ὁ τῆς Νηρῇδος ἔστι παῖς ἔτι;

Ορ. οὐκ ἔστιν· ἄλλως λέκτρ' ἔγημ' ἐν Αὐλίδι.   140

Ιφ. δόλια γάρ, ὡς ἴσασιν οἱ πεπονθότες.

Ορ. τίς εἶ ποθ'; ὡς εὖ πυνθάνῃ τἀφ' Ἑλλάδος.

Ιφ. ἐκεῖθέν εἰμι· παῖς ἔτ' οὖσ' ἀπωλόμην.

Ορ. ὀρθῶς ποθεῖς ἄρ' εἰδέναι τἀκεῖ, γύναι.

Ιφ. τί δ' ὁ στρατηγός, ὃν λέγουσ' εὐδαιμονεῖν;   145

Ορ. τίς; οὐ γὰρ ὅν γ' ἐγῷδα τῶν εὐδαιμόνων.

Ιφ. Ἀτρέως ἐλέγετο δή τις Ἀγαμέμνων ἄναξ.

Ορ. οὐκ οἶδ'· ἄπελθε τοῦ λόγου τούτου, γύναι.

Ιφ. μὴ πρὸς θεῶν, ἀλλ' εἴφ', ἵν' εὐφρανθῶ, ξένε.

Ορ. τέθνηχ' ὁ τλήμων, πρὸς δ' ἀπώλεσέν τινα.   150

Ιφ. τέθνηκε; ποίᾳ συμφορᾷ; τάλαιν' ἐγώ.

Ορ. τί δ' ἐστέναξας τοῦτο; μῶν προσῆκέ σοι;

Ιφ. τὸν ὄλβον αὐτοῦ τὸν πάροιθ' ἀναστένω.

Ορ. δεινῶς γὰρ ἐκ γυναικὸς οἴχεται σφαγείς.

Ιφ. ὦ πανδάκρυτος ἡ κτανοῦσα . . . χὠ κτανών.   155

Ορ. παῦσαί νυν ἤδη μηδ' ἐρωτήσῃς πέρα.

Ιφ. τοσόνδε γ', εἰ ζῇ τοῦ ταλαιπώρου δάμαρ.

Ορ. οὐκ ἔστι· παῖς νιν ὃν ἔτεχ', οὗτος ὤλεσεν.

Ιφ. ὦ συνταραχθεὶς οἶκος. ὡς τί δὴ θέλων;

Ορ. πατρὸς θανόντος τήνδε τιμωρούμενος.   160

Ιφ. φεῦ·
ὡς εὖ κακὸν δίκαιον εἰσεπράξατο.

Ορ. ἀλλ' οὐ τὰ πρὸς θεῶν εὐτυχεῖ δίκαιος ὤν.

Ιφ. λείπει δ' ἐν οἴκοις ἄλλον Ἀγαμέμνων γόνον;

Ορ. λέλοιπεν Ἠλέκτραν γε παρθένον μίαν.

Ιφ. τί δέ; σφαγείσης θυγατρὸς ἔστι τις λόγος;   165

Ορ. οὐδείς γε, πλὴν θανοῦσαν οὐχ ὁρᾶν φάος.

Ιφ. τάλαιν' ἐκείνη χὠ κτανὼν αὐτὴν πατήρ.

IPHIGENIA IN TAURIS 31

Ορ. κακῆς γυναικὸς χάριν ἄχαριν ἀπώλετο.
Ιφ. ὁ τοῦ θανόντος δ' ἔστι παῖς "Αργει πατρός;
Ορ. ἔστ', ἄθλιός γε, κοὐδαμοῦ καὶ πανταχοῦ.   170
Ιφ. ψευδεῖς ὄνειροι, χαίρετ'· οὐδὲν ἦτ' ἄρα.

*Iphigenia now proposes that she should allow Orestes to escape if
he will take to Argos a letter telling her brother that she is
alive and asking him to come and save her. Orestes says that
Pylades must go instead, whereupon Iphigenia praises
Orestes' generosity on behalf of his friend and promises to
tend his grave after his death on the altar. She goes off to get
the letter, and Pylades tries to persuade Orestes to take his
place and escape, but Orestes reminds him that it is he
(Orestes) who is polluted by the blood-guilt of his mother's
murder and so he must stay and die.*
    *Lines 172–272. Iphigenia returns with the letter and
exchanges oaths of mutual good faith with Pylades. As an
additional safeguard in case the letter is lost in a shipwreck
she tells him its contents so that he can take them by word of
mouth to Orestes at Argos. The message reveals her name,
and Orestes at last realizes that his long-lost sister stands
before him. At first she cannot believe that he is really
Orestes, but his mention of some incidents connected with her
past life at home convinces her. Brother and sister greet each
other with tears of joy.*

Ιφ. δέλτου μὲν αἵδε πολύθυροι διαπτυχαί,
ξένοι, πάρεισιν· ἃ δ' ἐπὶ τοῖσδε βούλομαι,
ἀκοῦσατ'. οὐδεὶς αὐτὸς ἐν πόνοις τ' ἀνὴρ
ὅταν τε πρὸς τὸ θάρσος ἐκ φόβου πέσῃ.   175
ἐγὼ δὲ ταρβῶ μὴ ἀπονοστήσας χθονὸς
θῆται παρ' οὐδὲν τὰς ἐμὰς ἐπιστολὰς
ὁ τήνδε μέλλων δέλτον εἰς "Αργος φέρειν.
Ορ. τί δῆτα βούλῃ; τίνος ἀμηχανεῖς πέρι;
Ιφ. ὅρκον δότω μοι τάσδε πορθμεύσειν γραφὰς   180

πρὸς "Αργος, οἷσι βούλομαι πέμψαι φίλων.
Ορ. ἦ κἀντιδώσεις τῷδε τοὺς αὐτοὺς λόγους;
Ιφ. τί χρῆμα δράσειν ἢ τί μὴ δράσειν; λέγε.
Ορ. ἐκ γῆς ἀφήσειν μὴ θανόντα βαρβάρου.
Ιφ. δίκαιον εἶπας· πῶς γὰρ ἀγγείλειεν ἄν;   185
Ορ. ἦ καὶ τύραννος ταῦτα συγχωρήσεται;
Ιφ. ναί.
πείσω σφε, καὐτὴ ναὸς εἰσβήσω σκάφος.
Ορ. ὄμνυ· σὺ δ' ἔξαρχ' ὅρκον ὅστις εὐσεβής.
Ιφ. δώσω, λέγειν χρή, τήνδε τοῖσι σοῖς φίλοις.
Πυ. τοῖς σοῖς φίλοισι γράμματ' ἀποδώσω τάδε.   190
Ιφ. κἀγὼ σὲ σώσω κυανέας ἔξω πέτρας.
Πυ. τίν' οὖν ἐπόμνυς τοισίδ' ὅρκιον θεῶν;
Ιφ. "Αρτεμιν, ἐν ἧσπερ δώμασιν τιμὰς ἔχω.
Πυ. ἐγὼ δ' ἄνακτά γ' οὐρανοῦ, σεμνὸν Δία.
Ιφ. εἰ δ' ἐκλιπὼν τὸν ὅρκον ἀδικοίης ἐμέ;   195
Πυ. ἄνοστος εἴην· τί δὲ σύ, μὴ σώσασά με;
Ιφ. μήποτε κατ' "Αργος ζῶσ' ἴχνος θείην ποδός.
Πυ. ἐξαίρετόν μοι δὸς τόδ', ἤν τι ναῦς πάθῃ,
χἠ δέλτος ἐν κλύδωνι χρημάτων μέτα
ἀφανὴς γένηται, σῶμα δ' ἐκσώσω μόνον,   200
τὸν ὅρκον εἶναι τόνδε μηκέτ' ἔμπεδον.
Ιφ. ἀλλ' οἶσθ' ὃ δράσω; πολλὰ γὰρ πολλῶν κυρεῖ·
τἀνόντα κἀγγεγραμμέν' ἐν δέλτου πτυχαῖς
λόγῳ φράσω σοι πάντ' ἀναγγεῖλαι φίλοις.
ἐν ἀσφαλεῖ γάρ· ἢν μὲν ἐκσώσῃς γραφήν,   205
αὐτὴ φράσει σιγῶσα τἀγγεγραμμένα·
ἢν δ' ἐν θαλάσσῃ γράμματ' ἀφανισθῇ τάδε,
τὸ σῶμα σώσας τοὺς λόγους σώσεις ἐμοί.
Πυ. καλῶς ἔλεξας τῶν τε σῶν ἐμοῦ θ' ὕπερ.
σήμαινε δ' ᾧ χρὴ τάσδ' ἐπιστολὰς φέρειν   210
πρὸς "Αργος ὅ τι τε χρὴ κλύοντα σοῦ λέγειν.

Ιφ. ἄγγελλ' Ὀρέστῃ, παιδὶ τῷ Ἀγαμέμνονος·
'Η 'ν Αὐλίδι σφαγεῖσ' ἐπιστέλλει τάδε
ζῶσ' Ἰφιγένεια, τοῖς ἐκεῖ δ' οὐ ζῶσ' ἔτι ...
Ορ. ποῦ δ' ἔστ' ἐκείνη ; κατθανοῦσ' ἥκει πάλιν;   215
Ιφ. ἥδ' ἣν ὁρᾷς σύ· μὴ λόγοις ἔκπλησσέ με.
Κόμισαί μ' ἐς Ἄργος, ὦ σύναιμε, πρὶν θανεῖν,
ἐκ βαρβάρου γῆς καὶ μετάστησον θεᾶς
σφαγίων, ἐφ' οἷσι ξενοφόνους τιμὰς ἔχω.
Ορ. Πυλάδη, τί λέξω; ποῦ ποτ' ὄνθ' ηὑρήμεθα;   220
Ιφ. ἢ σοῖς ἀραία δώμασιν γενήσομαι,
Ὀρέστ'—ἵν' αὖθις ὄνομα δὶς κλύων μάθῃς.
Πυ. ὦ θεοί. Ιφ. τί τοὺς θεοὺς ἀνακαλεῖς ἐν τοῖς ἐμοῖς;
Πυ. οὐδέν· πέραινε δ'· ἐξέβην γὰρ ἄλλοσε.
Ιφ. λέγ' οὕνεκ' ἔλαφον ἀντιδοῦσά μου θεὰ   225
Ἄρτεμις ἔσωσέ μ', ἣν ἔθυσ' ἐμὸς πατήρ,
δοκῶν ἐς ἡμᾶς ὀξὺ φάσγανον βαλεῖν,
ἐς τήνδε δ' ᾤκισ' αἶαν. αἵδ' ἐπιστολαί,
τάδ' ἐστὶ τἀν δέλτοισιν ἐγγεγραμμένα.
Πυ. ὦ ῥᾳδίοις ὅρκοισι περιβαλοῦσά με,   230
κάλλιστα δ' ὀμόσασ', οὐ πολὺν σχήσω χρόνον,
τὸν δ' ὅρκον ὃν κατώμοσ' ἐμπεδώσομεν.
ἰδού, φέρω σοι δέλτον ἀποδίδωμί τε,
Ὀρέστα, τῆσδε σῆς κασιγνήτης πάρα.
Ορ. δέχομαι· παρεὶς δὲ γραμμάτων διαπτυχὰς   235
τὴν ἡδονὴν πρῶτ' οὐ λόγοις αἱρήσομαι.
ὦ φιλτάτη μοι σύγγον', ἐκπεπληγμένος
ὅμως σ' ἀπίστῳ περιβαλὼν βραχίονι
ἐς τέρψιν εἶμι, πυθόμενος θαυμάστ' ἐμοί.
ὦ συγκασιγνήτη τε κἀκ ταὐτοῦ πατρὸς   240
Ἀγαμέμνονος γεγῶσα, μή μ' ἀποστρέφου,
ἔχουσ' ἀδελφόν, οὐ δοκοῦσ' ἕξειν ποτέ.
Ιφ. ἐγώ σ' ἀδελφὸν τὸν ἐμόν; οὐ παύσῃ λέγων;

τὸ δ' "Αργος αὐτοῦ μεστὸν ἤ τε Ναυπλία.

Ορ. οὐκ ἔστ' ἐκεῖ σός, ὦ τάλαινα, σύγγονος. 245

Ιφ. ἀλλ' ἡ Λάκαινα Τυνδαρίς σ' ἐγείνατο;

Ορ. Πέλοπός γε παιδὶ παιδός, οὗ 'κπέφυκ' ἐγώ.

Ιφ. τί φῄς; ἔχεις τι τῶνδέ μοι τεκμήριον;

Ορ. ἔχω. πατρῴων ἐκ δόμων τι πυνθάνου.

Ιφ. οὐκοῦν λέγειν μὲν χρὴ σέ, μανθάνειν δ' ἐμέ. 250

Ορ. λέγοιμ' ἂν ἀκοῇ πρῶτον Ἠλέκτρας τάδε·
'Ατρέως Θυέστου τ' οἶσθα γενομένην ἔριν;

Ιφ. ἤκουσα· χρυσῆς ἀρνὸς ἦν νείκη πέρι.

Ορ. ταῦτ' οὖν ὑφήνασ' οἶσθ' ἐν εὐπήνοις ὑφαῖς;

Ιφ. ὦ φίλτατ', ἐγγὺς τῶν ἐμῶν κάμπτεις φρενῶν. 255

Ορ. εἰκώ τ' ἐν ἱστοῖς ἡλίου μετάστασιν;

Ιφ. ὕφηνα καὶ τόδ' εἶδος εὐμίτοις πλοκαῖς.

Ορ. καὶ λούτρ' ἐς Αὖλιν μητρὸς ἀνεδέξω πάρα;

Ιφ. οἶδ'· οὐ γὰρ ὁ γάμος ἐσθλὸς ὤν μ' ἀφείλετο.

Ορ. τί γάρ; κόμας σὰς μητρὶ δοῦσα σῇ φέρειν; 260

Ιφ. μνημεῖά γ' ἀντὶ σώματος τοὐμοῦ τάφῳ.

Ορ. ἃ δ' εἶδον αὐτός, τάδε φράσω τεκμήρια·
Πέλοπος παλαιὰν ἐν δόμοις λόγχην πατρός,
ἣν χερσὶ πάλλων παρθένον Πισάτιδα
ἐκτήσαθ' Ἱπποδάμειαν, Οἰνόμαον κτανών, 265
ἐν παρθενῶσι τοῖσι σοῖς κεκρυμμένην.

Ιφ. ὦ φίλτατ', οὐδὲν ἄλλο, φίλτατος γὰρ εἶ,
ἔχω σ', Ὀρέστα, τηλύγετον ἀπὸ πατρίδος
Ἀργόθεν, ὦ φίλος.

Ορ. κἀγώ σε τὴν θανοῦσαν, ὡς δοξάζεται. 270
κατὰ δὲ δάκρυα, κατὰ δὲ γόος χαρά θ' ἅμα
τὸ σὸν νοτίζει βλέφαρον, ὡσαύτως δ' ἐμόν.

*Iphigenia learns that Pylades has married her sister Electra and
that Orestes was pursued by the avenging Furies for killing*

PELOPS AND HIPPODAMIA.

From a fifth-century B.C. Attic vase at Arezzo. Pelops rides in his chariot over the sea (indicated by the dolphin on the right), carrying off his newly-won bride Hippodamia. Two of Aphrodite's doves, symbolic of love, fly before her.

his mother and was tried for matricide at the court of the Areopagus at Athens, where he was acquitted by the aid of Apollo and Athena. But he was still harried by some of the Furies and was sent by Apollo to fetch the image of Artemis from among the Tauri, after which he would have relief from his Fury-inspired madness. Iphigenia suggests telling Thoas, king of the country, that both the strangers are defiled by blood-guilt of slaying their mother, which she must cleanse from them and from the image by purifying them in the sea. She will take them to the shore near where the ship is hidden and then all can escape together. Orestes and Pylades now enter the temple. The Chorus agrees to help in the deception, and sings an ode of longing for Greece, to which Iphigenia will soon return, though they must remain in captivity.

Lines 273–318. Enter King Thoas, who finds Iphigenia with the image of Artemis in her hands. She tells him the story already arranged about the need for cleansing it and the strangers from the pollution of blood by washing them in the sea, with which he is satisfied.

35

ΘΟΑΣ

ἔα·
τί τόδε μεταίρεις ἐξ ἀκινήτων βάθρων,
Ἀγαμέμνονος παῖ, θεᾶς ἄγαλμ' ἐν ὠλέναις;

Ιφ. ἄναξ, ἔχ' αὐτοῦ πόδα σὸν ἐν παραστάσιν.　　　275

Θο. τί δ' ἔστιν, Ἰφιγένεια, καινὸν ἐν δόμοις;

Ιφ. ἀπέπτυσ'· Ὁσίᾳ γὰρ δίδωμ' ἔπος τόδε.

Θο. τί φροιμιάζῃ νεοχμόν; ἐξαύδα σαφῶς.

Ιφ. οὐ καθαρά μοι τὰ θύματ' ἠγρεύσασθ', ἄναξ.

Θο. τί τοὐκδιδάξαν τοῦτό σ'; ἢ δόξαν λέγεις;　　　280

Ιφ. βρέτας τὸ τῆς θεοῦ πάλιν ἕδρας ἀπεστράφη.

Θο. αὐτόματον, ἤ νιν σεισμὸς ἔστρεψε χθονός;

Ιφ. αὐτόματον· ὄψιν δ' ὀμμάτων ξυνήρμοσεν.

Θο. ἡ δ' αἰτία τίς; ἢ τὸ τῶν ξένων μύσος;

Ιφ. ἥδ', οὐδὲν ἄλλο· δεινὰ γὰρ δεδράκατον.　　　285

Θο. ἀλλ' ἦ τιν' ἔκανον βαρβάρων ἀκτῆς ἔπι;

Ιφ. οἰκεῖον ἦλθον τὸν φόνον κεκτημένοι.

Θο. τίν'; εἰς ἔρον γὰρ τοῦ μαθεῖν πεπτώκαμεν.

Ιφ. μητέρα κατειργάσαντο κοινωνῷ ξίφει.

Θο. Ἄπολλον, οὐδ' ἐν βαρβάροις ἔτλη τις ἄν.　　　290

Ιφ. πάσης διωγμοῖς ἠλάθησαν Ἑλλάδος.

Θο. ἦ τῶνδ' ἕκατι δῆτ' ἄγαλμ' ἔξω φέρεις;

Ιφ. σεμνόν γ' ὑπ' αἰθέρ', ὡς μεταστήσω φόνου.

Θο. μίασμα δ' ἔγνως τοῖν ξένοιν ποίῳ τρόπῳ;

Ιφ. ἤλεγχον, ὡς θεᾶς βρέτας ἀπεστράφη πάλιν.　　　295

Θο. σοφήν σ' ἔθρεψεν Ἑλλάς, ὡς ᾖσθου καλῶς.

Ιφ. καὶ μὴν καθεῖσαν δέλεαρ ἡδύ μοι φρενῶν.

Θο. τῶν Ἀργόθεν τι φίλτρον ἀγγέλλοντέ σοι;

Ιφ. τὸν μόνον Ὀρέστην ἐμὸν ἀδελφὸν εὐτυχεῖν.

Θο. ὡς δή σφε σώσαις ἡδοναῖς ἀγγελμάτων.　　　300

Ιφ. καὶ πατέρα γε ζῆν καὶ καλῶς πράσσειν ἐμόν.

Θο. σὺ δ' ἐς τὸ τῆς θεοῦ γ' ἐξένευσας εἰκότως.

Ιφ. πᾶσάν γε μισοῦσ' Ἑλλάδ', ἥ μ' ἀπώλεσεν.
Θο. τί δῆτα δρῶμεν, φράζε, τοῖν ξένοιν πέρι;
Ιφ. τὸν νόμον ἀνάγκη τὸν προκείμενον σέβειν.   305
Θο. οὔκουν ἐν ἔργῳ χέρνιβες ξίφος τε σόν;
Ιφ. ἁγνοῖς καθαρμοῖς πρῶτά νιν νίψαι θέλω.
Θο. πηγαῖσιν ὑδάτων ἢ θαλασσίᾳ δρόσῳ;
Ιφ. θάλασσα κλύζει πάντα τἀνθρώπων κακά.
Θο. ὁσιώτερον γοῦν τῇ θεῷ πέσοιεν ἄν.   310
Ιφ. καὶ τἀμά γ' οὕτω μᾶλλον ἂν καλῶς ἔχοι.
Θο. οὔκουν πρὸς αὐτὸν ναὸν ἐκπίπτει κλύδων;
Ιφ. ἐρημίας δεῖ· καὶ γὰρ ἄλλα δράσομεν.
Θο. ἄγ' ἔνθα χρῄζεις· οὐ φιλῶ τἄρρηθ' ὁρᾶν.
Ιφ. ἁγνιστέον μοι καὶ τὸ τῆς θεοῦ βρέτας.   315
Θο. εἴπερ γε κηλὶς ἔβαλέ νιν μητροκτόνος.
Ιφ. οὐ γάρ ποτ' ἄν νιν ἠράμην βάθρων ἄπο.
Θο. δίκαιος ηὐσέβεια καὶ προμηθία.

Iphigenia tells Thoas to proclaim that everyone must remain indoors to avoid the pollution of the Greek strangers ; he must purify the temple and not be surprised if she stays on the sea-shore for some time. Thoas then enters the temple and Iphigenia goes down to the shore with the two Greeks. The Chorus sings an ode in honour of the oracle of Apollo at Delphi, and a messenger enters to say that the strangers have made off with the image. The Chorus tries to delay the pursuit by saying that Thoas is not in the temple, but he has heard voices and comes out to learn what has happened.

Lines 319–448. The messenger describes how Iphigenia went away out of sight with the strangers as though to purify them. After waiting a long time he and his companions followed to see what was going on, because they feared that she had been killed by the captives. A Greek ship was about to take the party on board, so the Taurians seized Iphigenia, but they were worsted in the fight that followed and the ship put out to sea. In spite of Iphigenia's prayers to Artemis it could not clear the harbour mouth and was thrown on to the rocks, where the Taurians secured it with ropes. Thoas sends a party to bring back the Greeks for execution, but the goddess Athena at this moment appears suspended above the stage as dea ex machina (see Introduction, page xxiv) and tells Thoas to call off his pursuit because Orestes is obeying the commands of Apollo. (Orestes is to institute at Halae and Brauron in Attica the worship of Artemis Tauropolos, of whom Iphigenia will be the priestess at Brauron, but the former human sacrifices are to cease; this part of Athena's speech is omitted.) Thoas accepts the goddess's commands (which include the sending back of the Chorus to Greece) and Athena promises to escort the fugitives, together with the image of Artemis, to Athens.

ΑΓΓΕΛΟΣ

ἡ νεᾶνις ἡ .'νθάδε

βωμοῖς παρίστατ', 'Ιφιγένει', ἔξω χθονὸς   320
σὺν τοῖς ξένοισιν οἴχεται, σεμνὸν θεᾶς
ἄγαλμ' ἔχουσα· δόλια δ' ἦν καθάρματα.

Θο. πῶς φής; τί πνεῦμα συμφορᾶς κεκτημένη;

Αγ. σώζουσ' Ὀρέστην· τοῦτο γὰρ σὺ θαυμάσῃ.

Θο. τὸν ποῖον; ἆρ' ὃν Τυνδαρὶς τίκτει κόρη;   325

Αγ. ὃν τοῖσδε βωμοῖς θεὰ καθωσιώσατο.

Θο. ὦ θαῦμα—πῶς σε μεῖζον ὀνομάσας τύχω;

Αγ. μὴ 'νταῦθα τρέψῃς σὴν φρέν', ἀλλ' ἄκουέ μου·
σαφῶς δ' ἀθρήσας καὶ κλύων ἐκφρόντισον
διωγμὸς ὅστις τοὺς ξένους θηράσεται.   330

Θο. λέγ'· εὖ γὰρ εἶπας· οὐ γὰρ ἀγχίπλουν πόρον
φεύγουσιν, ὥστε διαφυγεῖν τοὐμὸν δόρυ.

Αγ. ἐπεὶ πρὸς ἀκτὰς ἤλθομεν θαλασσίας,
οὗ ναῦς Ὀρέστου κρύφιος ἦν ὡρμισμένη,
ἡμᾶς μέν, οὓς σὺ δεσμὰ συμπέμπεις ξένων   335
ἔχοντας, ἐξένευσ' ἀποστῆναι πρόσω

Ἀγαμέμνονος παῖς, ὡς ἀπόρρητον φλόγα
θύουσα καὶ καθαρμὸν ὃν μετῴχετο,
αὐτὴ δ᾽ ὄπισθε δέσμ᾽ ἔχουσα τοῖν ξένοιν
ἔστειχε χερσί. καὶ τάδ᾽ ἦν ὕποπτα μέν,   340
ἤρεσκε μέντοι σοῖσι προσπόλοις, ἄναξ.
  χρόνῳ δ᾽, ἵν᾽ ἡμῖν δρᾶν τι δὴ δοκοῖ πλέον,
ἀνωλόλυξε καὶ κατῇδε βάρβαρα
μέλη μαγεύουσ᾽, ὡς φόνον νίζουσα δή.
ἐπεὶ δὲ δαρὸν ἦμεν ἥμενοι χρόνον,   345
ἐσῆλθεν ἡμᾶς μὴ λυθέντες οἱ ξένοι
κτάνοιεν αὐτὴν δραπέται τ᾽ οἰχοίατο.
φόβῳ δ᾽ ἃ μὴ χρῆν εἰσορᾶν καθήμεθα
σιγῇ· τέλος δὲ πᾶσιν ἦν αὐτὸς λόγος
στείχειν ἵν᾽ ἦσαν, καίπερ οὐκ ἐωμένοις.   350
  κἀνταῦθ᾽ ὁρῶμεν Ἑλλάδος νεὼς σκάφος
ταρσῷ κατήρει πίτυλον ἐπτερωμένον,
ναύτας τε πεντήκοντ᾽ ἐπὶ σκαλμῶν πλάτας
ἔχοντας, ἐκ δεσμῶν δὲ τοὺς νεανίας
ἐλευθέρους. πρύμνηθεν ἑστῶτες νεὼς   355
σπεύδοντες ἦγον διὰ χερῶν πρυμνήσια,
κοντοῖς δὲ πρῷραν εἶχον, οἱ δ᾽ ἐπωτίδων
ἄγκυραν ἐξανῆπτον, οἱ δὲ κλίμακας
πόντῳ διδόντες τοῖν ξένοιν καθίεσαν.
  ἡμεῖς δ᾽ ἀφειδήσαντες, ὡς ἐσείδομεν   360
δόλια τεχνήματ᾽, εἰχόμεσθα τῆς ξένης
πρυμνησίων τε, καὶ δι᾽ εὐθυντηρίας
οἴακας ἐξηροῦμεν εὐπρύμνου νεώς.
λόγοι δ᾽ ἐχώρουν· Τίνι λόγῳ πορθμεύετε
κλέπτοντες ἐκ γῆς ξόανα καὶ θυηπόλους;   365
τίνος τίς ὢν σὺ τήνδ᾽ ἀπεμπολᾷς χθονός;
ὁ δ᾽ εἶπ᾽· Ὀρέστης, τῆσδ᾽ ὅμαιμος, ὡς μάθῃς,
Ἀγαμέμνονος παῖς, τήνδ᾽ ἐμὴν κομίζομαι

λαβὼν ἀδελφήν, ἣν ἀπώλεσ' ἐκ δόμων.
ἀλλ' οὐδὲν ἧσσον εἰχόμεσθα τῆς ξένης   370
καὶ πρὸς σ' ἔπεσθαι διεβιαζόμεσθά νιν·
ὅθεν τὰ δεινὰ πλήγματ' ἦν γενειάδων.
κεῖνοί τε γὰρ σίδηρον οὐκ εἶχον χεροῖν
ἡμεῖς τε· πυγμαί τ' ἦσαν ἐγκροτούμεναι,
καὶ κῶλ' ἀπ' ἀμφοῖν τοῖν νεανίαιν ἅμα   375
ἐς πλευρὰ καὶ πρὸς ἧπαρ ἠκοντίζετο,
ὡς τῷ ξυνάπτειν καὶ συναποκαμεῖν μέλη.
δεινοῖς δὲ σημάντροισιν ἐσφραγισμένοι
ἐφεύγομεν πρὸς κρημνόν, οἱ μὲν ἐν κάρᾳ
κάθαιμ' ἔχοντες τραύμαθ', οἱ δ' ἐν ὄμμασιν·   380
ὄχθοις δ' ἐπισταθέντες εὐλαβεστέρως
ἐμαρνάμεσθα καὶ πέτρους ἐβάλλομεν.
ἀλλ' εἶργον ἡμᾶς τοξόται πρύμνης ἔπι
σταθέντες ἰοῖς, ὥστ' ἀναστεῖλαι πρόσω.
κἂν τῷδε—δεινὸς γὰρ κλύδων ὤκειλε ναῦν   385
πρὸς γῆν, φόβος δ' ἦν παρθένῳ τέγξαι πόδα—
λαβὼν Ὀρέστης ὧμον εἰς ἀριστερόν,
βὰς ἐς θάλασσαν κἀπὶ κλίμακος θορών,
ἔθηκ' ἀδελφὴν ἐντὸς εὐσήμου νεώς,
τό τ' οὐρανοῦ πέσημα, τῆς Διὸς κόρης   390
ἄγαλμα. ναὸς δ' ἐκ μέσης ἐφθέγξατο
βοή τις· Ὦ τῆσδ' Ἑλλάδος ναῦται νεώς,
λάβεσθε κώπης ῥόθιά τ' ἐκλευκαίνετε·
ἔχομεν γὰρ ὧνπερ οὕνεκ' ἄξενον πόρον
Συμπληγάδων ἔσωθεν εἰσεπλεύσαμεν.   395
οἱ δὲ στεναγμὸν ἡδὺν ἐκβρυχώμενοι
ἔπαισαν ἅλμην. ναῦς δ', ἕως μὲν ἐντὸς ἦν
λιμένος, ἐχώρει, στόμια διαπερῶσα δὲ
λάβρῳ κλύδωνι συμπεσοῦσ' ἠπείγετο·
δεινὸς γὰρ ἐλθὼν ἄνεμος ἐξαίφνης νεὼς   400

ὠθεῖ παλίμπρυμν' ἐστί· οἱ δ' ἐκαρτέρουν
πρὸς κῦμα λακτίζοντες· ἐς δὲ γῆν πάλιν
κλύδων παλίρρους ἦγε ναῦν. σταθεῖσα δὲ
'Αγαμέμνονος παῖς ηὔξατ'· *Ω Λητοῦς κόρη
σῶσόν με τὴν σὴν ἱερέαν πρὸς 'Ελλάδα   405
ἐκ βαρβάρου γῆς καὶ κλοπαῖς σύγγνωθ' ἐμαῖς.
φιλεῖς δὲ καὶ σὺ σὸν κασίγνητον, θεά·
φιλεῖν δὲ κἀμὲ τοὺς ὁμαίμονας δόκει.
ναῦται δ' ἐπευφήμησαν εὐχαῖσιν κόρης
παιᾶνα, γυμνὰς ἐκ πέπλων ἐπωμίδας   410
κώπῃ προσαρμόσαντες ἐκ κελεύσματος.
μᾶλλον δὲ μᾶλλον πρὸς πέτρας ᾖει σκάφος·
χὠ μέν τις ἐς θάλασσαν ὡρμήθη ποσίν,
ἄλλος δὲ πλεκτὰς ἐξανῆπτεν ἀγκύλας.
κἀγὼ μὲν εὐθὺς πρὸς σὲ δεῦρ' ἀπεστάλην,   415
σοὶ τὰς ἐκεῖθεν σημανῶν, ἄναξ, τύχας.
ἀλλ' ἕρπε, δεσμὰ καὶ βρόχους λαβὼν χεροῖν·
εἰ μὴ γὰρ οἶδμα νήνεμον γενήσεται,
οὐκ ἔστιν ἐλπὶς τοῖς ξένοις σωτηρίας.
Θο. ὦ πάντες ἀστοὶ τῆσδε βαρβάρου χθονός,   420
οὐκ εἷα πώλοις ἐμβαλόντες ἡνίας
παράκτιοι δραμεῖσθε κἀκβολὰς νεὼς
'Ελληνίδος δέξεσθε, σὺν δὲ τῇ θεῷ
σπεύδοντες ἄνδρας δυσσεβεῖς θηράσετε,
οἳ δ' ὠκυπομποὺς ἕλξετ' ἐς πόντον πλάτας;   425
ὡς ἐκ θαλάσσης ἔκ τε γῆς ἱππεύμασι
λαβόντες αὐτοὺς ἢ κατὰ στύφλου πέτρας
ῥίψωμεν, ἢ σκόλοψι πήξωμεν δέμας.

ΑΘΗΝΑ
ποῖ ποῖ διωγμὸν τόνδε πορθμεύεις, ἄναξ
Θόας; ἄκουσον τῆσδ' 'Αθηναίας λόγους.   430

παῦσαι διώκων ῥεῦμά τ' ἐξορμῶν στρατοῦ·
πεπρωμένος γὰρ θεσφάτοισι Λοξίου
δεῦρ' ἦλθ' Ὀρέστης, τόν τ' Ἐρινύων χόλον
φεύγων ἀδελφῆς τ' Ἄργος ἐσπέμψων δέμας
ἄγαλμά θ' ἱερὸν εἰς ἐμὴν ἄξων χθόνα,   435
τῶν νῦν παρόντων πημάτων ἀναψυχάς.
πρὸς μὲν σ' ὅδ' ἡμῖν μῦθος· ὃν δ' ἀποκτενεῖν
δοκεῖς Ὀρέστην ποντίῳ λαβὼν σάλῳ,
ἤδη Ποσειδῶν χάριν ἐμὴν ἀκύμονα
πόντου τίθησι νῶτα πορθμεύειν πλάτῃ.   440
Θο. ἄνασσ' Ἀθάνα, τοῖσι τῶν θεῶν λόγοις
ὅστις κλύων ἄπιστος, οὐκ ὀρθῶς φρονεῖ.
ἐγὼ δ' Ὀρέστῃ τ', εἰ φέρων βρέτας θεᾶς
βέβηκ', ἀδελφῇ τ' οὐχὶ θυμοῦμαι· τί γὰρ
πρὸς τοὺς σθένοντας θεοὺς ἀμιλλᾶσθαι καλόν;   445
ἴτωσαν ἐς σὴν σὺν θεᾶς ἀγάλματι
γαῖαν, καθιδρύσαιντό τ' εὐτυχῶς βρέτας.
παύσω δὲ λόγχην ἣν ἐπαίρομαι ξένοις
ναῶν τ' ἐρετμά, σοὶ τάδ' ὡς δοκεῖ, θεά.
Ἀθ. αἰνῶ· τὸ γὰρ χρεὼν σοῦ τε καὶ θεῶν κρατεῖ.   450
ἴτ', ὦ πνοαί, ναυσθλοῦσθε τὸν Ἀγαμέμνονος
παῖδ' εἰς Ἀθήνας· συμπορεύσομαι δ' ἐγὼ
σῴζουσ' ἀδελφῆς τῆς ἐμῆς σεμνὸν βρέτας.

[Exeunt omnes

NOTES

IPHIGENIA IN AULIS

Line 1. ἐγένοντο, 'there were born to ...'. Phoebe is not usually mentioned in the legends as being one of Leda's daughters. For the spelling of Κλυταιμήστρα see note on *I.T.* 22.

l. 3. ταύτης μνηστῆρες ἦλθον, 'came as her suitors', or 'came to court her'. οἱ ... ὠλβισμένοι (from ὀλβίζω), 'those who were deemed the first in fortune in Greece'. τὰ πρῶτα is adverbial, lit. thought to be fortunate to the first, i.e. greatest, extent. The noun ὄλβος can mean either good fortune or wealth.

l. 5. δειναὶ ἀπειλαὶ καὶ φόνος is 'hendiadys' (the use of two nouns connected by 'and' instead of a noun and an adjective, like 'bread and butter', which usually means 'buttered bread') for 'dreadful threats of death'.

l. 6. ξυνίστατο, from ξυνίσταμαι, singular with φόνος but to be taken also with ἀπειλαί. ὅστις, the antecedent must be understood from the previous clause; 'threats of death were uttered (lit. arose) by each man against one another, if he did not obtain ...', lit. whoever did not obtain. μὴ λάβοι is an indefinite clause.

l. 7. ἀπόρως εἶχε = ἄπορον ἦν, 'was perplexing'; ἔχω with an adverb often equals εἰμί with the corresponding adjective.

l. 8. δοῦναί τε μὴ δοῦναί τε, 'whether to give her or not'; a double deliberative question would be more usual here. ὅπως ἅψαιτο (from ἅπτομαι) is probably another indirect deliberative question; '(for he wondered) how best he should lay hold of fortune'.

l. 9. νυν εἰσῆλθεν τάδε, 'this (idea) occurred to him, that the suitors should take an oath...'.

l. 10. δεξιὰς συμβαλεῖν ἀλλήλοισι (=ἀλλήλοις, as often in poetry), 'clasp one another's right hand'.

l. 11. δι' ἐμπύρων, 'with burnt sacrifices'.

l. 12. καθεῖναι, aorist infinitive of καθίημι, 'pour out'. The

43

sacrifices and drink-offerings were part of the ceremony of taking a solemn pledge. κἀπαράσασθαι = καὶ ἐπαράσασθαι ; this combination of words is called ' crasis '. τάδε, ' take this oath '.

l. 13. ὅτου, genitive of ὅστις ; the antecedent is τούτῳ in l. 14 ; ' to join in aiding the man whose wife the maiden . . . became '. γένοιτο is indefinite, as in l. 6, i.e. whoever he was.

l. 15. τὸν ἔχοντα, lit. him who possessed her, i.e. ' her husband '. ' If anyone should . . . and oust her husband from his marriage with her.'

l. 16. The future infinitives still depend on ἐπαράσασθαι in l. 12. κἀπιστρατεύσειν = καὶ ἐπιστρατεύσειν.

l. 17. Ἕλληνα is a feminine adjective here ; ' Greek or barbarian (i.e. non-Greek) city alike '. ὅπλων μέτα, a preposition often follows its noun at the end of a line of poetry and has its accent thrown back to the first syllable.

l. 18. εὖ πως, lit. somehow well, ' by a fine trick indeed '.

l. 20. δίδωσι, historic present, ' he allowed his daughter to choose '. ἐλέσθαι is from αἱρέω, of which εἵλετο in l. 22 is the aorist.

l. 21. ὅτου . . . φέροιεν, indefinite, as in l. 13 ; ' him whose sweet breath of love should carry her away '.

l. 22. ἢ δέ, ' and she '. ὅς σφε . . . , ' and would that he had never taken her '. The aorist of ὀφείλω with the infinitive expresses a wish for the past. Take Μενέλαον before ὅς . . .

l. 23. ὁ τὰς θεὰς κρίνας ὅδε, ' that man who judged the goddesses ', i.e. Paris, son of Priam of Troy. When invited to award the golden apple as the prize of beauty to the fairest of the three goddesses, Hera, Athena and Aphrodite, he gave it to Aphrodite, who had promised him the loveliest woman in Greece as his bride. This was Helen, with whom he eloped and thus caused the Trojan war.

l. 24. ἔχει almost equals λέγει. So in English we say ' the story has it that. . .'.

l. 25. Λακεδαίμονα, accusative of motion towards, after ἐλθών.

l. 27. ἐρῶν ἐρῶσαν, ' with mutual love ', lit. loving her who loved him.

l. 28. Ἴδης βούσταθμα. Paris had been left to die by his

parents on Mount Ida, but he survived and grew up as a shepherd (or, as here, an ox-herd) until he was acknowledged by Priam as his son. In the usual version of the story he returned to his parents at Troy after the Judgment of Paris and before his elopement with Helen. ἔκδημον λαβών, 'finding Menelaus away from home'.

l. 29. ὁ δέ, 'and he', i.e. Menelaus. οἰστρήσας δρόμῳ, 'rushing in mad haste throughout all Greece', lit. raving at a run.

l. 31. ὡς..., 'saying that they must help the injured husband', lit. those who had been wronged. τοῖσιν = τοῖς.

l. 32. τοὐντεῦθεν = τὸ ἐντεῦθεν, 'after that', or 'thereupon', accusative of respect, lit. with regard to (the thing that came) afterwards. ᾄξαντες (from ἄσσω) δορί, 'rushing out spear in hand', or 'with the spear'.

l. 33. βάθρα, accusative of motion towards, lit. to the foundations of this Aulis with the narrow strait, i.e. 'to Aulis here built near the narrow strait'. The Euripus is a wind-swept strait, at one place only 40 yards wide, separating the island of Euboea from the coast of Boeotia, where Aulis was.

l. 35. ἠσκημένοι, from ἀσκέω, 'equipped with ships and...'.

l. 36. κἀμέ = καὶ ἐμέ, 'and they chose me as supreme general', lit. to be general over all. Μενέλεω χάριν, 'for the sake of', i.e. 'out of respect for Menelaus'. When used as a preposition χάριν follows the genitive case.

l. 37. σύγγονόν γε, supply ὄντα, 'because, of course, I am his brother'. ἀξίωμα = τὸ ἀξίωμα.

l. 38. ὤφελε, see note on l. 22 : 'I wish that another had received this honour'.

l. 39. The verbs are both genitive absolute, from ἀθροίζω and ξυνίσταμαι (contracted perfect participle) respectively.

l. 40. ἥμεσθα = ἥμεθα, from ἧμαι ; this form is often found in poetry ; 'we sat idle'. ἀπλοίᾳ χρώμενοι, lit. using weather unfit for sailing, i.e. 'unable to sail', or 'weather-bound'.

l. 41. ἀπορίᾳ κεχρημένοις (from χράομαι) is a similar phrase ; 'in our perplexity'; the participle agrees with ἡμῖν understood.

l. 42. ἀνεῖλεν, from ἀναιρέω, 'announced the will of heaven

to us ', is followed first by an indirect command θῦσαι, ' that I must sacrifice ', and then by an indirect statement ἔσεσθαι, ' that there would be a voyage ', i.e. ' that the fleet would sail '.

l. 46. εἶπον with the accusative sometimes means ' I ordered '. ἀφιέναι, from ἀφίημι.

l. 47. ὡς οὔποτ' ἂν τλάς, ' for I should never bring myself to. . .'. The participle with ἄν represents οὔποτ' ἂν τλαίην of his original words, ' I should never bring myself ', a ' potential ' optative with ἄν which is frequently used as a less vivid future tense, or a polite future, like the Latin velim, which corresponds to our ' I should like '; in Greek velim would be βουλοίμην ἄν See also l. 63, note. ὡς is literally ' as ', but cannot be translated literally. κτανεῖν, aorist infinitive of κτείνω.

l. 48. οὗ δή, ' whereupon '. πάντα λόγον, ' all kinds of arguments '.

l. 49. τλῆναι δεινά, ' to bring myself to do the terrible deed '. καὶ ἐν δέλτου πτυχαῖς. A δέλτος consisted of two (or more) wooden tablets coated on the inside with wax and tied up with string, the knot of which was sealed.

l. 50. γράψας, ' having written a message ', on the wax surface.

l. 51. πέμπειν, ' bidding her send '. ὡς γαμουμένην, ' in the belief that she would marry '. lit. as though about to marry.

l. 52. τε . . . τε, ' both . . . and '. τἀνδρός = τοῦ ἀνδρός, i.e. Achilles.

l. 53. συμπλεῖν τε . . . , ' and saying that (οὔνεκα = ὅτι) he refused to sail with the Achaeans '. θέλοι is optative in indirect speech for θέλει.

l. 54. εἶσιν, from εἶμι (= ibo) ; this verb also could be optative, like θέλοι ; ' unless a bride from my family (lit. a marriage from us) went to Phthia ', the home of Achilles.

l. 55. πειθώ, accusative, ' I have this means of persuasion (to use) upon my wife ', i.e. the hope of a good marriage for her daughter.

l. 56. τολμᾷς, ' you are venturing to do '. χρεών, supply ἐστι ; the phrase is equivalent to χρή and governs σε, ' which you ought not to do '.

l. 57. ἄπελθε, ' stand back '; the old servant is trying to

snatch the letter away from Menelaus. δεσπόταισι = δεσπόταις, ' to your master ', plural for singular.

l. 58. τοὔνειδος = τὸ ὄνειδος ; ' yes (γε), the reproach that you have uttered against me is a credit to me ', because he was defending his master's property. The combination of opposite ideas in καλὸν ὄνειδος is called ' oxymoron '.

l. 59. κλαίοις ἄν, ' you would rue it ', lit. you would weep. μή is ' generic ', i.e. the sentence means ' such things as you ought not to do ', but is best translated simply as ' what you ought not to do '.

l. 60. χρῆν = ἐχρῆν, the past tense, ' you ought not to have. . . '. *φερον = ἔφερον ; this elision of a vowel at the beginning of a word is called ' prodelision '.

l. 61. οὐδέ, supply ἐχρῆν ; ' nor ought you to have been carrying (what will cause) evil to all the Greeks '. He refers to the contents of the letter, for if Clytemnestra received Agamemnon's message and kept Iphigenia at home the Greeks would never sail to Troy.

l. 62. ἀμιλλῶ, imperative. ταῦτα is adverbial accusative ; ' quarrel about this with others ', i.e. with Agamemnon. ἄφες, aorist imperative of ἀφίημι.

l. 63. οὐκ ἂν μεθείμην (from μεθίημι), ' I will not give it up '. For this ' potential ' optative with ἄν, see note on l. 47 : here the meaning is almost the same as a future indicative.

l. 64. ἄρα = ἄρα, ' then '.

l. 65. ἀλλὰ . . . τοι, ' but indeed '. εὐκλεές, supply ἐστι. For the position of ὕπερ, which governs δεσποτῶν, see note on l. 17.

l. 66. μέθες, Menelaus probably finally snatches the letter away at this point. δοῦλος ὤν . . . , ' for a slave, your words are very big '.

l. 67. ἀδικούμεσθα = ἀδικούμεθα ; the 1st person plural is often used for the singular.

l. 69. οὐδέν, adverbial accusative, ' is in no way willing to act justly '.

l. 70. τίς . . . , ' what is this. . . ? ' λόγων ἀκοσμία, lit. disorder of words, i.e. ' wrangling '. The trochaic metre (see Introduction, page xxxii) shows a more excited conversation, as in ll. 238–279.

l. 71. οὑμός = ὁ ἐμός, 'my words, not this man's, have a better right to be spoken ', lit. are more right (for me) to speak. λέγειν is ' epexegetic ' or explanatory infinitive.

l. 72. ἀφῖξαι, 2nd singular perfect of ἀφικνέομαι ; ' why have you quarrelled with this man and are dragging him away by force?' Agamemnon perhaps thought that his brother was trying to drag the slave away, letter and all.

l. 73. βλέψον, aorist imperative of βλέπω. ἡμᾶς = ἐμέ, as often in poetry. ἵν' ἀρχὰς λάβω, ' that I may make a beginning '. ταύτας is best omitted in translation.

l. 74. τρέσας, from τρέω. ἀνακαλύψω is deliberative subjunctive ; ' am I then to be afraid and not open my eyes, I who am sprung from Atreus? ' γεγώς is the contracted perfect participle of γίγνομαι, and 'Ατρέως is genitive of origin. The name Atreus is here taken to mean ' fearless ', the negative of τρέσας.

l. 76. ἀπάλλαξον, aorist imperative, ' give it up from your hands '.

l. 77. οὔ, πρὶν ἄν . . . , ' no, not until I have shown. . . '. πρὶν ἄν with the subjunctive refers to indefinite future time when there is a negative in the main clause. δείξω, aorist subjunctive of δείκνυμι. τἀγγεγραμμένα = τὰ ἐγγεγραμμένα, from ἐγγράφω.

l. 78. ἦ γάρ is a surprised question ; ' have you really opened (from ἀνίημι) the seal and do you know what (it is) not right for you to know? ' For this ' generic ' μή, see note on l. 59.

l. 79. γε often means ' yes ' or ' no ' in dialogue. ' Yes, to your sorrow (lit. so that it grieves you), for I have exposed the evils which you have done '; i.e. in telling Iphigenia not to come to Aulis. εἰργάσω, 2nd singular aorist of ἐργάζομαι.

l. 80. ποῦ δὲ καὶ ἔλαβές νιν ; ' and where then (καί) did you find him? ' νιν probably means the slave, not the letter. σῆς ἀναισχύντου φρενός is causal genitive in an exclamation ; ' Heavens! what a shameless heart you have!' θεοί is here scanned as one long syllable.

l. 81. The main verb is understood from l. 80 ; ' (I found him) while waiting to see if your daughter would come to the host.' A well-known example of this common Greek idiom, by which the subject of the indirect question is made the object of the main verb, is ' I know thee who thou art ' in St. Mark, i, 24.

l. 82. τί σε δεῖ, 'why should you...?' τὰ ἐμά, 'my affairs'. ἀναισχύντου is ' characteristic ' genitive ; ' is not this the mark of a shameless man? '

l. 83. τὸ βούλεσθαι is the subject ; ' because the wish to do so urged me on '.

l. 84. οὐχὶ δεινά, supply ἐστι ; ' is it not monstrous? ' οἰκεῖν οἶκον, ' to manage my own household ', or ' my own affairs '. ἐάσομαι is future passive, not middle, from ἐάω.

l. 85. πλάγια γάρ..., ' no, for your thoughts are shifty, now here, now there, now somewhere else,' lit. you think shifty things, some now, some formerly, some presently.

l. 86. κεκόμψευσαι, 2nd singular perfect middle of κομψεύω ; ' you have cleverly made your wicked conduct (i.e. in opening the letter) seem fine ; a clever tongue is a hateful thing.' A similar use in Latin of a neuter adjective is triste lupus stabulis (Virgil, Eclogue III, 80), ' a wolf in the cattle-stalls is a terrible thing '.

l. 87. νοῦς δέ γε, ' yes, but an inconstant mind is a possession unjust and not to be trusted by friends '.

l. 88. σ' εἰπεῖν κακῶς αὖ, ' to upbraid you in my turn '. βραχέα, adverbial accusative, ' briefly '. μή is used because of the preceding infinitive.

l. 89. τἀναιδές = τὸ ἀναιδές, ' not raising (aorist participle of ἄγω) my eyebrows (lit. eyes) too high in disdain ', lit. to shamelessness. Note the unusual ending of the comparative adverb.

l. 90. ὡς ἀδελφὸν ὄντα, in apposition to σε in l. 88 ; ' since you are...'. αἰδεῖσθαι φιλεῖ, ' is wont to show consideration for others '.

l. 91. εἰπέ, imperative. τί δεινὰ φυσᾷς ; ' why do you breathe (so) angrily? ' αἱματηρὸν ὄμμα, either ' bloodshot eyes ' or ' a face flushed with anger '.

l. 92. τοῦ (=τίνος) κέχρησαι (2nd singular perfect middle of χράομαι), ' what do you want? ' λαβεῖν means ' get ', not ' get back ', because Helen was not ' a good wife ' (χρηστὰ

λέκτρα, lit. a marriage) ; Agamemnon refers to his getting
another wife.

l. 93. οὐκ ἔχοιμι ἀν παρασχεῖν (from παρέχω), 'I could not
provide you with one ' ; another ' potential ' optative with ἄν,
for which see note on l. 47. ὧν is ' relative attraction ' for
ἐκείνων ἅ ; ' you managed badly the wife whom you did
possess ', from κτάομαι.

l. 94. δῶ, deliberative aorist subjunctive from δίδωμι ; ' am
I to pay the penalty for. . .? ' ὁ μὴ σφαλείς, ' I, one who has
not been deceived ', i.e. by his wife, as Menelaus had been.
μή is generic, as in l. 59.

l. 95. τὸ φιλότιμον τὸ ἐμόν, ' my advancement ' to be leader
of the expedition.

l. 96. γυναῖκα, governed by ἔχειν. τὸ λελογισμένον, from
λογίζομαι, lit. that which is reckoned (good) ; ' casting aside
(aorist participle, from παρίημι) discretion and honour '.

l. 97. κακαί, supply εἰσι ; ' the desires of . . . are evil '.

l. 98. γνούς, from γιγνώσκω, ' having decided wrongly
before '. μετετέθην, from μετατίθεμαι, ' have changed my
mind through good counsel '.

l. 99. σὺ μᾶλλον, supply μαίνει. ὅστις . . ., ' because you,
having lost (from ἀπόλλυμι) a bad wife, wish to recover her '.

l. 100. θεοῦ διδόντος, genitive absolute, ' though heaven
kindly gives you good fortune (to be rid of her) '.

l. 101. ὤμοσαν, from ὄμνυμι. ὅρκον is ' cognate ' accusative,
one that contains the same sense as the preceding intransitive
verb, like the English ' to run a race ' ; ' swore the oath
demanded by Tyndareus '. See also l. 420.

l. 102. φιλόγαμοι, ' in their eagerness to win the bride '.
'Ελπίς . . ., ' Hope, a goddess, I suppose '. The δέ clause is
omitted.

l. 103. καὶ ἐξέπραξεν αὐτό, ' has indeed (καί) brought it
to pass '. αὐτό is the fulfilment of the oath to recover Helen,
which each suitor carried out in the hope of still getting Helen
as his wife, according to Agamemnon's argument.

l. 104. οὕς refers to μνηστῆρες in l. 102 ; ' take them and
go on your expedition '. μωρίᾳ, ' in the folly '.

l. 105. τὸ θεῖον = οἱ θεοί, 'the gods are not ...; they are able (ἔχει) to ...'.

l. 106. κακῶς παγέντας (from πήγνυμι), 'sworn to no good purpose'.

l. 107. τὰ ἐμὰ τέκνα, plural but meaning only Iphigenia. 'γώ = ἐγώ. The οὐ in κοὐ negatives both the μέν and the δέ clauses; 'your fortunes (τὸ σόν) will not prosper (εὖ ἔσται), contrary to justice, in your vengeance on ..., while nights and days make me pine away with tears'. κοὐ = καὶ οὐ.

l. 110. ἄνομα κοὐ δίκαια and παῖδας are double accusatives after δρῶντα, ' doing (i.e. having done, a historic present) lawless ... things to the children whom I begot (from γεννάω).'

l. 111. λέλεκται, from λέγω; tr. 'I have spoken these words'. ῥάδια, 'easy to understand'.

l. 112. φρονεῖν εὖ, 'to be wise', lit. to think well. βούλῃ = βούλει. τὰ ἐμὰ θήσω (from τίθημι), 'I shall manage my own affairs'.

l. 113. τοὐμοῦ = τοῦ ἐμοῦ.

l. 114. ἐκλήθη, from καλέω. τὸν τεκόντα (from τίκτω) τ' 'Ατρέα, 'and by Atreus who begat (him)'.

l. 115. ἦ μήν is used after oaths; 'verily', or it can be omitted. τἀπό (= τὰ ἀπό) καρδίας, 'the thoughts of my heart'. ἐρεῖν is used as the future of εἰπεῖν.

l. 116. μὴ ... μηδέν, note the double negative, and the use of μή with a verb of swearing. 'πίτηδες = ἐπίτηδες. ὅσον φρονῶ, 'what I (really) think '.

l. 118. ὤκτιρα, from οἰκτίρω. καὐτός = καὶ αὐτός. ἀντάφῆκα, from ἀνταφίημι; supply δάκρυ as the object. πάλιν, 'in turn'.

l. 119. λόγων, 'arguments', in favour of Iphigenia's execution.

l. 120. οὐκ ... δεινός, supply ὤν, 'not being hostile towards you'. εἰμί ..., 'I now stand where you are', i.e. I have come over to your side in the argument.

l. 122. μήτ' ἀνθελέσθαι (from ἀνθαιρέομαι) τὸ ἐμόν, 'and not to put my interests before yours'. οὐ γὰρ ἔνδικον, 'for (it is) not right that you should lament and that my fortunes (τὰ ἐμά) should be prosperous '. An adverb with ἔχειν often equals the corresponding adjective with εἶναι.

l. 124. τοὺς σούς, 'your children', again referring to Iphigenia alone. ὁρᾶν φάος, a common phrase for ' to be alive '. Menelaus and Helen had a daughter called Hermione, who eventually married Orestes.

l. 126. Note the ' mixed ' condition, with the indicative in the ' if ' clause and the optative with ἄν in the main clause : ' could I not make (lit. take) another splendid marriage, if I desire a marriage? ' The plural γάμοι is often used in the singular sense.

l. 127. ἀπολέσας, ' after ruining ', i.e. by making him sacrifice his daughter. χρῆν = ἐχρῆν, ' whom I ought least of all to ruin '.

l. 128. ἕλωμαι, deliberative aorist subjunctive, from αἱρέω ; ' am I to recover Helen, a bad thing in exchange for good (= τοῦ ἀγαθοῦ) '.

l. 129. νέος ἦ, ' I was thoughtless '. πρίν in a positive sentence takes the infinitive, but ἄφρων νέος τε contains a negative idea (' not wise ') so that the indicative is used as though the sentence were negative ; ' until, considering the matter from close at hand, I saw what a (terrible) thing it was to slay one's children '.

l. 131. ἄλλως τε, ' besides '. τῆς . . . κόρης, objective genitive, ' pity for the maiden '.

l. 132. ἐννοουμένῳ, a change of case, as though μοι instead of με had preceded it ; ' as I thought about. . .'.

l. 133. The antecedent of ἥ is of course κόρης in l. 131.

l. 134. μέτα = μέτεστι, ' how is your daughter concerned with Helen? ', lit. in what (adverbial accusative) is there a share of Helen to your daughter?

l. 135. ἴτω, imperative of εἶμι (=ibo), ' let the host be disbanded and go '.

l. 136. παῦσαι, aorist imperative middle, used with the participle ; ' stop moistening. . .'.

l. 137. κἀμέ = καὶ ἐμέ.

l. 138. εἰ δέ . . . , ' if you are concerned at all in the oracles about (lit. of) your daughter, let them not concern me '. The construction with μέτεστι is the same as in l. 134. μετέστω, imperative of μέτεστι. 'μοί = ἐμοί.

l. 139. σοὶ νέμω..., 'I give up to you my part in them'.

l. 140. ἀλλά or ἀλλὰ γάρ often introduces a supposed objection ; ' but, you will say, have I made a change from those cruel arguments of mine ?'

l. 141. εἰκὸς πέπονθα (from πάσχω), lit. I have suffered what is natural, i.e. ' my change of attitude is natural '.

l. 142. μετέπεσον, from μεταπίπτω, 'I have changed my mind because I love him who was born (from φύω) from the same parents '.

l. 143. τοιοίδε..., 'such (are) the ways of..., always to follow (lit. use) the best course '. τοῖσι (=τοῖς) βελτίστοις is neuter.

l. 144. ὅτι, ' because '. παρὰ γνώμην ἐμήν, ' contrary to my expectation '.

l. 145. ὑπέθηκας, from ὑποτίθημι, lit. you have suggested words rightly and worthily of yourself, i.e. ' you have made a suggestion that is honourable and worthy of yourself'.

l. 146. ἀλλὰ ... γάρ, ' but (your words are useless) for I have come...'. Such an ' ellipse ' (omission of a sentence) is not uncommon with ἀλλὰ γάρ.

l. 148. τήν γε σήν, 'your own daughter '. κτανεῖν, from κτείνω.

l. 150. οὔκ, ἤν (= ἐάν)..., ' not if you send her...'.

l. 151. τοῦτο and ἐκεῖνο are both accusatives of respect ; ' in this matter I might act secretly (potential optative), but in the other (lit. that) I shall not '. ἐκεῖνο refers to what he is about to say in l. 153. Both verbs are from λανθάνω.

l. 152. τὸ ποῖον; ' what is that? ' οὔτοι χρή, ' you should not '.

l. 154. οὔκ, ἤν..., see note on l. 150. εὐμαρές, supply ἐστι. Menelaus' cold-blooded proposal to murder Calchas is in keeping with the character of a man who was willing to see his niece sacrificed so that he could get his wife back. It has been suggested that his sudden change of attitude about the sacrifice was not genuine but only assumed because he knew that Agamemnon was afraid of the opposition of the army and would stubbornly resist advice when he had finally made up his mind to sacrifice his daughter; readers may judge for themselves.

l. 155. πολλῷ χρόνῳ, ' after (lit. in) a long time '.

l. 156. καὶ γὰρ πατὴρ σέ, ' yes, and your father gladly (sees) you too '. τόδ' ἴσον . . . , ' what you say applies equally to us both ', lit. you say this equal on behalf of both.

l. 157. χαῖρε, ' greetings '. εὖ δέ . . . , ' you did well to send for (from ἄγω) me ', i.e. I am glad that you did.

l. 158. φῶ, from φημί, is deliberative subjunctive ; ' I do not know whether I am to say this (i.e. that I have done well) or not,' lit. how I am to say this and not say it.

l. 159. ὡς οὐ . . . , ' how troubled you look in spite of being glad to see me '. ἔκηλον is adverbial accusative, lit. not calm.

l. 160. πόλλα μέλει, ' many cares beset a man who is. . .'.

l. 161. γενοῦ, aorist imperative of γίγνομαι ; ' give yourself to me ', lit. be beside me. μὴ 'πί = μὴ ἐπί, ' do not surrender (lit. turn) yourself to cares '.

l. 162. ' my thoughts are (lit. I am) now entirely with you and nowhere else '.

l. 163. μέθες and ἔκτεινον are aorist imperatives of μεθίημι and ἐκτείνω. νυν without an accent means ' well then '. ' Relax your frown and smooth your countenance (ὄμμα) to a loving aspect'. φίλον is ' proleptic ' or anticipatory, lit. smooth your face (so that it becomes) loving.

l. 164. γέγηθα (from γηθέω), ' I rejoice as indeed I do rejoice at seeing you '.

l. 165. καὶ ἔπειτα, ' and even then '. σέθεν is a poetical form of σοῦ.

l. 166. γάρ, ' yes, for our coming absence (will be) long '. ἐπιοῦσα is from ἔπειμι. He means her to understand his absence from her when he goes to Troy, not her absence in death.

l. 167. ἐπί, ' with '.

l. 168. θέλω μέν, ' I wish (I could stay), and I grieve at not having what I wish '.

l. 169. ὄλοιντο, aorist optative of ὄλλυμι, ' a curse upon wars ', lit. may spears perish.

l. 170. ἀμέ = ἃ ἐμέ. The antecedent of ἃ is the subject of ὀλεῖ ; ' the evils which have already (πρόσθε) ruined me will also ruin others '. The aorist participle with ἔχω often has the force of a perfect indicative. Both verbs come from ὅλλυμι. This reference to her father's ruin must have puzzled Iphigenia.

l. 171. ὡς πολὺν χρόνον, 'what a long time'. ἀπῆσθα, 2nd singular imperfect of ἄπειμι. μυχοῖς, there are two bays at Aulis suitable for ships.

l. 172. καὶ νῦν γε, 'yes, and something now prevents me from sending off the host'. μή is the 'redundant' (unnecessary) negative used with verbs of preventing.

l. 173. ποῦ λέγουσι, 'where do men say that the Phrygians live? ', lit. have been settled, from οἰκίζω.

l. 174. οὗ ..., 'where I wish that Paris the (son) of Priam had never lived '. For ὤφελον, see note on l. 22.

l. 175. μακράν, 'a long way'; the feminine adjective (agreeing with ὁδόν understood) is used as an adverb. ἀπαίρεις governs ναῦν understood ; 'you are sailing' or 'departing'. λιπών, from λείπω.

l. 176. ταὐτόν = τὸ αὐτόν, 'you will meet your father once again ', lit. you will come to the same (place) as your father. He means in Hades, but she thinks he means that they will soon meet again in this world.

l. 177. εἴθε ἦν, a wish for present time, 'I wish it were possible (lit. right) for you and me that you should take me as your fellow-voyager '.

l. 178. ἔτ' ἔστι καὶ σοί ..., 'indeed you still have (before you) a voyage (i.e. across the river of death) where you will remember your father '. ἀμνήσῃ, poetic future of ἀναμιμνήσκω, and person singular.

l. 179. πλεύσασα, from πλέω.

l. 180. ἀπό, away from, i.e. 'without'. Note the uncontracted genitive of μήτηρ.

l. 181. οὔ που ..., 'can it be that you are sending me to live in ...? '

l. 182. ἔασον, aorist imperative, 'ask no more ', lit. allow it.

l. 183. σπεῦδέ μοι, 'hasten back to me '. θέμενος (from τίθημι) εὖ τὰ ἐκεῖ, 'after arranging matters there well ', i.e. victoriously.

l. 184. θῦσαι θυσίαν, 'make a sacrifice '.

l. 185. ἀλλά ..., 'well, you must pay heed to sacred things with the aid of holy rites '.

l. 186. εἴσῃ, future of οἶδα, ' you will know (what I do), for you will stand near. . .'. ἐστήξῃ, future perfect middle of ἵστημι with future simple sense.

l. 187. στήσομεν, plural for singular, ' shall I then lead the dance . . .? ', lit. set up, also from ἵστημι.

l. 188. 'μέ (ἐμέ) = ἐμαυτόν. τοῦ μηδὲν φρονεῖν, causal genitive, ' because you do not understand '. μή is always used with the infinitive except in indirect speech.

l. 189. χώρει, imperative. ὀφθῆναι, from ὀράω ; ' (it is) unpleasant for maidens to be seen (by men) '. The great gulf that existed between the sexes in heroic Greece is illustrated by this remark and by Achilles' modesty on seeing Clytemnestra in ll. 204–205 and 216–217.

l. 190. δεξιάν, lit. right hand ; tr. ' an embrace '. δοῦσα, from δίδωμι.

l. 191. μέλλουσα, ' you who are destined soon to. . .'.

l. 193. ὡς ἄχθος . . ., ' what a sorrow has the city . . . been to you '.

l. 195. διώκει με, ' overwhelms me '. ὀμμάτων, ' from my eyes ', with νοτίς.

l. 196. ἴθι, imperative of εἶμι (=ibo). σὲ παραιτοῦμαι τάδε, ' I beg you to forgive these (tears) ', on a day that ought to have been happy.

l. 199. ἀποστολαὶ . . ., ' the sending away of a daughter in marriage (is) a happy event '. ἀλλά not δέ, follows μέν here.

l. 200. τοὺς τεκόντας, ' the parents ', from τίκτω.

l. 201. πολλὰ μοχθήσας, ' after taking (so) much trouble (in bringing her up) '.

l. 203. ἐξέβην, from ἐκβαίνω.

l. 204. ὦ πότνι' αἰδώς, ' O Modesty ', lit. O queen Modesty. For Achilles' attitude to a woman, see note on l. 189. τίνα . . ., ' what lady is this that I see, possessing (from κτάομαι) beauty (so) fair? '

l. 206. οὐ θαῦμα . . ., ' (it is) not strange that you. . .'. ἡμᾶς =ἐμέ. μή is ' generic ', i.e. she was the kind of person whom he had not met before ; tr. ' since you have not met me before '.

l. 207. αἰνῶ, supply σε. τὸ σωφρονεῖν, ' modesty '.

l. 208. τί, ' why? '

l. 209. πεφραγμένους, from φράσσω.

l. 211. μοῦστίν = μοι ἐστίν, ' my husband is. . .'.

l. 212. ἐν βραχεῖ, ' in brief '. τὰ καίρια, ' the main facts ', lit. the timely things.

l. 213. αἰσχρὸν δέ μοι, ' but (it is) unfitting for me to join in conversation with a woman ', lit. with women.

l. 214. μεῖνον and σύναψον are aorist imperatives from μένω and συνάπτω.

l. 215. ἀρχήν is accusative in apposition to the preceding sentence ; ' as a happy prelude to. . .'.

l. 216. ἐγώ σοι . . . , ' I (give) my hand to you? I should be ashamed to meet Agamemnon if I were to touch what it is not right for me to touch '. ὧν μή, another ' generic ' μή ; the antecedent is ἐκείνων understood ; ' those things which (such as) it is not right. . .'.

l. 218. θέμις μάλιστα, ' it is indeed right '. γαμεῖς, future.

l. 219. θεᾶς ποτνίας, ' the queenly goddess ', i.e. Thetis.

l. 220. ἀφασία μ' ἔχει, ' I am struck dumb (with wonder) '.

l. 221. ' Unless you utter strange words because you are somewhat (τι) out of your mind '. A very ungallant remark, especially after his previous exaggerated respect.

l. 222. ἐμπέφυκεν, from ἐμφύω, ' this is natural for everyone, to be shy when seeing (i.e. meeting) new friends and speaking of marriage '.

l. 225. οὐδ' ἐξ . . . , ' nor did any talk of marriage come to me from. . .'.

l. 226. τί δῆτ' ἂν εἴη, ' what then could it be? ' σὺ πάλιν . . . , ' you in your turn may wonder at. . .'. πάλιν αὖ are sometimes thus combined.

l. 227. τὰ παρὰ σοῦ, ' your words are strange to me '.

l. 228. κοινόν . . . , ' to guess at this is a task shared by us both ', lit. common.

l. 229. ἄμφω . . . , ' perhaps we are both not mistaken in what we say ', and so between us we may learn the whole truth.

l. 230. ἀλλὰ ἤ, an indignant question, ' have I then suffered (from πάσχω) disgraceful treatment? ' μνηστεύω usually means ' to woo ' but here means ' to arrange a marriage '.

l. 231. οὐκ ὄντας..., 'that does not exist, as it seems'. εἴξασιν, 3rd plural from ἔοικα.

l. 232. κἀμέ..., 'both you and me'.

l. 233. ἀμελίᾳ δὸς αὐτά, 'disregard them ', lit. give it to disregard.

l. 234. ὀρθοῖς ὄμμασιν, 'straight in the face', lit. with straight eyes.

l. 235. γενομένη, 'being proved to be ', lit. having become. ἀνάξια is neuter plural, not feminine singular as the accent shows. The phrase is similar to πέπονθα δεινά in l. 230. Clytemnestra now realizes that she has been tricked by her husband, but she does not yet know the worst.

l. 236. τόδε, i.e. the word χαῖρε ; 'farewell from me to you also'

l. 237. ματεύσων, a purpose clause, ' to look for '.

l. 238. The next 42 lines are again in ' trochaic tetrameters ' (see Introduction, page xxxii), like ll. 70–112, and show a more excited conversation. μεῖνον, aorist imperative of μένω. ὦ, σέ τοι λέγω, ' O sir, it is you that I address '. ὦ by itself is unusual.

l. 239. γεγῶτα, contracted perfect participle of γίγνομαι, ' born from '.

l. 240. παροίξας, from παροίγω ; ' who is it who calls, having half-opened...? ' ὡς τεταρβηκώς, ' with what fear he calls us ', lit. how having feared.

l. 241. ' A slave ; I have no pride about that ', i.e. I am not ashamed to admit it.

l. 242. τίνος..., ' whose? not mine ; my slaves (τὰ ἐμά) and Agamemnon's are separate '. He means that the slaves who accompanied him have not gone into the tent and so this man cannot belong to him. κἀγαμέμνονος = καὶ Ἀγαμέμνονος.

l. 243. τῆσδε..., ' (I am the property) of her who is now in front of the tent (i.e. Clytemnestra), given by her father ', lit. her father having given.

l. 244. ἕσταμεν, perfect of ἵστημι with present meaning ; ' I am remaining ', plural for singular as με in the relative clause shows. φράζε ὧν = φράζε ἐκεῖνα ὧν οὕνεκα, lit. speak those things for which you held me back (from ἐπέχω), i.e. ' tell me why... '.

l. 245. There are three duals in this line; 'are you two really (ἢ δῆτα) standing (perfect of ἐφίσταμαι) alone beside this door? ', lit. being present at.

l. 246. λέγοις ἄν, the 'potential' optative with ἄν meaning 'you will speak '; see notes on ll. 47 and 63. ὡς μόνοιν, lit. as to (us) alone, i.e. 'to us alone '. δέ, almost like our ' so '.

l. 247. δεξιᾶς ἕκατι ..., 'do not hesitate (to speak) as far as my right hand is concerned '; she refers either to the protection of her right hand, which she now promises him, or to his kneeling to touch her hand.

l. 248. Lit. do you know me then, being who I am well-disposed ...?, i.e. 'do you know then who I am and how well-disposed...? ' For the subject of the indirect question appearing also as the object of the main verb, see note on l. 81.

l. 249. οἶδά σ' ὄντα, the usual construction of a participle instead of an infinitive after a verb of perception : ' I know that you are...'.

l. 250. χὥτι = καὶ ὅτι, ' and that ...'; verbs of perception can also take ὅτι. ἔλαβεν, 'received '.

l. 251. ἐμὸς ἦσθ' ἀεί ποτε, ' you have been my servant ever since '. κἀμός = καὶ ἐμός.

l. 252. ὧδ' ἔχει, ' that is so '. ἧσσον, ' less well-disposed ', or ' less so ', though he showed great loyalty to Agamemnon in the struggle with Menelaus over the letter.

l. 253. νῦν ποτε, ' now at last '. οὕστινας (from ὅστις) ..., ' whatever words you (intend to) say '.

l. 254. ὁ φύσας, ' who beget her '. κτενεῖν, the future infinitive is often used after μέλλω, ' to intend '.

l. 255. πῶς, ' what! ' ἀπέπτυσα, aorist with present meaning, as often with verbs expressing emotion ; ' I reject your words ', i.e. I refuse to believe them. οὐ γάρ ..., ' for you are not in your right mind '.

l. 256. There is no main verb because the slave continues his statement as if there has been no interruption.

l. 257. μεμηνὼς (from μαίνομαι) τυγχάνει, ' is he mad? ', lit. does he happen to be mad.

l. 258. τοῦτο, accusative of respect, ' on this point '.

l. 259. ἐκ τίνος λόγου, ' for what reason? ' οὑπάγων = ὁ

ἐπάγων, 'which of the avenging deities is it that drives him on? '

l. 260. θέσφατα, understand ἐπάγει αὐτόν, ' an oracle (drives him on) '.

l. 261. τάλαινα ἦν..., 'wretched (is she) whom her father...'.

l. 262. Δαρδάνου πρὸς δώματα, i.e. to Troy, which was founded by Dardanus. λάβῃ, ' recover '.

l. 263. εἰς ἄρα..., ' was the return of Helen then fated to be fraught with ruin for Iphigenia? ', lit. fated against Iphigenia.

l. 264. πάντ' ἔχεις, ' you know it all '.

l. 265. τίνα πρόφασιν, ' what was the reason for the (false) marriage by which ...? ', lit. what pretext did the marriage have?

l. 266. ἵν' ἀγάγοις (from ἄγω), ' so that you should gladly bring ... to marry her to Achilles '.

l. 267. ἐπ' ὀλέθρῳ, ' to meet your ruin '. καὶ... καί, ' both ... and '.

l. 268. πάσχετον, dual, ' you are both (lit. being two) suffering...'. δεινὰ ἔτλη, supply ποιεῖν, ' has brought himself to do...'.

l. 269. οἴχομαι, ' I am undone '. στέγει, the subject is ὄμματα, ' my eyes no longer restrain their tears '.

l. 270. τὸ στερόμενον, the article with the participle is here (and in l. 342) used, like the article with infinitive, as a noun ; ' if being deprived of your children (is) painful, shed your tears '. The old servant tries to persuade his mistress to relieve her sorrow by weeping.

l. 271. πόθεν φῄς..., ' whence do you say that you learnt and know this? ' πεπυσμένος, from πυνθάνομαι.

l. 272. ᾠχόμην, ' I went '. πρός..., ' to cancel the former message '. γεγραμμένα, from γράφω.

l. 273. οὐκ ἐῶν (from ἐάω), as though the slave who bore the letter were himself giving the order : ' forbidding me or joining in ordering me...? ' θανουμένην, ' to her death ', lit. about to die.

l. 274. μὲν οὖν, ' no, (telling you) not to bring her '. φρονῶν ἔτυχε τότ' εὖ, ' was then in his right mind '.

l. 275. κᾆτα = καὶ εἶτα. δίδως, historic present, 'why did you not give it to me so that I should receive it?' λαβεῖν is an infinitive of purpose after a verb of giving. φέρων γε, 'if you brought it'.

l. 276. ἀφείλετο, from ἀφαιρέω, takes two accusatives of which one ('it', i.e. the letter) is understood. ἡμᾶς = ἐμέ. ὅς, supply ἐστι.

l. 278. ἔκλυον, imperfect for present, 'yes, I hear that you are...'. τὸ δ' ἐμόν..., 'and I do not regard with indifference my own part in the matter'. Achilles is naturally vexed at having been made the bait in the supposed marriage.

l. 279. σοῖς..., 'having beguiled her with (the hope of) marriage to you'.

l. 280. εἰ εἶχον λόγον, 'if I had the voice'. This is an 'unfulfilled' condition, εἰ with the imperfect indicative followed by the aorist indicative with ἄν 'Ορφέως is her ea spondee.

l. 281. πείθειν ἐπᾴδουσα, 'to (be able to) persuade by my song', lit. while singing.

l. 282. οὖς, the antecedent is ἐκείνους understood, 'those whom I wished'.

l. 283. ἐνταῦθ' ἂν ἦλθον, 'I should have had recourse to it', lit. I should have gone there. νῦν δέ 'but as it is'. τἀπ' ἐμοῦ = τὰ ἐπ' ἐμοῦ, 'I will offer my tears, the only skill that is in my power'.

l. 284. δυναίμεθ' ἄν, potential optative with ἄν; 'for these I can (offer)'.

l. 285. ἱκετηρίαν..., 'I throw myself (lit. fasten my body) at your knees as though I were a suppliant's olive branch'. She kneels before him and clasps his knees in the usual attitude of a suppliant, who would also place an olive branch twined with fillets (wisps) of wool on the altar of a deity; she was as it were performing both actions at once. τοὐμόν = τὸ ἐμόν.

l. 286. ἥδε, 'my mother here'; she points to Clytemnestra

l. 287. ἀπολέσῃς, aorist subjunctive of ἀπόλλυμι. ἡδύ, supply ἐστι. τὸ φῶς βλέπειν, i.e. to be alive.

l. 288. τὰ ὑπὸ γῆς, 'the underworld'.

l. 289. πρώτη..., 'I was the first to call you father'; she was the eldest child.

l. 290. γόνασι..., 'climbing on to your knees', lit. having given my body to your knees.

l. 291. φίλας χάριτας, 'sweet pleasures', i.e. kisses and embraces.

l. 292. λόγος..., 'these were your words'.

l. 293. ὄψομαι, future of ὁράω. ἀνδρός, 'of a husband'.

l. 295. ἐξαρτωμένης agrees with the genitive implied in οὑμός (=ὁ ἐμός); 'this was my reply (λόγος understood from l. 292) as I clung to your beard', lit. of me hanging round your beard.

l. 296. οὗ νῦν..., 'which I now touch with my hand'. It was the custom for suppliants to touch the beard of the man to whom they were appealing.

l. 297. τί...σέ; supply ὄψομαι from l. 293; 'how then shall I see you (faring)?' πρέσβυν, 'you, when old'.

l. 299. πόνων..., 'repaying to you the tender care with which you brought me up', lit. the nursing upbringing (consisting) of your labours. He himself referred to this in l. 201, though not in Iphigenia's hearing.

l. 300. μνήμην ἔχω, 'I remember'.

l. 301. ἐπιλέλησαι, 2nd singular perfect of ἐπιλανθάνομαι.

l. 302. μή, supply ποιήσῃς τοῦτο. πρός σε Πέλοπος, note the order of words, in which πρός ('in the name of') governs Πέλοπος, and σε is governed by ἱκετεύω ('I beg') understood: Horace (Odes I, viii, 1) has the same order, per omnes te deos oro.

l. 303. καὶ τῆσδε μητρός..., 'and in the name of my mother here, who once bore me in travail and now feels this second agony'. ὠδίνουσα is historic present participle.

l. 305. τί μοι..., 'what have I to do with...?'

l. 306. πόθεν ἦλθε..., 'why (lit. whence) did he (i.e. Paris) come to cause my ruin?' τὠμῷ = τῷ ἐμῷ.

l. 307. Both verbs are aorist imperative. ὄμμα δός..., 'turn your face and give me a kiss'.

l. 308. ἀλλὰ τοῦτο..., 'this at least as a remembrance of you'.

l. 310. μικρός..., 'you (are) but a little ally to those who love you'. Orestes is lying in the arms of one of the Chorus.

l. 311. ἱκέτευσον here governs the genitive. Both verbs are aorist imperative.

l. 312. τὴν ... μὴ θανεῖν, indirect petition, 'that your sister should not be slain '.

l. 313. κἀν = καὶ ἐν, 'even in infants there is an inborn perception. ...'.

l. 314. σιωπῶν λίσσεται σε, 'he silently entreats you '.

l. 315. The verbs are again aorist imperative.

l. 316. ναί, πρὸς γενείου, 'indeed, by your beard '; see note on l. 301. ἀντόμεσθα = ἀντόμεθα. φίλω, nominative dual, ' we two loved ones '.

l. 317. ὁ μὲν ... ἢ δέ, 'the one ..., the other is now grown up '. ηὐξημένη, from αὐξάνω ; Iphigenia was probably 15 or 16 years old.

l. 318. ἐν συντεμοῦσα ..., 'summing up everything in one (word), I shall win the argument '.

l. 319. βλέπειν is 'epexegetic' or explanatory infinitive ; '(is) most sweet for men to look upon '.

l. 320. τὰ νέρθε δ' οὐδέν, 'and what is below is nothingness '. μαίνεται ..., 'he who wishes for death is a madman'.

l. 321. κρεῖσσον, supply ἐστί ; 'it is better to live in dishonour than to die gloriously '. This plea for life at any cost is forgotten by Iphigenia when she later resolves to die willingly for her country.

l. 322. συνετός εἰμι is treated as though it were the verb συνίημι and is followed by the accusative ; ' I understand both what arouses pity and what does not '. μή is ' generic ', i.e. such things as do not arouse pity.

l. 323. φιλῶ τε almost means ' because I love '. μαινοίμην γὰρ ἄν, ' for (otherwise) I should be mad '.

l. 324. δεινῶς ἔχει = δεινόν ἐστι ; ' it is terrible for me to bring myself to do this, lady (i.e. Clytemnestra), and terrible also not to do it '. μή here is the normal negative with an infinitive.

l. 326. ὁρᾶθ' = ὁρᾶτε, addressed to his wife and daughter ; ' you see (or it may be imperative) how great (is) this. ...'.

l. 327. ' and how many of the Greeks, lords of brazen arms, (are here) '. χαλχέων is scanned as two long syllables.

l. 328. οἷς νόστος ..., ' who cannot voyage to. ..'. For πύργους ἔπι, see note on l. 17.

l. 330. ἐστι = ἔξεστιν, 'it is possible'; 'nor can they capture'. βάθρον, 'city'.

l. 331. μέμηνε is from μαίνομαι; 'some passion rages in . . . , to sail'.

l. 333. παῦσαι τε, 'and to put a stop to the theft of Greek wives', though only one such theft, that of Helen, had taken place.

l. 334. οἵ, the antecedent is Ἑλλήνων in l. 331; 'and they will slay my daughters', i.e. Electra and Chrysothemis (I.T., 164, n.)

l. 335. ὑμᾶς, Clytemnestra and Iphigenia. λύσω, 'make void', or 'bring to naught'.

l. 336. οὐ Μενέλεως . . . , 'it is not Menelaus who has. . .'.

l. 337. ἐπὶ τὸ κείνου βουλόμενον, 'to satisfy his wishes'; for this use of the article with the participle as a substantive, see also l. 275. ἐλήλυθα, from ἔρχομαι.

l. 338. ἀλλ' Ἑλλάς, 'but it is Greece'; the verb is καταδεδούλω-ται in l. 336. ᾗ δεῖ (με) . . . , 'for which I must sacrifice you, whether I want to or not'. κἂν = καὶ ἐάν, lit. and if.

l. 339. καθέσταμεν, perfect of καθίσταμαι, 'I am bound by this (necessity)', lit. we stand weaker than this.

l. 340. νιν is Greece; 'she must be free'. ὅσον (ἐστὶν) ἐν σοὶ κἀμοί, 'as far as it concerns you and me', or 'as far as it rests in the power of you and me'.

l. 341. μηδὲ . . . , 'nor must they (i.e. our fellow-country-men), being Greeks, be robbed of their wives'. συλᾶν takes two accusatives when active and λέκτρα is one of the accusa-tives which remains when the verb becomes passive.

l. 343. εἰσακούσατε, aorist imperative plural, though μῆτερ is singular, because she addresses Achilles as well. The metre from ll. 343–376 is trochaic tetrameters again; see Introduc-tion, page xxxii.

l. 345. οὐ ῥᾴδιον (ἐστί), 'it is not easy for us to bear patiently what cannot be resisted', lit. the impossible.

l. 346. δίκαιον (ἐστί), 'it is right that we should thank (lit. praise) this stranger (i.e. Achilles) for his kindness'. προθυμίας is causal genitive.

l. 347. ἀλλὰ καί . . . , 'but you must consider this point also, that he should not be. . .'. διαβληθῇ is from διαβάλλω Although about to be killed, Iphigenia is anxious that no harm, or even slander through misrepresentation of his motives, should come upon Achilles for his offer to champion her.

l. 348. καὶ πλέον..., 'and that we get no advantage, while he meets with misfortune'. διαβληθῇ and πράξωμεν οὐδέν depends on (ὅπως) μή after ὁρᾶν, the construction of a verb of precaution, which can be the same as that of a verb of fearing ; hence the μή... οὐδέν.

l. 349. οἷα..., 'hear what (thoughts) entered my mind as I pondered '.

l. 350. μοι δέδοκται, from δοκέω, ' I am resolved ', lit. it has seemed (good) to me. τοῦτο αὐτό, ' I want to do this (i.e. to die) nobly '.

l. 351. παρεῖσα, from παρίημι, ' putting aside dishonour '.

l. 352. δεῦρο σκέψαι, aorist imperative of σκέπτομαι ; ' consider this point, how true my words are ', lit. look hither, how well I speak. ἡμῶν = ἐμοῦ.

l. 353. εἰς ἐμέ, ' mighty Greece all looks towards me '.

l. 354. καὶ ἐν ἐμοί, ' and upon me depends...'. ἐστι is understood. ναῶν = νεῶν, ' the ships '.

l. 356. μηκέθ' ἁρπάζειν ἐᾶν is another subject of ἐν ἐμοί ἐστι ; ' and if the barbarians (try to) do anything, upon me it depends to prevent them from seizing (lit. no longer to allow them to seize) our women in the future (τὰς μελλούσας) from...'.

l. 357. τὸν..., ὄλεθρον, ' when they have atoned for (from τίνω) the ruin of Helen '.

l. 358. κατθανοῦσα, ' by my death '.

l. 359. ὡς depends on κλέος, ' my fame, in that I have freed '.

l. 360. καὶ γάρ..., 'and indeed (it is) not right that I should be in any way (τι) too fond of life '.

l. 361. με κοινὸν ἔτεκες (from τίκτω), ' you bore me (as a possession) common to...'.

l. 362. πεφραγμένοι, from φράσσω.

l. 363. πατρίδος ἠδικημένης (from ἀδικέω), genitive absolute.

l. 364. δρᾶν governs τι and ἐχθρούς ; ' to strike a blow against (lit. do something to) the enemy '. χὐπέρ = καὶ ὑπέρ.

l. 365. ἡ δ' ἐμή..., ' and shall my life, mine alone...? ', lit. being one.

66   NOTES

l. 366. τί τὸ δίκαιον τοῦτο, 'how (lit. in what respect) is this
just?' ἆρ' ἔχοιμ' ἄν, 'would I be able to . . .?'; 'potential'
optative with ἄν.

l. 367. καὶ ἐπ' ἐκεῖν' ἔλθωμεν, 'and let me come to the next
point'. τόνδε is Achilles, who was willing to fight the other
Greeks to try to save Iphigenia's life. διὰ μάχης μολεῖν =
μάχεσθαι.

l. 369. εἷς ἀνὴρ κρείσσων (ἐστί) . . . , 'it is better that one
man should live than countless women', lit. one man (is) better
to see the light than. . . . γυναικῶν is genitive of comparison.

l. 371. ἐμποδὼν γενήσομαι 'γώ (ἐγώ) . . . , 'shall I, a mortal,
oppose the goddess?', lit. shall I become in the way of the
goddess?

l. 372. ἀλλ' ἀμήχανον (ἐστί), 'no, it is impossible'. τοὐμὸν = τὸ
ἐμόν.

l. 373. θύετε, supply ἐμέ as the object. ταῦτα and οὗτοι are
each 'attracted' to agree with the noun ; 'this (i.e. the story
of my willingness to die) shall be my memorial for ever (lit.
through a long time), this shall be my children. . .'. The verb
is ἔσται understood.

l. 375. εἰκός . . . , '(it is) right that Greeks should rule
barbarians, but not that barbarians should rule Greeks ; for the
one are slaves, the others free '. Note the neuter singular in
τὸ μέν, followed by the masculine plural οἱ δέ ; there is no
particular reason for this, except perhaps convenience of
scansion. The Greeks of the classical era (500–330 B.C.) thought
that all barbarians, i.e. non-Greeks, were φύσει δοῦλοι, 'slaves
by nature '.

l. 378. ἔμελλε . . . εἰ τύχοιμι, a 'mixed' conditional clause ;
'some god intended to make (from τίθημι) me happy, if I
were to obtain you in marriage ', lit. your marriage.

l. 379. ζηλῶ . . . , 'I envy Greece because of you, and you
because of Greece '. The genitives are causal.

l. 381. μᾶλλον δὲ λέκτρων . . . , 'a longing to marry you
comes over me all the more now that I have looked upon your
character '.

l. 383. ὅρα, imperative, 'consider '.

l. 384. ἄχθομαι, present for future, 'I shall be vexed—let

Thetis be my witness (lit. let her know ; imperative of οἶδα)—
if I do not. . .'.

l. 385. διὰ μάχης ἐλθών = μαχεσάμενος, as in l. 367.

l. 386. ἄθρησον . . . , ' consider ; death (is) a dreadful evil '.

l. 387. ἡ Τυνδαρὶς παῖς . . . , ' it is enough that the daughter
of Tyndareus (Helen) should cause battles . . . because of her
beauty (σῶμα) , lit. she suffices causing battles.

l. 389. The present imperative and the aorist subjunctive,
both with μή, are here used in the same line to express negative
commands.

l. 390. ἔα, imperative of ἐάω. ἢν δυνώμεθα = ἐὰν δύνωμαι.

l. 391. ὦ λῆμ' ἄριστον, ' o heroic heart '. οὐκ ἔχω = οὐ δύναμαι.
πρὸς τοῦτο, ' in reply to this '.

l. 392. σοι τάδε δοκεῖ, ' this is your resolve ' ; see also l. 350.
γενναῖα is neuter accusative, as the accent shows (in l. 382
γενναία is feminine) ; ' your intention is noble ', lit. you think
noble things.

l. 393. τί γὰρ τὸ ἀληθές . . . , ' why should one not speak the
truth? ' ; a ' potential ' optative with ἄν, as also is μεταγνοίης
in l. 394.

l. 394. κἄν = καὶ ἄν, ' you might perhaps still (καί) change your
mind (aorist optative of μεταγιγνώσκω) about this '.

l. 396. ὡς οὐκ ἐάσων, expressing an intention in the future,
' ready, not to allow you, but to prevent you from being slain '.

l. 397. χρήσῃ = χρήσει, from χράομαι, ' perhaps (τάχα) even
then you will accept my offer ', lit. use my words.

l. 398. πέλας of course governs σῆς δέρης.

l. 399. κόρας, ' your eyes '. Elsewhere in this book it means
' maiden ' or ' daughter '.

l. 400. πρόφασιν ὥστε . . . , ' a good reason to. . .'. φρένα, ' in
my heart ' ; accusative of respect, like τάδε and οὐδέν in the
next two lines.

l. 401. παῦσαι (' stop weeping ') and πιθοῦ (from πείθω) are
aorist imperatives. 'μέ = ἐμέ. τάδε . . . , ' obey me in this '.

l. 402. ὡς παρ' ἡμῶν . . . , ' for you will not be wronged in
anything by me ', although she has been so terribly wronged
by her father. ἀδικήσῃ is future middle used as passive.

l. 403. ἐκτέμῃς, aorist subjunctive of ἐκτέμνω. In English

we should take σόν with τριχός (from θρίξ) instead of with
πλόκαμον, ' a lock of your hair '. It was customary to cut off
a lock of one's hair and lay it on the tomb of a loved one as a
mark of sorrow. The second μήτε does not appear because
Iphigenia is interrupted by her mother's question.

l. 404. τί δή . . . , ' what do you mean by this? (Must I not
mourn for you) after I have lost you? '

l. 405. οὐ σύ γε, ' no, you (will not lose me) '. σέσωσμαι,
from σώζω. κατ' ἐμέ = τὸ κατ' ἐμέ, ' as far as I am concerned ',
i.e. as far as I can make you. ἔση = ἔσει, from εἰμί.

l. 406. πῶς εἶπας, ' what do you mean? Must I not . . . ?'
ψυχήν, we should say ' mourn for your death ', not ' your life '.

l. 407. χωσθήσεται, from χόω. Her body is to be burnt on
the altar after the sacrifice, so that there will be no tomb.

l. 408. τί δαί, ' what then? It is the death, not the burial,
that is remembered ', lit. is considered.

l. 409. μοι μνῆμα, supply ἔσται . . . , ' shall be my memorial '.
Διός, from Ζεύς ; he was the father of Artemis. τῆς . . . κόρης
is in apposition to θεᾶς.

l. 410. ἀλλά, ' well, then '.

l. 411. ὡς . . . γε . . . , ' yes, (I speak) as one who is happy
and . . .'.

l. 412. τί ἀγγελῶ, ' what message shall I give? '

l. 413. ἐξάψῃ, from ἐξάπτω, ' do not put black robes even
(μηδέ) on them '.

l. 414. εἴπω, deliberative subjunctive, ' am I to say? '

l. 415. χαίρειν γε, ' yes, bid them farewell, and bring up
Orestes here to manhood, I pray you '. ἄνδρα is used in a
' proleptic ' or anticipatory sense, i.e. bring him up so that he
becomes a man. μοι is dative of advantage.

l. 416. προσέλκυσαι, aorist imperative of προσέλκω ; ' take
him in your arms, looking upon him for the last time '. ὕστατον
is an adverb.

l. 417. ὅσον εἶχες, ' as far as you could '. φίλοις, ' those
who love you ', i.e. herself.

l. 418. ἔσθ' ὅ τι . . . , ' is there anything that I can do at
Argos to please you? ', lit. doing which I please you.

l. 419. στύγει, imperative. πόσιν γε σόν, ' for he is your husband '.

l. 420. δεινοὺς ἀγῶνας, ' cognate ' accusative (see note on l. 101) with δραμεῖν ; ' he must run a dreadful race because of you ' ; she refers to the remorse that Agamemnon will always feel at having sacrificed his beloved daughter ; to the audience there is also the thought of his eventual murder by Clytemnestra, to which no doubt his treatment of Iphigenia contributed.

l. 421. διώλεσεν, aorist used for present ; ' he is killing me '.

l. 422. δόλῳ δέ, ' yes, but by trickery '.

l. 423. εἶσιν, from εἶμι (=ibo). ἄξων is a final clause ; ' who will come to lead me (to the altar), before I am seized by the hair ', i.e. for the actual sacrifice. Or it may mean ' to prevent me from being dragged along by my hair '. The genitive is often used of the thing by which a person is grasped.

l. 424. ἔγωγε, supply εἶμι ; ' I shall go with you '. μὴ σύ γε, ' no, do not (come with me) ; what you say is wrong '.

l. 425. ἐχομένη, ' holding on to ', with the genitive.

l. 426. ὡς τόδε ..., ' for this (is) better. ..'.

l. 427. τίς is not interrogative, but is indefinite with the accent thrown back from με. ' Let one of the attendants here . . . escort me '.

l. 428. σφαγήσομαι, from σφάζω.

l. 429. οἴχῃ = οἴχει, ' have you gone? ' καί ...γε, ' yes, and I shall never come back again '. οὐ μή with the aorist subjunctive is a strong negative future statement.

l. 430. ὡς ὁρᾷς γε, ' yes, as you see, a cruel fate '; lit. undeservedly.

l. 431. σχές, aorist imperative of ἔχω ; ' wait '. προλίπῃς, aorist subjunctive of προλείπω. οὐκ ἐῶ, ' I forbid you '.

l. 432. The phrase ἐπευφημήσατε (aorist imperative) παιᾶνα is equivalent to a verb and governs κόρην ; ' sing a chant in honour of the daughter. ..'. ὦ νεάνιδες, she now addresses the chorus of Chalcidian maidens.

l. 433. τἠμῇ = τῇ ἐμῇ, ' at my unhappy fate ; the dative is governed by the ἐπι in ἐπευφημήσατε.

l. 434. ἴτω (from εἶμι =ibo) and the next four verbs are all

3rd person imperative ; 'let there go forth solemn silence among the Greeks '.

l. 435. κανᾶ..., 'let someone begin the rite with the baskets of barley '. Barley-meal was sprinkled on the altar and on the victim and was thrown on the fire as a purification before the sacrifice began.

l. 437. ἐνδεξιούσθω, 'let my father walk round the altar towards the right ', i.e. clockwise, as the rite required. ὡς... δώσουσ' ἔρχομαι, ' for I come to give ', a final clause.

IPHIGENIA IN TAURIS

Lines 1-5. The Prologue opens with a list of Iphigenia's ancestors, which was useful to remind the audience of the background of the legend. An account of the story of the family of Pelops and a family tree is given in the Introduction, pages xi ff.

l. 2. θοαῖσιν ἵπποις, probably to be taken with μολών ; ' arriving with his swift mares '. γαμεῖ, historic present, often used in verbs denoting relationship, like τίκτει in l. 23. Οἰνομάου κόρην, Hippodamia.

l. 3. ἀπο governs 'Ατρέως. When a preposition comes after the noun it governs, at the end of a line, the accent is thrown back to the first syllable. Some verb, like ἐγένοντο, meaning ' were sprung ' must be understood.

l. 4. τοῦ, ' from him ', genitive of origin ; the article is often used as a pronoun in Homer, sometimes in Attic Greek.

l. 6. ἀμφὶ δίναις..., ' beside the eddies which the Euripus often whirls round with frequent gusts of wind and ruffles the dark-blue sea '. The Euripus is the wind-swept strait, at one place only 40 yards wide, separating the island of Euboea from the coast of Boeotia, where Aulis was.

l. 8. ὡς δοκεῖ, ' as he thought ', because she really escaped death ; historic present. Or perhaps, ' as is (still) thought '.

l. 10. ναῶν = νεῶν, ' ships '.

l. 11. συνήγαγε, from συνάγω.

l. 12. καλλίνικον...'Ιλίου, ' the crown of glorious victory

over Ilium '. 'Ἰλίου is objective genitive governed by the verbal part of the adjective.

l. 13. τοὺς ὑβρισθέντας ... μετελθεῖν, ' to avenge the insult to Helen's marriage ', lit. the insulted marriage, i.e. her elopement with Paris to Troy.

l. 14. χάριν φέρων, ' doing a favour to. . .'.

l. 15. δεινῆς ... , ' meeting with terrible weather, unfit for sailing, and (contrary) winds '.

l. 16. ἦλθε, ' he had recourse to . . .'.

l. 17. ὦ ἀνάσσων, ' O you who are in command of . . .'. 'Ἑλλάδος is a feminine adjective here, not a noun.

l. 18. οὐ μή with the aorist subjunctive (or future indicative) expresses a strong negative statement ; ' you shall not unmoor . . . from the land '.

l. 19. πρὶν ἄν with the subjunctive refers to indefinite future time when there is a negative in the main clause and means ' before ' or ' until '.

l. 20. σφαγεῖσαν, from σφάζω. ὅ τι with the optative is another indefinite clause, this time in historic sequence ; ' whatever the year should produce most fair '. The ' year ' was the year of, or perhaps from, Iphigenia's birth, so that the fulfilment of the vow was being demanded at least 15 years later.

l. 21. ηὔξω, 2nd singular aorist of εὔχομαι. φωσφόρῳ θεᾷ, Artemis, the moon-goddess.

l. 22. οὖν, ' well then '. Κλυταιμήστρα is spelt correctly in Greek without the ν after the μ. In Latin and English it has become ' Clytemnestra '.

l. 23. τίκτει, historic present, as in l. 2. The parenthesis, of course, refers to Calchas ; ' said Calchas, ascribing the title of " fairest " to me '.

l. 25. παρείλοντο is from παραιρέομαι ; ' they (i.e. the Greeks) took me away from my mother to marry Achilles ', lit. for the marriage of Achilles. Odysseus devised the scheme of a pretended marriage to get her away from her mother to be sacrificed.

l. 26. Αὐλίδα, accusative of motion towards, without a preposition. ἡ τάλαινα, ' I, unhappy one '.

l. 27. μεταρσία ... , ' raised up (lit. taken ; from λαμβάνω) on high above the pyre I was about to be slain '. The imperfect is sometimes used for an unsuccessful attempt to do something.

l. 28. ἐξέκλεψεν, supply ἐμέ as object. μου is governed by the ἀντι- of ἀντιδοῦσα (from ἀντιδίδωμι) ; ' giving a deer instead of me '.

l. 30. πέμψασα, ' conveying '. ᾤκισεν, from οἰκίζω.

l. 31. οὗ, ' where '. βαρβάροισι = βαρβάροις, a common form of the dative plural in poetry ; it is dative of advantage ; for, i.e. ' among barbarians '.

l. 32. ὠκὺν ... πτεροῖς, ' moving (lit. placing) his foot swiftly, as fast as (lit. equal to) wings '. Note the pun on the name Θόας, from θοός, 'swift '.

l. 33. τοὔνομα = τὸ ὄνομα ; ' received (lit. came to) this name '. χάριν following a genitive case is used as a preposition, ' on account of '.

l. 34. τίθησι, the subject of this historic present is Artemis, not Thoas ; ' she made me. . .'. ναοῖσι, plural for singular.

l. 35. καινὰ φάσματα, though inside the relative clause, is the antecedent of ἃ and the object of λέξω. ' I will tell to the air the strange visions which the night came and brought '. It was thought to be ' healing ' (ἄκος) to tell bad dreams aloud to the open air. εἴ τι ..., ' if indeed (as I think is so) there is any healing in this '.

l. 37. ἔδοξα, ' I seemed ', is followed by οἰκεῖν and εὕδειν, but must be understood to change to ἔδοξε for νῶτα in l. 39 and then back again to the 1st person for φεύγειν. Such change of construction is called ' anacoluthon '. Tr. ' it seemed that I dwelt . . . and that the surface of the earth . . . and that I fled. . .'. ἀπαλλαχθεῖσα, from ἀπαλλάσσω.

l. 38. παρθένοισι = παρθένοις, as in l. 31.

l. 40. κἄξω = καὶ ἔξω. στᾶσα, strong aorist participle of ἵστημι, ' standing '.

l. 41. ἐρείψιμον goes predicatively with βεβλημένον (from βάλλω) ; ' thrown down in ruin from its topmost pillar '. The σταθμός, here used in the plural for the singular, was the main support of a house.

l. 43. λελεῖφθαι, perfect infinitive passive of λείπω.

l. 44. καθεῖναι, aorist infinitive active of καθίημι, ' to put forth '.

l. 46. κἀγώ =καὶ ἐγώ ; the verb ἔδοξα must now be supplied from ἔδοξε in l. 43.

l. 47. τιμῶσα, ' duly observing ', not ' honouring '. It was her duty to observe the rite (τέχνη) of preparing strangers for sacrifice (κατάρχεσθαι with the genitive) by sprinkling their heads with holy water ; she did not actually kill the victims herself.

l. 48. τοὔναρ =τό ὄναρ.

l. 49. The relative clause explains the main clause ; ' Orestes is dead, for it is he whom I prepared for sacrifice '.

l. 51. οὖς ἄν is indefinite ; ' any one upon whom my holy water falls is slain '.

l. 53. παροῦσ' ἀπόντι, ' though we are far away from each other ', lit. I being present to him who is absent ; both verbs are present participles of εἰμί (sum). ταῦτα γὰρ δυναίμεθ' ἄν, ' for this (at least) I can do '. Iphigenia refers to herself in the 1st person plural, as often in Greek. The ' potential ' optative with ἄν is frequently used as a less vivid future tense, or as a polite future ; lit. I should be able to do it. Both the optative and a past tense of the indicative with ἄν correspond to our ' I should like ', ' I should have liked ', and to the Latin velim and other subjunctive tenses.

l. 55. 'Ελληνίδας γυναῖκας is ' attracted ' into the relative clause, but should really be dative in apposition to προσπόλοισιν : ' with my attendants, the Greek women, whom. . .'. She had presumably already sent for them to meet her in front of the temple. ἐξ αἰτίας τίνος, ' for what reason? '

l. 56. εἶμι with this accent is ' I shall go '.

l. 57. ἀνακτόρων, descriptive genitive, ' in which I live, consisting of this temple ' ; or it may be ' within this temple '.

l. 58. ποῖ, lit. whither, i.e. ' why? ' αὖ, the first time he had been led into the snare was when Phoebus ordered him to kill his mother. ἤγαγες is from ἄγω, and χρήσας in l. 59 from χράω, ' having given a reply from your oracle '.

l. 59. ἐπεισάμην, from τίνω.

l. 60. κατακτάς, strong aorist participle from κατακτείνω.

διαδοχαῖς 'Ερινύων, lit. by successions of Furies, i.e. ' by troop after troop of Furies '.

l. 61. ἠλαυνόμεσθα, a common poetical form of ἠλαυνόμεθα. The 1st person plural is again used for the singular, as in l. 53 ; ' I was pursued as an exile. . . '.

l. 62. δρόμους καμπίμους is probably a metaphor from the race-course, where competitors had to run one lap down the track, turn sharply round a καμπή, turning-post, and then run up the other lap back to the starting-place. Tr. ' many races, doubling back on my track '. ἐξέπλησα, from ἐκπίμπλημι.

l. 63. τροχηλάτου μανίας, lit. whirling madness, i.e. ' the madness that drives me round in circles '.

l. 64. πῶς ἂν ἔλθοιμι, ' how I should come ' ; an indirect question in the form of a ' potential ' optative ; see note on l. 53.

l. 66. εἶπας με, ' you ordered me '. ὅρους, accusative of motion towards.

l. 67. ἔχοι, a subordinate clause in indirect command ; the indicative could also be used.

l. 68. φασιν, ' men say '. θεᾶς is here scanned as one long syllable.

l. 69. ἄπο governs οὐρανοῦ ; the accent is thrown back to the first syllable when a preposition follows its noun and ends a line ; see l. 3.

l. 70. λαβόντα, repeat εἶπας με from l. 66 ; ' you ordered me to take it . . . and give it (δοῦναι, from δίδωμι) '.

l. 71. ἐκπλήσαντα, from ἐκπίμπλημι.

l. 72. τὸ ἐνθένδε is adverbial accusative : lit. as to afterwards, i.e. ' after that, no further order was given '. ἐρρήθη is used as the aorist passive of εἶπον.

l. 73. ἕξειν, from ἔχω, is now indirect statement, no longer indirect command : ' after doing this, (you said that) I should have. . .'.

l. 76. σύ, supply εἶ.

l. 77. τί δρῶμεν, deliberative subjunctive, ' what are we to do? ' τοίχων is descriptive genitive, lit. the lofty encirclements consisting of the walls, i.e. ' the lofty encircling walls '.

l. 78. πότερα here introduces a single, not a double, question. δωμάτων, ' of the temple '.

l. 79. ἐμβησόμεσθα = ἐμβησόμεθα, from ἐμβαίνω. πῶς ἄν . . . ,
' how then should we escape being seen? ', another potential
optative.

l. 80. There is an ' anacoluthon ' or change of construction
after μοχλοῖς ; ' or forcing with crowbars the bronze barriers—
of which we know nothing? ' κλῇθρα were the cross-bars that
kept the double doors of the temple shut. ἴσμεν is from οἶδα.

l. 81. ἤν (= ἐάν) is used with the subjunctive, ληφθῶμεν
(from λαμβάνω), for a future condition ; ' if we are caught
opening. . .'.

l. 83. πρὶν θανεῖν, lit. before being killed, i.e. ' to avoid
death '. νεὼς ἔπι, ' to the ship ' ; for the order of words and
the accent on ἔπι, see note on l. 3.

l. 85. ἀνεκτόν, supply ἐστι ; ' to flee is intolerable, and we
are not accustomed (to behave like that) '.

l. 86. κακιστέον is the neuter verbal adjective, governing
χρησμόν ; ' we must not bring reproach on . . .'; ἐστί must be
supplied as the verb. Note that δέ is here the fourth word.

l. 87. ἀπαλλαχθέντε, nominative dual of the aorist participle
passive of ἀπαλλάσσω, ' having withdrawn from the temple, let
us conceal ourselves (lit. our body) in the caves '.

l. 88. μέλας, ' dark ', perhaps because it was stormy.

l. 89. μή = ὅπως μή, a final clause.

l. 90. βασιλεῦσιν, plural for singular. κᾆτα = καὶ εἶτα.

l. 91. νυκτὸς ὄμμα = νύξ, not the moon.

l. 92. τολμητέον (ἐστί), ' we must dare to take. . .'.

l. 93. προσφέροντε, another dual participle, ' using every
device '.

l. 94. ἆρα is ' inferential ' ; ' which then of you two? '
ἐνθάδε, she had heard the name mentioned in the herdsman's
narrative ; ' having been thus addressed (upon the shore)
here ' ; κέκληται, from καλέω.

l. 96. εἴ τι . . . , ' if indeed (it is) any pleasure (lit. in pleasure) for you to know this '.

l. 97. Ἕλληνος is a feminine adjective here. γεγώς contracted
perfect participle of γίγνομαι, ' being a citizen of what. . .? '

l. 98. τί ἂν πλέον λάβοις, ' what advantage would you get? '
μαθοῦσα is the ' if-clause ' ; ' if you learnt this '.

l. 99. πότερον here introduces a single question, not the usual double one ; ' are you . . .? ' ἀδελφώ and ἐστον are both 2nd person dual.

l. 100. γε in ' stichomuthia ', i.e. lines spoken by alternate characters often means ' yes ' or ' no ', according to the context ; ' yes, in friendship.' Orestes and Pylades were in fact cousins.

l. 101. ἔθετο, from τίθημι, ' gave '. ὁ γεννήσας πατήρ, ' the father who begot you '.

l. 102. τὸ δίκαιον is adverbial accusative ; ' in justice I should be called Unhappy '. The optative with ἄν is ' potential ' ; see note on l. 53. The verb is plural again, though the subject is singular, as also is the complement of the verb.

l. 103. τοῦτο, ' that question (i.e. what your name ought to be) '. δός, aorist imperative of δίδωμι ; ' put that down to fortune '.

l. 104. θανόντες is equivalent to the protasis (if-clause) of a conditional, as in l. 98 ; ' if I were to die without a name, I should not be a laughing-stock (to my enemies) '. Orestes refuses to tell his name so that his enemies may not exult over him by name when he is dead.

l. 105. ἤ, an interrogative particle, not ' or ', as the accent shows. μέγα is adverbial ; ' are you so proud? '

l. 106. τοὐμόν = τὸ ἐμόν and τοὔνομα = τὸ ὄνομα. Such combination of words is called ' crasis '.

l. 107. οὐδ' ἂν φράσειας, the potential optative in a polite question ; ' would you not say what is your city? ' Note the position of πόλιν, lit. say your city, what it is ; a familiar instance in English of this common Greek idiom is ' I know thee who thou art ' in St. Mark, i, 24.

l. 108. γάρ in stichomuthia (see note on l. 100) often means ' yes, for . . .' or ' no, for. . .'. Here it is ' no, for you are asking what is no advantage (to me) since I am about to die '.

l. 109. χάριν is a ' favour ' to her rather than an ' advantage ' (κέρδος) to him, so he gives way and names his city. Iphigenia's cross-examination of the man whose sacrifice she is about to arrange is tactless to say the least, though excusable because of her anxiety to learn news of her home.

l. 110. πατρίδ' ἐμήν, supply εἶναι ; ' I boast that Argos is my native land '.

l. 111. πρὸς θεῶν, ' in heaven's name ', introducing a surprised question. θεῶν is here scanned as one long syllable. εἰ κεῖθεν γεγώς, ' are you sprung from there? ' For γεγώς, see note on l. 97.

l. 112. γε, ' yes, from Mycenae '. Argos was the name both of a city and of the whole district.

l. 113. φυγάς is nominative, and ἀπῆρας (from ἀπαίρω) governs ναῦν understood ; ' did you depart (lit. set sail) as an exile from...? '

l. 114. τρόπον τινα, adverbial accusative, ' in a way '. φεύγειν here means ' to be an exile '. He was ' willing but yet not willing ' because the Furies had driven him out for having murdered his mother, but the city had not officially banished him.

l. 115. ποθεινός, Iphigenia means ' welcome to me ', because he was a Greek with news of her home, to which Orestes replies ' not welcome to myself ' because he was doomed to die.

l. 116. εἰ δὲ σοί ..., ' if I am welcome to you, you may enjoy it '. ἔρα is imperative.

l. 117. τί is not interrogative but has the accent thrown back from μοι. ὧν is ' relative attraction ' for ἐκείνων ἅ ; ' would you tell me any of the things which I want (to know)? '

l. 118. ' (I will tell you), for it is a small point compared with my (present) misfortune ', lit. for it is in a secondary consideration of my misfortune.

l. 119. οἶσθα, 2nd singular of οἶδα ; not ' you know Troy ', but ' you know of Troy '. λόγος, supply ἐστί, ' the renown of which is everywhere '.

l. 120. ὤφελον (from ὀφείλω) with the infinitive, here εἰδέναι understood, expresses a wish for the past ; ' how I wish I had never known of it, not even (μηδέ) seeing it in a dream '.

l. 121. φασίν νιν οἴχεσθαι, ' men say that it no longer exists and has been destroyed ', lit. has gone.

l. 122. ἔστιν γὰρ οὕτως, ' yes, for it is so, and you (plural) have heard of what has come to pass ', lit. not unfulfilled.

l. 123. δῶμα, motion towards without a preposition. Here it

means ' household ', not ' home ', because if Helen were at home, i.e. in Sparta, the question in l. 125 would be pointless. ' Has she come back to the household of Menelaus again? '

l. 124. κακῶς τῶν ἐμῶν τινι, ' with evil result for one of my own family '. He means Agamemnon, because the return of Helen meant the end of the war and his home-coming to be killed by his wife Clytemnestra.

l. 125. καὶ ἐμοί, ' to me too ', because Helen's elopement was the original cause of the Trojan war and Iphigenia's sacrifice at Aulis. For 'στι (=ἐστι) see note on l. 319.

l. 126. πάρος, an adverb with the article sometimes equals an adjective ; ' with her former husband '.

l. 127. ὦ μῖσος . . . , ' O hateful creature to (all) the Greeks '.

l. 128. ἀπέλαυσα, used ironically ; ' I too have had some benefit ', meaning ' some misfortune '. γάμων, plural but with singular meaning ; it refers only to her marriage with Paris.

l. 129. νόστος ἐγένετο, ' did the return take place? '

l. 130. συλλαβοῦσα governs πάντα, ἀνιστορεῖς governs με. ' How you question me, including everything at once! '

l. 131. γάρ, ' yes, for before you die, I want to get the advantage of this ', i.e. of your answers. Iphigenia's extreme tactlessness in referring again to Orestes' approaching death shows her eagerness to learn news of home.

l. 135. πότνια, i.e. Artemis. ὡς εὖ, ' how just that is ', because Calchas had demanded her sacrifice, as she relates in lines 16 ff. τί γάρ . . . , ' How then does the son of Laertes (Odysseus) fare? ', or ' what of the son of Laertes? '

l. 136. ἐστι, ' he is alive '. ὡς λόγος, ' as the story (goes) '.

l. 137. ὄλοιτο (from ὄλλυμι), a wish, ' may he perish ', hence the μήποτε with τυχών, which is equal to καὶ μήποτε τύχοι.

l. 138. μηδὲν κατεύχου, ' utter no curse (on him) ; everything of his (τὰ ἐκείνου) is amiss ', because he had to wander about for ten years after the fall of Troy before reaching home.

l. 139. ὁ παῖς, Achilles, the greatest warrior of the Greeks, whom Iphigenia was told she would marry at Aulis.

l. 140. οὐκ ἔστιν, ' he is not alive '. λέκτρα, cognate accusative, i.e. one that continues the sense of the verb ; lit. he

married a marriage, i.e. ' he married '. The supposed marriage
of course never took place.

l. 141. δόλια agrees with λέκτρα from l. 140 ; ' yes, for it
was a false marriage, as those who suffered (from πάσχω) from
it know '. She means herself.

l. 142. ὡς εὖ . . . , ' how aptly you enquire about affairs in
Greece '. τἀφ' 'Ελλάδος = τὰ ἀπὸ 'Ελλάδος, lit. affairs from
Greece. A similar phrase occurs in l. 298 and l. 416. πυνθάνῃ, in
this book the second person singular of the middle always ends
in -ῃ instead of -ει.

l. 143. ἀπωλόμην, ' I was lost (to Greece) ', as though her
removal from Aulis were really her death. She was probably
15 or 16 years old at the time. ἀπωλόμην, from ἀπόλλυμι.

l. 144. τὰ ἐκεῖ, ' what has happened there '.

l. 145. τί ὁ στρατηγός, see note on l. 135. λέγουσι, ' men say '.

l. 146. ἐγᾦδα = ἐγὼ οἶδα. ' For the one whom I know is not
among the fortunate '.

l. 147. ἐλέγετό τις, ' there was one called. . .'. 'Ατρέως, ' son
of Atreus '.

l. 148. ἄπελθε . . . , ' depart from this subject '.

l. 149. μὴ πρὸς θεῶν, ' in heaven's name, do not (say this),
but tell me '. εἴφ' = εἰπέ.

l. 150. πρός, an adverb, ' in addition '. τινα, ' another ',
meaning Orestes himself, who avenged his father's murder and
was pursued by the Furies. ἀπώλεσεν, from ἀπόλλυμι.

l. 152. τί . . . τοῦτο, ' why did you utter this lament? ' (not
' why did you lament at this? ') μῶν προσῆκέ σοι, ' was he
related to you? '

l. 153. τὸν πάροιθ' ὄλβον, ' his former prosperity ' ; see note
on l. 126.

l. 154. γάρ justifies Iphigenia's lament ; ' (you are right
to lament), for. . .'. δεινῶς . . . σφαγείς, ' cruelly slain by the
hand of (ἐκ) his wife '.

l. 155. ὦ introduces an exclamation, not a vocative ; ' Oh,
most wretched is she who slew him—and he who slew me '.
χὡ = καὶ ὁ. She cannot forget her father's willingness to sacrifice her, even when she hears of his death.

l. 156. παῦσαι, aorist imperative, ' cease asking ', followed by μή with the aorist subjunctive, ' and do not enquire further '.

l. 157. τοσόνδε γε, ' yes, (but I will ask) only this (lit. so much), whether. . .'.

l. 158. ἔτεχ' = ἔτεκε, from τίκτω ; ' the son whom she bare, he slew her '.

l. 159. ὡς is best omitted in translation ; ' with what purpose (did he kill her)? ', lit. as wishing what.

l. 160. πατρὸς θανόντος . . . , ' taking vengeance on her for the murder of his father '.

l. 161. ' How well he exacted an evil justice .' Note the ' oxymoron ' (combination of opposite ideas) in εὖ and κακόν, and also in κακόν and δίκαιον.

l. 162. τὰ πρὸς θεῶν, adverbial accusative ; ' he does not prosper as far as the gods are concerned (lit. in the things from the gods), although he is righteous '. θεῶν, one long syllable.

l. 163. λείπει, historic present. λέλοιπεν in the next line is the perfect of λείπω.

l. 164. γε, ' yes, he left. . .'. In *Iphigenia in Aulis*, l. 334, a third daughter Chrysothemis, is referred to. Electra was now married to Pylades.

l. 165. τί δέ, ' what then? Is there any news of. . .? '

l. 166. οὐδείς γε, ' no, none, except that she is dead and. . .'. αὐτήν is understood as the subject of ὁρᾶν.

l. 167. χὠ = καὶ ὁ.

l. 168. χάριν ἄχαριν, another example of ' oxymoron ' (see note on l. 161). χάριν is used as a preposition, as in l. 33, but also has an adjective agreeing with it ; ' for the worthless sake of a bad woman '.

l. 169. ἔστι παῖς "Αργει, ' is the son . . . alive at Argos? '

l. 170. ' He is alive, poor wretch, both nowhere (=καὶ οὐδαμοῦ) and everywhere ', because he has no home and is driven everywhere by the Furies.

l. 171. She realizes that her interpretation of her dream (ll. 35 ff.), which she took to mean the death of Orestes, was incorrect and bids farewell to the vision. οὐδὲν ἦτ' ἄρα, ' you were as nothing, then '.

l. 172. αἴδε πάρεισιν, ' here are. . .'. A δέλτος consisted of two or more wooden tablets coated on the inside with wax and

tied up with string, the knot of which was sealed. A message
was written on the wax surface with a metal pen. πολύθυροι
must be an exaggeration, for the ten-line message (given in
ll. 213–228) would not have needed more than the minimum
two tablets, unless the writing was very big.

l. 174. ἀκούσατε, aorist imperative, 'hear what I want in
addition to this'. αὐτός = ὁ αὐτός; 'no man is the same both
in troubles and when....'. ὅταν πέσῃ is indefinite, 'whenever',
but is better translated here as ' when he changes', lit. falls.

l. 176. μὴ ἀπονοστήσας is scanned as if μή and ἀ were one
long syllable. χθονός, 'from this land', genitive of separation.

l. 177. θῆται (aorist subjunctive middle of τίθημι) παρ' οὐδέν,
'will regard as of no value', or 'forget'.

l. 179. βούλῃ, 2nd singular, present indicative. τίνος πέρι,
'about what?'; see note on l. 69.

l. 180. δότω, aorist imperative of δίδωμι, 'let him give me
an oath'.

l. 181. οἷσι φίλων = ἐκείνοις φίλων οἷς, 'to those of my
friends to whom'.

l. 182. ἦ καὶ ἀντιδώσεις, 'and will you also give the same
oath to him?'

l. 183. The infinitives in this and the next line depend on
the verb of swearing understood in l. 182 : ' to do or not to do—
what?' μή is the usual negative in oaths.

l. 184. μὴ θανόντα, 'alive'; supply αὐτόν as the object of
ἀφήσειν (from ἀφίημι). βαρβάρου is here a feminine adjective.

l. 185. δίκαιον εἶπας, 'your words are reasonable, for how
(else) could he take the message?'

l. 187. καὶ αὐτὴ . . . , 'and I myself will put him (Pylades) on
board his ship', lit. the hull of the ship. εἰσβαίνω here takes
two accusatives, one of which is understood. ναός = νεώς.

l. 188. ὄμνυ (imperative) is addressed to Pylades, the rest of
the line to Iphigenia. ὅστις εὐσεβής, 'whatever oath (is)
sacred in your eyes'.

l. 189. Iphigenia dictates the oath for Pylades to swear.
'You must say " I will give this letter..."'.

l. 191. καὶ ἐγὼ σὲ σώσω, 'and I will send you safely'. The

' blue rock ' (usually plural) was the Symplegades, the Clashing Rocks, at the northern end of the Bosporus, the entrance to the Euxine Sea (the Black Sea); see also note on l. 395.

l. 192. τοισίδε = τοῖσδε, ' which of the gods do you swear by as a witness to this? '

l. 193. τιμάς, ' my sacred task '.

l. 194. ἐγώ, supply ἐπόμνυμι.

l. 195. The main clause is omitted; ' and (what penalty would you suffer) if you were to break your oath and wrong me? '

l. 196. εἴην, a wish, not the main verb of a conditional clause, which would require ἄν; ' may I never return '. μή is used with σώσασα, not οὐ, because the participle is equivalent to an if-clause ; ' if you do not send me away safely '.

l. 197. θείην, from τίθημι ; ' never may I set foot in Argos ', lit. the print of my foot.

l. 198. ἐξαίρετον . . . , ' give me this as an exception (to the terms of the oath) '. πάθῃ τι, i.e. is wrecked ; in modern speech, ' if anything happens to the ship '.

l. 199. χἤ = καὶ ἤ. χρημάτων μέτα, ' with everything on board '.

l. 200. σῶμα μόνον, ' myself alone '.

l. 201. ' That this oath should no longer be binding.' This is an indirect command, depending on ἐξαίρετον δὸς τόδε.

l. 202. οἶσθ' ὃ δράσω, ' do you know (from οἶδα) what I shall do? ' πολλὰ γὰρ . . . , ' many plans obtain many ends ', a proverbial saying implying that if one plan fails another may succeed.

l. 203. τἀνόντα κἀγγεγραμμένα = τὰ ἐνόντα (from ἔνειμι) καὶ ἐγγεγραμμένα (from ἐγγράφω) ; ' I will tell you in words all that is contained and written in. . . '. ἀναγγεῖλαι, supply ὥστε σε δυνησέσθαι, ' so that you will be able to take the message '.

l. 205. ἐν ἀσφαλεῖ γάρ, supply ἔσται ; ' for thus it will be safe '.

l. 206. αὐτὴ σιγῶσα, ' though silent it will itself say '.

l. 208. τὸ σῶμα, ' yourself ', as in l. 200.

l. 209. τῶν τε σῶν . . . , ' for your own sake and mine '. τὰ σά, lit. your own affairs.

l. 210. ᾧ, the relative is used instead of the interrogative τίνι, though the interrogative ὅ τι follows in the next line ; ' tell me to whom I must ', lit. the person to whom.

l. 211. πρὸς ᾿Αργος must be translated ' at Argos ' in this context. ὅ τι..., ' and what I must say, hearing it from you '.

l. 213. The message begins here. 'Η 'ν = ἡ ἐν ; ' Iphigenia, slain at Aulis, but now alive ..., though no longer alive to those in Argos ', lit. to those there.

l. 215. Orestes cannot help interrupting when he hears his sister's name. ἥκει πάλιν, ' has she come back (to life) when dead? '

l. 216. ἥδ' ἣν ὁρᾷς σύ, ' it is she whom you now see '.

l. 217. The message begins again after Orestes' interruption. κόμισαι, aorist imperative middle of κομίζω. πρὶν θανεῖν, ' before I die '.

l. 218. μετάστησον, aorist imperative of μεθίστημι, ' take me away from '.

l. 219. ἐφ' οἷσι, ' at which I have the sacred task of slaying strangers '.

l. 220. τί λέξω, deliberative aorist subjunctive ; ' what am I to say? ' ὅπως is dual, though combined with a plural verb : lit. where ever being have we been found? i.e. ' in what situation do we find ourselves? ' This line of Orestes again interrupts the message, which is continued in l. 221 and in 222 down to 'Ορέστα ; it then goes on after λεγ' οὕνεκα in l. 225 and ends at l. 228.

l. 221. ἀραία γενήσομαι, ' I shall bring a curse upon....'.

l. 222. ἵν' αὖθις ..., ' (I say this) that you may hear the name a second time (αὖθις δίς) and remember it '. The name was first mentioned in l. 213 ; in this line 'Ορέστα is vocative.

l. 223. ἐν τοῖς ἐμοῖς, ' in my affairs '. θεοί and θεούς are here each scanned as one long syllable.

l. 224. οὐδέν, ' for no reason ' ; adverbial accusative, like τί in l. 223, ' for what reason? ' ἐξέβην (from ἐκβαίνω) ἄλλοσε, ' my thoughts had turned to another direction ', lit. I went out.

l. 225. οὕνεκα = ὅτι, ' say that...'. The message here continues. μου is governed by ἀντι in ἀντιδοῦσα.

84 NOTES

l. 226. ἥν, the antecedent is of course ἔλαφον.

l. 227. ἡμᾶς = ἐμέ, as often in poetry ; ' thinking that he had plunged into me. . .'.

l. 228. αἴδε, ' here (is) the letter'.

l. 229. τάν = τὰ ἐν, ' this is what is written in. . .'.

l. 230. ὦ περιβαλοῦσά με, ' O you who have bound me '.

l. 231. κάλλιστα δέ . . . , ' and have sworn (from ὄμνυμι) to me a noble oath '. σχήσω is from ἔχω, ' I will not restrain (myself) a long time ', i.e. ' I will not delay long '. Note the combination of singular and plural in the verbs in l. 232 ; both should be translated as singular.

l. 233. ἀποδίδωμι, not ' I give back ', but ' I duly deliver '.

l. 234. κασιγνήτης πάρα ; for the order of words, see note on l. 3.

l. 235. παρείς, aorist participle, from παρίημι. γραμμάτων διαπτυχάς, lit. the folds of the letter, i.e. ' the letter ', as in l. 172.

l. 236. ' I will take my joy, not in words (i.e. in reading the letter, but in embracing you) '.

l. 237. ἐκπεπληγμένος, from ἐπλήσσω, ' though bewildered, yet (ὅμως). . .'.

l. 238. ἀπίστῳ βραχίονι, ' in my unbelieving arms ' ; this transference of an adjective from the person with which it really agrees to another word is called ' hypallage ' ; e.g. ' a cowardly blow ' is a blow struck by a coward.

l. 239. εἶμι, lit. I shall go into joy, i.e. ' I am full of joy, having learnt (from πυνθάνομαι) what is marvellous to me '.

l. 240. καὶ ἐκ ταὐτοῦ πατρὸς γεγῶσα, ' and sprung from the same father '. γεγῶσα is contracted perfect participle from γίγνομαι. ταὐτοῦ = τοῦ αὐτοῦ.

l. 242. οὐ δοκοῦσα is historic present, ' though you thought that you would never have him (again) '. ἕξειν is from ἔχω.

l. 243. ἐγώ, supply ἔχω, ' I have you?' οὐ παύσῃ . . . , ' will you not stop. . .? '

l. 244. This means literally ' Argos and Nauplia are full of him ', which presumably means ' he lives at Argos or Nauplia'.

l. 246. ' The Spartan daughter of Tyndareus ' was Clytemnestra. ἀλλά introduces a surprised question ; ' did the . . . really bear you? '

l. 247. γε, 'yes, (she bore me) to the son of Pelops' son, from whom I...'. ἐκπέφυκα is from ἐκφύω.

l. 249. πυνθάνου, 'ask some question about (lit. of) our father's house'.

l. 250. οὐκοῦν = οὖν ; ' (no), *you* must speak, *I* must hear the answer'. She means that he must give some proof of his identity, unprompted by her.

l. 251. λέγοιμ' ἄν, a polite future, almost =' I will tell this '. ἀκοῇ Ἠλέκτρας, ' having heard it from Electra,' lit. by hearing from. Electra was Orestes' elder sister, mentioned in l. 164. She was married to Pylades.

l. 252. οἶσθα . . . , ' do you remember (lit. know) the quarrel that arose between Atreus and Thyestes? ' For the story, see Introduction, page xii.

l. 253. νείκη, plural for singular. πέρι governs χρυσῆς ἀρνός. The ' golden lamb ' (see Introduction, page xii) gave to its possessor the kingship of Mycenae and the troubles it caused were part of the curse on the family of Pelops.

l. 254. ὑφῆνασ' οἶσθα. . ., ' do you remember weaving (from ὑφαίνω) the story of this quarrel in . . .? '

l. 255. κάμπτεις is a metaphor from chariot-racing, in which competitors had to run one lap down the track, turn sharply round a καμπή, turning-post, and then run the other lap back to the starting-place. ' You turn your chariot near my heart ', i.e. you touch a chord in my memory.

l. 256. εἰκώ is accusative ; both it and μετάστασιν, which is in apposition, are governed by ὑφήνασα in l. 254. Tr. ' and a picture of the changing course of the sun in the woven work? '

l. 257. καί, ' yes, I did weave this. . .'. She now remembers it.

l. 258. ἀνεδέξω, 2nd singular aorist middle from ἀναδέχομαι ; ' did you receive ceremonial water at (lit. to) Aulis from your mother? ' The water for a ceremonial bath before a wedding was sent from a sacred spring, in this case from Argos.

l. 259. οἶδα . . . , ' I remember, for the marriage was not a happy one and has not deprived me (of this memory) '. She means that the preliminaries to the false wedding are all that she has and have not been swallowed up by memories of a

happy married life. οὐ negatives both ἐσθλὸς ὤν and ἀφείλετο
(from ἀφαιρέω).

l. 260. τί γάρ introduces another point ; ' well, then '.
With δοῦσα (from δίδωμι) supply οἶσθα again ; ' do you remember giving a lock of your hair (to someone) to take to your
mother? ' φέρειν is infinitive of purpose after a verb of sendinք

l. 261. γε, ' yes, as a memorial. . .'. She expected her body
to be burnt at Aulis after the sacrifice and sent her mother a
lock of hair for her cenotaph, instead of her body. τοὐμοῦ = τοῦ
ἐμοῦ.

l. 262. The relative clause is placed first ; ' I will mention
the proofs which. . .'.

l. 263. λόγχην is accusative in apposition to τεκμήρια in
l. 262 ; it depends on Πέλοπος, and δόμοις depends on πατρός.
κεκρυμμένην (from κρύπτω) in l. 266 agrees with λόγχην.

l. 264. ἦν χερσί . . . , ' which he brandished . . . and won
Hippodamia '. In this version of the story, Pelops killed
Oenomaus with his spear and won the hand of his daughter.
The usual version of the legend is given in the Introduction,
page xii.

l. 267. οὐδὲν ἄλλο, ' I can call you nothing else '. Iphigenia
at last acknowledges her brother, whom she half doubtfully
called φίλτατε in l. 255.

l. 268. τηλύγετον . . . , this perhaps means ' far away from
your native-land, from Argos ', though the exact sense is
doubtful.

l. 269. ὦ φίλος, nominative for vocative. The metre of
this line is ' dochmiac ', i.e. $-\cup\cup-\cup-$.

l. 270. καὶ ἐγώ, supply ἔχω. ὡς δοξάζεται, historic present,
' as was thought '.

l. 271. κατά each time belongs to νοτίζει in l. 272, forming
one word κατανοτίζει ; this division into two parts is called
' tmesis '. ' Tears and weeping and at the same time joy
bedew your eyes, and also mine.'

l. 273. τί, ' why? ' In. l. 274 θεᾶς is one long syllable.

l. 275. ἔχ' αὐτοῦ . . . , ' keep your foot there ', i.e. do not enter.

l. 277. ἀπέπτυσα, ' I avert the evil omen ', lit. I have spat,
to avert the omen ; she says the word instead of actually

spitting. 'Οσίᾳ is ceremonial Purity ; ' I say this for the sake of Purity '. This line is not a reply to Thoas' question in l. 276, but is intended to express her supposed horror at the imaginary pollution of the shrine.

l. 278. τί . . . , ' what strange prelude do you utter?' φροιμιάζῃ = φροιμιάζει.

l. 279. οὐ καθαρά . . . , ' it is no pure sacrifice that you (plural, i.e. your people) have caught for me '.

l. 280. τοὐκδιδάξαν = τὸ ἐκδιδάξαν ; ' what was it that taught you this? ' δόξαν λέγεις, ' do you speak of what is (only) your own idea? '

l. 281. πάλιν . . . ἀπεστράφη (from ἀποστρέφω), ' was turned round from its place '. θεοῦ is scanned as one long syllable.

l. 283. ὄψιν ὀμμάτων = ' its eyes '. ξυνήρμοσεν, from ξυναρμόζω.

l. 284. ἦ, interrogative ; ' was it the pollution. . .? '

l. 285. ἥδε agrees with αἰτία, ' that is the reason '. δεδράκατον, dual perfect of δράω.

l. 286. ἦ, interrogative again ; ' but did they. . .? ' ἔκανον is from καίνω. Notice how Euripides makes the barbarian Thoas refer to his own people as ' barbarians ' both here and, more strangely, in l. 290. ἀκτῆς ἔπι, ' on the shore '.

l. 287. κεκτημένοι, from κτάομαι, ' having incurred blood-guilt of their own kindred '. Pylades was of course innocent, but in Iphigenia's story to Thoas he too had to appear as a murderer with his supposed brother.

l. 288. εἰς ἔρον . . . , ' I want to know ', lit. we have fallen (from πίπτω) into a desire of learning.

l. 290. "Απολλον, vocative, invoking the god. οὐδέ . . . , ' not even among barbarians would anyone have dared (from τλάω) to do this '.

l. 291. ἠλάθησαν, from ἐλαύνω. πάσης 'Ελλάδος, genitive of separation ; ' out of the whole of Greece '.

l. 292. ἦ δῆτα, ' is it then because of this that you are taking. . .? '

l. 293. γε, ' yes, out under the sky '. μεταστήσω, aorist subjunctive of μεθίστημι, ' to free it from the stain of. . .'.

l. 294. ἔγνως, 2nd singular aorist of γιγνώσκω. τοῖν ξένοιν, genitive dual.

88 NOTES

l. 295. ἤλεγχον, supply αὐτούς. ὡς, 'when'. θεᾶς is here
scanned as one long syllable.

l. 296. ἔθρεψεν, from τρέφω. ὡς = ὅτι οὕτως, 'clever, in
that you discovered (from αἰσθάνομαι) it so well'.

l. 297. καὶ μήν, 'yes, and they held out (from καθίημι) an
attractive bait to catch my heart'.

l. 298. ἀγγέλλοντε, dual participle, 'telling you some news
(τι) from Argos (lit. of affairs from Argos) as an inducement (to
win you over)?' Note the change of metaphor from δέλεαρ to
φίλτρον, lit. a charm.

l. 299. εὐτυχεῖν, indirect statement depending on ἀγγέλλοντε;
'saying that...'.

l. 300. 'So that you should of course (δή) spare them in your
joy at the news'.

l. 301. καὶ ... γε, 'yes, and (they said) that my father...'.
Perhaps Iphigenia tells this falsehood because she is afraid
that her mention of Orestes may arouse Thoas' suspicions,
which she now tries to allay.

l. 302. ἐς τὸ τῆς θεοῦ, 'you naturally inclined towards the
(side) of the goddess', i.e. you took her side and rejected the
offered bait. θεοῦ is here scanned as one long syllable.

l. 303. πᾶσαν γε, 'yes, because I hate...'. Poor Iphigenia
had good cause to hate all the Greeks until now.

l. 304. τί δρῶμεν, deliberative subjunctive, 'what are we
to do?'

l. 305. ἀνάγκη, supply ἐστί; 'we must respect...'.

l. 306. οὔκουν = οὐκ οὖν, whereas οὐκοῦν (l. 250) = οὖν. 'Is
not then your holy water ... ready (ἐν ἔργῳ)?', i.e. for the
sacrifice. ξίφος σόν, though she only prepared the victims for
sacrifice, leaving the actual slaughter to the attendants.

l. 307. νιν, 'them', i.e. the strangers. νίψαι, from νίζω.

l. 308. ὑδάτων, from ὕδωρ, 'fresh water'. δρόσος, lit. dew,
here 'sea-water'.

l. 309. τἀνθρώπων = τὰ ἀνθρώπων.

l. 310. γοῦν, 'then they would be a purer sacrifice', lit. they
would fall more purely, i.e. if they were first cleansed in the sea.

l. 311. τἀμά = τὰ ἐμά; 'yes, and my own fortunes would
thus turn out better'. To Thoas she means her priestly

duties ; to herself and to the audience she means her escape with Orestes.

l. 312. οὔκουν, 'well, does not...?' πρὸς αὐτὸν ναόν, 'against the very foundations of the temple '.

l. 313. δεῖ here governs the genitive, ' there is need of '. ἀλλα δράσομεν, ' I shall perform other things as well ' ; again a double meaning, referring to (imaginary) religious rites and also to her escape.

l. 314. ἄγε, supply αὐτούς ; ' take them '. τἄρρητα = τὰ ἄρρητα.

l. 315. καί, ' I must also purify...'. μοι is dative of agent after the verbal adjective, with which ἐστί is understood.

l. 316. εἴπερ γε..., ' yes, indeed, if...'. ἔβαλε, ' has touched it '.

l. 317. γάρ, ' (it has touched it), for (otherwise) I should not have moved it from its pedestal.' ἠράμην, from αἴρω.

l. 318. ηὐσέβεια = ἡ εὐσέβια, ' your piety '. δίκαιος, ' proper ', is sometimes an adjective of two terminations only, here feminine. Supply ἐστί as the verb.

l. 319. ἢ 'νθάδε = ἢ ἐνθάδε. This elision of a vowel at the beginning of a word is called ' prodelision '.

l. 320. παρίστατ', the elided vowel is -ο, imperfect indicative ; ' who stood beside the altar here ', i.e. presided over it.

l. 323. πῶς, ' what? ' τί πνεῦμα..., ' what breeze of fortune did she catch (from κτάομαι)? ' The exact meaning of the phrase is uncertain ; it may mean ' ill-wind ', or ' influence of fortune '.

l. 324. σώζουσ', the elided vowel is -α ; ' trying to save '. θαυμάσῃ, ' you will marvel at this '.

l. 325. τὸν ποῖον, agreeing with 'Ορέστην ; ' what Orestes? do you mean the one whom...? ' Thoas must have heard about her family from Iphigenia. τίκτει is historic present.

l. 326. ὅν..., ' the one whom the goddess had dedicated to this altar '. θεά is here scanned as one long syllable.

l. 327. πῶς σε..., lit. how can I be right (deliberative subjunctive) in calling you by a greater name?, i.e. ' what stronger name can I find for you? ' He thinks that ' marvel ' does not do justice to the strange news.

90 NOTES

l. 328. 'νταῦθα by 'prodelision' = ἐνταῦθα, 'in that direction'. The messenger quickly brings Thoas back to the point and will not allow him to find a stronger word than θαῦμα.

l. 329. ἀθρήσας and κλύων should be translated as if they were imperatives, like ἐκφρόντισον ; 'consider clearly, listen and decide'.

l. 330. ὅστις must be taken before διωγμός, 'what pursuit'; indirect question.

l. 331. ἀγχίπλουν πόρον is cognate or internal accusative with the intransitive verb φεύγουσιν ; 'it is no short voyage on which they flee', lit. they flee a journey not near by sea. A good example of a cognate accusative in English is 'to run a race'. Thoas means that he can afford to listen to the messenger's story because so long a voyage allows him to waste a little time before starting the pursuit.

l. 332. ὥστε . . . τὸ ἐμὸν δόρυ, 'so as to escape my spear', or it may be 'ship'.

l. 334. οὗ, 'where'. κρύφιος, adverbial, 'moored (from ὁρμίζω) in a hidden place'.

l. 335. ἡμᾶς, governed by ἐξένευσε ; 'signalled to us to stand far away'. ἀποστῆναι is strong aorist infinitive of ἀφίστημι. δεσμὰ ξένων ἔχοντας, 'holding the fetters of the strangers'. συμπέμπεις, historic present, 'you sent with her'.

l. 337. ὡς . . . θύουσα, 'as though she wished to light the sacred (lit. ineffable) cleansing fire for which she had come '. φλόγα καὶ καθαρμόν, 'fire and cleansing ' = ' cleansing fire ', by 'hendiadys' (two nouns connected by 'and' instead of an adjective and a noun ; e.g. 'bread and butter', which is usually 'buttered bread '). θύειν is really 'to sacrifice' and φλόγα is cognate accusative, 'to make a sacrifice with the flame ' ; see note on l. 331.

l. 339. τοῖν ξένοιν, genitive dual. χεροί of course goes with ἔχουσα.

l. 342. χρόνῳ, 'some time later'. ἵν' ἡμῖν . . . , 'that she should of course (δή) seem to us to be doing something important', lit. something more.

l. 343. κατῇδε, from κατᾴδω, governs βάρβαρα μέλη, which here means 'unintelligible', though the word is used by a 'bar-

barian ', i.e. a non-Greek. μαγεύουσα is intransitive, ' performing her magic rites '.

l. 344. ὡς δή, ' pretending to cleanse the blood-guilt '.

l. 345. ἦμεν ἥμενοι, ' we had been sitting there '.

l. 346. ἐσῆλθεν, an impersonal verb followed by the construction of a verb of fearing, as though φόβος were the subject ; tr. ' the fear came upon us that . . . would kill her and
depart as fugitives '. οἰχοίατο = οἴχοιντο.

l. 348. φόβῳ . . . , ' through fear of seeing what we ought not
to see '. εἰσορᾶν is infinitive with φόβῳ, as though it were
φοβούμενοι, ' being afraid to see '. μή is ' generic ', i.e. ' such
things as we ought not to see '. χρῆν = ἐχρῆν, imperfect.

l. 349. πᾶσιν ἦν . . . , ' all said the same thing (lit. the same
word was to all), that we should go (to the place) where they
were '. στείχειν is infinitive as though λόγος ἦν were a verb
like ἐκέλευον.

l. 350. οὐκ ἐωμένοις, ' forbidden '.

l. 351. κἀνταῦθα = καὶ ἐνταῦθα. ὁρῶμεν, historic present. Ἑλλάδος
(a feminine adjective) νεὼς σκάφος = Ἑλλάδα ναῦν, as in l. 187.

l. 352. πίτυλον, accusative of respect, lit winged in respect
of its sweep of oars with blade made ready, i.e. ' with the
blades of its sweep of oars made ready like wings '.

l. 353. ἐπὶ σκαλμῶν, ' seated at the tholes ', i.e. the pins in the
side of the ship to which the oars were made fast.

l. 355. ἐκ δεσμῶν in l. 354 goes with ἐλευθέρους. Note the
' asyndeton ' or absence of a connecting particle after the full
stop in this line. νεώς is partitive genitive after πρύμνηθεν, ' at
the stern of the vessel '. ἑστῶτες, contracted perfect participle
of ἵστημι.

l. 356. οἱ μέν must be understood with ἦγον, to correspond
with οἱ δέ in ll. 357 and 358 ; ' some, standing . . . , were
hastily (σπεύδοντες) hauling in . . . hand over hand (διὰ χερῶν)
and holding the bows (close to the shore) with poles '.

l. 357. οἱ δέ . . . , ' others were hauling up the anchor (lit.
suspending it from the catheads), others were letting down a
rope-ladder (plural for singular) into the sea, giving it to the
strangers '. Catheads were beams projecting from each side

of the bows, from which the anchor was suspended when not in use. τοῖν ξένοιν, dative dual.

l. 360. ἀφειδήσαντες, ' no longer respecting (her as a priestess) '.

l. 361. εἰχόμεσθα = εἰχόμεθα. The middle of ἔχω, with the genitive, means ' seize '. οἱ μέν and οἱ δέ is understood, for some seized Iphigenia, others the stern-cables.

l. 363. ἐξηροῦμεν, from ἐξαιρέω ; ' we tried to drag the steering-oars out through the stern-holes '. Ancient ships were steered by large oars, one on each side of the stern, passing through holes in the stern-bulwarks.

l. 364. ἐχώρουν, ' were being uttered ', or ' were passing '. τίνι λόγῳ, ' by what right? ' or ' on what pretext? '

l. 365. ξόανα καὶ θυηπόλους, plural used half-humorously by the messenger, who is evidently a ' character '; see l. 328, n.

l. 366. τίνος τίς ὤν, ' whose son and who are you, you who...? ' The Greeks had no surnames, so a full name included also the father's. χθονός, genitive of separation, ' out of this land '.

l. 367. ὡς μάθῃς, ' you must know ', lit. that you may know.

l. 369. λαβών..., ' having recovered her whom I lost '.

l. 370. οὐδὲν ἧσσον, adverbial accusative, ' none the less '.

l. 371. διεβιαζόμεσθα, a ' conative ' imperfect, ' we tried to compel her '.

l. 372. ὅθεν..., ' and from that struggle (lit. whence) came these terrible blows on our cheeks '. τά = τάδε ; he points to his bruises.

l. 373. κεῖνοί τε ... οὐκ ... ἡμεῖς τε = οὔτε κεῖνοι οὔτε ἡμεῖς.

l. 374. ἦσαν ἐγκροτούμεναι, ' were being dashed against us '.

l. 375. καὶ κῶλα..., lit. feet were aimed at our ... from both the ... ; i.e. ' we were kicked in the ribs and the stomach ', lit. liver.

l. 377. ὡς = ὥστε, ' so that as soon our limbs joined in the fray (lit. in the joining) they also became tired '. The Greeks were fighting for their lives and so managed to hold off the much larger number of Taurians.

l. 378. ἐσφραγισμένοι, from σφραγίζω, ' scarred '.

l. 379. οἱ μὲν ... οἱ δέ, ' some ... others '.

IPHIGENIA IN TAURIS   93

l. 380. ὄμμασιν, probably ' face ' rather than ' eyes '.

l. 381. ἐπισταθέντες, from ἐφίσταμαι, ' taking our stand ' ; like σταθέντες in l. 384. Note the unusual ending of the comparative adverb.

l. 384. ὥστ' ἀναστεῖλαι πρόσω, ' so that they checked us (and kept us away) at a distance '.

l. 385. καὶ ἐν τῷδε, ' meanwhile '. ὤκειλε, from ὀκέλλω.

l. 386. φόβος ἦν . . . , ' the maiden was afraid to wade through the water ', lit. to wet her foot. The ship could not come near enough to the shore for her to reach the rope-ladder without wading.

l. 387. λαβὼν εἰς . . . , ' lifting her up on to his. . .'. For the origin of ἀριστερός, see note on l. 395.

l. 388. βάς, from βαίνω. ἐπί, ' up '. θορών, from θρώσκω.

l. 389. ἔθηκε, from τίθημι, ' he put down '.

l. 390. τὸ οὐρανοῦ πέσημα, ' the object that fell from heaven ' ; compare the phrase ὅ φασιν οὐρανοῦ πεσεῖν ἄπο in ll. 68–69. ' The daughter of Zeus ' is of course Artemis.

l. 391. ναός = νεώς.

l. 393. λάβεσθε κώπης, aorist middle imperative, ' seize your oars ', singular for plural.

l. 394. ὧνπερ οὕνεκα, the antecedent is ἐκεῖνα understood, ' those things for which '.

l. 395. ἔσωθεν governs Συμπληγάδων, the Clashing Rocks at the entrance to the Euxine which used to crush ships that passed between them until the Argo got safely through and they were fastened in their present position. The legend no doubt arose from the storms that used to wreck ships passing through the Bosporus. The Black Sea was ἄξενος, ' inhospitable ', because of its storms, but by a ' euphemism ' the Greeks called it the Euxine Sea (Εὔξεινος), ' Hospitable ', hoping thus to avert the bad weather. In l. 387, ἀριστερός (' better ') is another euphemism to avert ill luck from the left hand.

l. 396. οἱ δέ, ' and they '. στεναγμὸν ἡδύν, ' a cry of joy '.

l. 398. ἐχώρει, ' made headway '. Note the position of δέ, after the second word, instead of after the first ; ' but while

it was passing through the mouth of the harbour, it met . . .
and was in difficulties '.

l. 401. ὤθει, ' drove the sails (i.e. the ship) astern ' ; historic
present. οἱ δέ, ' and they ', i.e. the crew.

l. 402. πρὸς κῦμα λακτίζοντες, ' struggling against the waves ',
an adaptation of the proverbial πρὸς κέντρα λακτίζειν,
' to kick against the pricks ', used originally of oxen kicking
against the ox-goad ; see Acts, ix, 5, where St. Paul heard
the phrase used by Christ in the vision that appeared to him
on the road to Damascus.

l. 404. Λητοῦς, genitive of Λητώ. Artemis was the daughter
of Leto.

l. 405. σῶσον, aorist imperative, ' bring me safely '.

l. 406. σύγγνωθι, aorist imperative of συγγιγνώσκω.

l. 407. καὶ σύ, ' you also '. κασίγνητον, i.e. Apollo.

l. 408. δόκει, imperative, ' think that I too love. . .'.
ὁμαίμονας, plural, but of course referring to Orestes.

l. 409. ἐπευφήμησαν . . . , ' sang a solemn chant to support
the prayers '. The ' paean ' was originally a song of triumph
raised to Apollo the Healer after a victory, then the battle-song,
and then a solemn chant before any undertaking, as here.

l. 410. γυμνὰς . . . ἐπωμίδας, ' their arms stripped of their
clothes '.

l. 411. προσαρμόσαντες, lit. fitting, i.e. ' moving their arms
with the oars, in time with (ἐκ) the word of command '. A
boatswain, κελευστής, used to give the time to the rowers, so
that all should pull together.

l. 412. μᾶλλον δὲ μᾶλλον, ' but nearer and nearer '. ᾔει,
imperfect of εἶμι (= ibo).

l. 413. καὶ ὁ μέν, ' and some (of us) '. ὡρμήθη, from ὁρμάω.

l. 414. ἐξανῆπτεν, ' others fastened twisted loops of rope (to
some object on the shore) '. The other end of the ropes were
to be made fast to the ship by the men who were wading out.

l. 415. ἀπεστάλην, from ἀποστέλλω. μέν is followed by ἀλλά in
l. 417, which is used in an exhortation.

l. 416. σημανῶν is a future participle expressing purpose, ' to
relate the events that happened there ', lit. from there ; see
note on l. 142.

l. 420. βαρβάρου, a feminine adjective.   For Thoas' use of the word, see note on l. 286.

l. 421. εἶα is an exclamation generally used with an imperative, but the questions here ('will you not ...? ') are equivalent to commands ; 'come ... run along the shore (παράκτιοι = παρὰ τὴν ἀκτήν) and wait for (lit. receive) the wreckage (ἐκβολάς) of the ship ', i.e. the people cast ashore.

l. 423. σὺν τῇ θεῷ, ' with the favour of the goddess '.

l. 425. οἱ δέ is vocative, as though οἱ μέν had appeared in l. 422 ; ' and others drag down. . .'.

l. 426. ὡς, ' for '. ἐκ θαλάσσης . . . , 'catching them by sea and (i.e. or) by riding on the land '.

l. 427. κατά, ' down from '. ἢ . . . ἤ, ' either . . . or '.

l. 428. ῥίψωμεν and πήξωμεν (from πήγνυμι) are aorist subjunctives in an exhortation, ' let us. . .'.

l. 430. ἄκουσον, lit. hear the words of this Athena, i.e. ' I am Athena ; hear my words '.

l. 431. παῦσαι . . . , ' cease . . . sending out the flood of your army ', a vivid metaphor.

l. 432. πεπρωμένος, ' fated ', i.e. almost ' sent '.

l. 433. τε . . . τε, ' both . . . and in order to take to Argos his sister ', lit. the body of his sister. ἐσπέμψων and ἄξων (from ἀγώ) are future participles of purpose.

l. 436. ἀναψυχάς is in apposition to the whole of the previous sentence ; ' (to get) relief from. . .'.

l. 437. ἡμῖν is a kind of possessive dative; 'these (are) my words'. 'Ορέστην is the antecedent of ὅν and should be taken first, though by an ' anacoluthon ' or change of construction the word has no grammatical part in the sentence. ' As for Orestes, whom you expect to kill . . . , Poseidon is already making the surface of the sea calm so that he can voyage over it in his ship '. πορθμεύειν = ὥστε αὐτὸν πορθμεύειν. χάριν ἐμήν ' for my sake '.   With this prepositional meaning χάριν governs a genitive case, but with a personal pronoun a possessive adjective agrees with it. So in Latin, regis causa, ' for the sake of the king ', mea causa, ' for my sake '.

l. 442. ἄπιστος, supply ἐστί, 'whoever hears and does not obey the words of the gods is mad '.

l. 443. τε ... τε ... οὐχὶ θυμοῦμαι, ' I am not angry with either ... or. ...'.

l. 444. βέβηκε, from βαίνω. τί γὰρ ..., ' for what good (is it) to fight against the powerful gods? ', lit. in what way (accusative of respect) is it good.

l. 445. θεούς is here scanned as one long syllable.

l. 446. ἴτωσαν, an unusual and late form of the 3rd plural imperative of εἶμι, ' let them go '.

l. 447. καθιδρύσαιντο, a wish, ' may they dedicate the image with good fortune '.

l. 448. λόγχην ..., lit. the spear which I am raising, i.e. ' the spearmen whom I am sending out '.

l. 449. ναῶν = νεῶν. σοὶ τάδ' ὡς δοκεῖ, ' since this is your will ', lit. seems (good) to you.

l. 450. αἰνῶ, ' I approve ', i.e. ' it is well '. χρεών, the present participle of χρή, is used with the article to make a noun ; ' necessity rules the gods as well as you '. It is here scanned as one long syllable.

l. 452. συμπορεύσομαι ..., ' I will travel with him, bringing safely. ...'.

l. 453. ἀδελφῆς τῆς ἐμῆς, Artemis and Athena were both daughters of Zeus.

APPENDIX ON THE TEXT

The text used is that of the Oxford Classical Text by Professor Gilbert Murray, with omissions and alterations as given below. The numbering of the lines in this book and the corresponding lines in the full O.C.T. are also given. Minor alterations in punctuation are not given.

IPHIGENIA IN AULIS

ll. 1–55 = 49–104, omitting l. 93.

l. 72. κρίνας for κρίνων.   l. 84. πᾶσι for κᾶτα.

ll. 56–112 = 303–334 and ll. 378–401.

l. 378. αὖ for εὖ.

ll. 113–154 = 473–519, omitting ll. 502–503 and ll. 508–510.

ll. 502–503. τροπυὶ τοιοίδε for τροπαὶ τοιαίδε.

ll. 155–201 = 640–690, omitting ll. 652–655.

l. 657. θέλω μέν, ὃ θέλω δ' for θέλω γε· τὸ θέλειν δ'.

l. 665. Insert αὖθις after ταὐτόν, ἥξεις for ἥκεις, and omit σῷ.

l. 671. ἔασον for ἐατέ'.

ll. 262–279 = 819–898, omitting ll. 864–865.

l. 888. δάκρυον ... στέγει for δακρύων ... στέγω.

ll. 280–342 = 1211–1275, omitting ll. 1253–1254.

l. 1274. βαρβάρων for βαρβάροις.

ll. 343–438 = 1368–1473, omitting ll. 1402–1403, 1408–1409, 1416, 1425, 1430–1432 and 1438.

Iphigenia in Tauris

ll. 1–57 = 1–66, omitting ll. 35–41 and ll. 59–60.

l. 3. Ἀτρέως δ' ἄπο for Ἀτρέως δὲ παῖς.

ll. 58–93 = 77–112.

l. 86. σὴ for σοι.

l. 98. ἐμβησόμεθα for ἐκβησόμεθα.

ll. 94–171 = 492–569, with ll. 515–516 placed after l. 512.

ll. 172–272 = 727–833, omitting ll. 753–754, l. 782 and ll. 798–799.

l. 766. τῶν τε σῶν for τῶν θεῶν. ll. 778–779 are punctuated differently.

l. 829, omit [χθονὸς].

l. 832. δάκρυα for δάκρυ, and χαρά θ' ἄμα for ἄμα χάρᾳ.

ll. 273–318 = 1157–1202.

ll. 319–453 = 1313–1489, omitting ll. 1420–1, 1431–1434, 1446–1474 and 1482–1483.

l. 1349. ἐστῶτες for ἐστῶτας.

l. 1352 comes after l. 1349, and ll. 1349–1352 are punctuated differently.

l. 1353. διδόντες for δὲ δόντες.

ll. 1386–1387. τῆσδ'... ναῦται νεώς, λάβεσθε κώπης, for γῆς... ναῦται, νεὼς λάβεσθε κώπαις.

l. 1392. Comma at ἐχώρει, not at στόμια.

VOCABULARY

(General rules for determining the length of vowels are given on page xxxiii. Vowels that do not come under those rules can be assumed to be short unless they are marked as being long.)

ABBREVIATIONS

acc.	accusative	*interj.*	interjection
adj.	adjective	*interrog.*	interrogative
adv.	adverb	*intr.*	intransitive
aor.	aorist	*m.*	masculine
c.	common	*mid.*	middle
comp.	comparative	*n.*	neuter
conj.	conjunction	*p.p.*	perfect participle
contr.	contracted	*p.p.p.*	perfect participle passive
dat.	dative	*part.*	participle
f.	feminine	*pass.*	passive
fut.	future	*perf.*	perfect
gen.	genitive	*pl.*	plural
imperf.	imperfect	*poss.*	possessive
impers.	impersonal	*prep.*	preposition
indecl.	indeclinable	*pron.*	pronoun
indef.	indefinite	*superl.*	superlative
infin.	infinitive	*tr.*	transitive

A

ἁβρύνομαι, *with dat.*, have pride in.

ἀγαθός, -ή, -όν, good, noble.

ἄγαλμα, -ατος, *n.*, image.

Ἀγαμέμνων, -ονος, *m.*, Agamemnon, king of Mycenae.

ἄγαν, *adv.*, too much, too.

ἀγγέλλω, ἀγγελῶ, ἤγγειλα, ἤγγελκα, announce, bring news, give a message.

ἄγγελμα, -ατος, *n.*, news, message.

ἄγγελος, -ου, *m.*, messenger.

ἀγεννῶς, *adv.*, dishonourably.

ἀγκάλη, -ης, *f.*, arm.

ἀγκύλη, -ης, *f.*, loop (of a rope).

99

ἄγκῡρα, -ας, f., anchor.

ἁγνιστέος, -α, -ον, verbal adj., must be purified.

ἀγνοέω, -ήσω, not to know.

ἁγνός, -ή, -όν, pure, holy.

ἄγνωστος, -ον, unknown.

ἀγρεύομαι, aor., ἠγρευσάμην, catch.

ἀγχίπλους, -ουν, near by sea, short.

ἄγω, ἄξω, ἤγαγον, lead, drag, take, bring, raise.

ἀγών, -ῶνος, m., race, contest.

ἀδελφή, -ῆς, f., sister.

ἀδελφός, -οῦ, m., brother.

Ἀίδης, -ου, m., Hades, the god of the underworld, death.

ἀδικέω, -ήσω, ἠδίκησα, -ηκα, wrong, injure.

ἄδικος, -ον, unjust.

ἀδύνατος, -ον, impossible.

ἀεί, adv., always.

Ἀθάνα, Ἀθηναία, -ας, f., the goddess Athena.

Ἀθῆναι, -ῶν, f. pl., Athens.

Ἀθηναῖοι, -ων, m. pl., the Athenians.

ἄθλιος, -α, -ον, wretched.

ἀθρέω, -ήσω, see, consider.

ἀθροίζω, -σω, ἤθροισα, perf. pass., ἤθροισμαι, collect.

αἶα, -ας, f., land.

Αἰακός, -οῦ, m., Aeacus, grandfather of Achilles.

αἰδέομαι, -έσομαι, ἠδέσαμην, be ashamed, be shy, have mercy on, be considerate.

αἰδώς, -οῦς, f., modesty.

αἰθήρ, -έρος, m., air.

αἴθω, light, kindle ; mid., burn.

αἷμα, -ατος, n., blood, murder.

αἱματηρός, -ά, -όν, bloody, bloodshot, flushed with anger.

αἰνέω, -έσω, ἤνεσα, approve, praise.

αἱρέω, -ήσω, εἷλον, take ; mid., take, choose, recover.

αἴρω, ἀρῶ, ἦρα, raise ; mid., rise.

αἰσθάνομαι, αἰσθήσομαι, ᾐσθόμην, perceive.

αἴσθημα, -ατος, n., perception, understanding.

αἰσχρός, -ά, -όν, unfitting.

αἰτία, -ας, f., reason.

αἴτιος, -α, -ον, responsible, responsible for, with gen.

ἀκίνητος, -ον, not to be touched, inviolable.

ἀκοή, -ῆς, f., hearing, report.

ἀκοντίζω, -ιῶ, aim.

ἄκος, ἄκους, n., healing, remedy.

ἀκοσμία, -ας, f., wrangling.

ἀκούω, ἀκούσομαι, ἤκουσα, with gen. or acc., hear.

ἄκραντος, -ον, unfulfilled.

ἄκρος, -α, -ον, topmost.

ἀκτή, -ῆς, f., shore.

ἀκύμων, -ονος, calm.

ἄκων, ἄκουσα, ἆκον, unwilling.

ἀλάστωρ, -ορος, m., avenging deity.

ἀλγεινός, -ή, -όν, painful.

ἀλγέω, -ήσω, grieve (intr.).

ἀλγύνω, -υνῶ, grieve (tr.) ; mid., grieve (intr.).

Ἀλέξανδρος, -ου, m., Paris.

ἀληθής, -ές, true ; τὸ ἀληθές, the truth ; adv., really.

ἀλλά, conj., but.

ἀλλήλους, -λων, each other.

ἄλλοθι, adv., elsewhere.

ἄλλος, -η, -ον, other, another.

ἄλλοσε, adv., in another direction.

ἄλλως, adv., in vain ; ἄλλως τε, besides.

ἅλμη, -ης, f., sea, sea-water.

ἅλς, ἁλός, f., sea.

ἅμα, adv., at the same time.

ἀμελία, -άς, f., disregard.

ἀμηχανέω, -ήσω, be puzzled, be in difficulties.

ἀμήχανος, -ον, adj., impossible.

ἀμιλλάομαι, -ήσομαι, fight.

ἀμός, -ή, -όν, my, mine.

ἀμπνοή, -ῆς, f., rest, respite.

ἀμφί, prep. with acc., around, on; with dat., on, beside.

ἀμφίβληστρον, -ου, n., encirclement.

ἄμφω, ἀμφοῖν, dual, both.

ἄν, particle used in indefinite sentences, ever; and in conditionals, would.

ἀνά, prep. with acc., throughout.

ἀναγγέλλω, aor. -ήγγειλα, report, take back a message.

ἀναγκάζω, -άσω, compel.

ἀναγκαῖος, -α, -ον, necessary, unavoidable.

ἀνάγκη, -ης, f., necessity; with ἐστί, one must.

ἀναδέχομαι, -δέξομαι, receive.

ἀναιδής, -ές, shameless; τὸ ἀναιδές, shamelessness.

ἀναιρέω, -ήσω, -εῖλον, give the reply of an oracle.

ἀναίσχυντος, -ον, shameless.

ἀνακαλέω, -έσω, call upon.

ἀνακαλύπτω, -ψω, open.

ἀνάκτορον, -ου, n., also pl., temple.

ἀναλαμβάνω, -λήψομαι, -έλαβον, recover.

ἀναμιμνήσκομαι, ἀναμνήσομαι or ἀμμνήσομαι, with gen., remember.

ἄναξ, ἄνακτος, m., king, lord.

ἀνάξιος, -α, -ον, unworthy, disgraceful.

ἀναρπάζω, -σω, carry off.

ἄνασσα, -ης, f., queen.

ἀνάσσω, -ξω, with gen., be in command of.

ἀναστέλλω, -στελῶ, -έστειλα, check, keep back.

ἀναστένω, grieve for.

ἀναφέρω, -οίσω, -ήνεγκα, ascribe.

ἀναψυχή, -ῆς, f., also pl., relief.

ἀνεκτός, -ή, -όν, tolerable.

ἄνεμος, -ου, m., wind.

ἀνήρ, ἀνδρός, m., man, husband.

ἀνθαιρέομαι, -ήσομαι, -ειλόμην, put first, choose first.

ἀνθηρός, -ά, -όν, bright, fresh.

ἄνθρωπος, -ου, m., man.

ἀνίημι, -ήσω, -ῆκα, aor. part., ἀνείς, open.

ἀνιστορέω, -ήσω, question.

ἀνοίγω, -οίξω, -έῳξα, open, expose.

ἀνολολύζω, -ξω, cry aloud.

ἄνομος, -ον, lawless, illegal.

ἄνοστος, -ον, without a return.

ἀνταφίημι, -ήσω, -ῆκα, shed (tears) in sympathy with.

ἀντεῖπον, aor., speak in contradiction.

ἀντί, prep. with gen., instead of.

ἀντιδέχομαι, -δέξομαι, receive in return.

ἀντιδίδωμι, -δώσω, -έδωκα, aor. part., ἀντιδούς, give instead of, give in return.

ἀντιλάζυμαι, with gen., take hold of, touch.

ἄντομαι, beg, beseech.

ἄντρον, -ου, n., cave.

ἄνω, adv., up, on high.

ἀνώνυμος, -ον, without a name.

ἄξενος, -ον, inhospitable.

ἀξίωμα, -ατος, n., glory, reputation.

ἀξίως, adv. with gen., worthily, as befits.

ἀπαίρω, -αρῶ, -ῆρα, with ναῦν understood, set sail, depart.
ἀπαλλάσσω, -ξω, remove, give up; aor. pass., ἀπηλλάχθην, depart.
ἀπανταχοῦ, adv., everywhere.
ἅπαξ, adv., once, at once.
ἅπᾱς, ἅπᾱσα, ἅπᾶν, all, the whole.
ἀπειλή, -ῆς, f., threat.
ἄπειμι, -έσομαι, -ῆν, be away, be absent.
ἀπεμπολάω, -ήσω, smuggle out.
ἀπέρχομαι, -ειμι, -ῆλθον, go away.
ἄπιστός, -όν, unbelieving, disobedient, with dat.
ἄπλοια, -ας, f., weather unfit for sailing.
ἀπό, prep. with gen., from, away from, by.
ἀποβλέπω, -βλέψομαι, look at.
ἀποδίδωμι, -δώσω, -έδωκα, give back, deliver, repay, duly give.
ἀποικέω, -ήσω, with gen., live far away from.
ἀποκτείνω, -κτενῶ, -έκτανον, -έκτονα, kill.
ἀπολαύω, -λαύσομαι, with gen., have benefit from.
ἀπόλλῡμι, -ολῶ, -ώλεσα, ruin, kill, lose ; intr., -όλλυμαι, -ωλόμην, -όλωλα, die, be ruined, be lost.
'Απόλλων, -ωνος, m., Phoebus Apollo, the sun-god.
ἀπονοστέω, -ήσω, return home.
ἀποπτύω, -ύσω, spit (upon), reject, avert an omen.
ἀπορέω, -ήσω, be in difficulties.
ἀπορία, -ας, f., distress, perplexity.
ἄπορος, -ον, perplexing ; ἀπόρως ἔχειν, be perplexing.
ἀπόρρητος, -ον, ineffable, sacred.
ἀπουτέλλω, -στελῶ, -έστειλα, send back.

ἀποστολή, -ῆς, f., also pl., sending away of a daughter in marriage.
ἀποστρέφω, -ψω, aor. pass., -εστράφην, turn round ; mid. with acc., turn away from.
ἀπουσία, -ας, f., absence.
ἅπτομαι, ἅψομαι, ἡψάμην, with gen., lay hold of.
ἄπωθεν, adv. with gen., away from.
ἀπωθέω, -ώσω, -έωσα, thrust away, drive out.
ἄρα, inferential particle, then.
ἆρα, interrog. particle ; also =ἄρα.
ἀραῖος, -α, -ον, with dat., bringing a curse upon.
'Αργεῖος, -α, -ον, Argive, Greek.
"Αργος, -ους, n., Argos, the city and country of Agamemnon ;
'Αργόθεν, from Argos.
ἀρέσκω, ἀρέσω, ἤρεσα, with dat., satisfy.
ἀριστερός, -ά, -όν, left, left-hand.
ἄριστος, -η, -ον, superl. of ἀγαθός, best, noble ; adv., ἄριστα.
ἀρκέω, ἀρκέσω, suffice, be enough.
ἄρκυς, -υος, f., net, snare.
ἅρμα, -ατος, n., chariot.
ἀρνός, f. gen. (no nom.), lamb.
ἁρπαγή, -ῆς, f., theft.
ἁρπάζω, -σω, snatch away.
ἄρρητος, -ον, ineffable, sacred ; τἄρρητα, sacred mysteries.
ἄρσην, ἄρσεν, male.
"Αρτεμις, -ιδος, f., Artemis, the goddess of hunting.
ἀρτίφρων, -ον, sane, sound of mind.
ἀρχή, -ῆς, f., also pl., beginning, prelude.
ἄρχω, -ξω, with gen., control, rule, manage.
ἀσκέω, -ήσω, equip.

ἄσμενος, -η, -ον, glad, happy.

ἀσπίς, -ίδος, f., shield.

ᾄσσω, ᾄξω, ᾖξα, rush out.

ἀστός, -οῦ, m., citizen.

ἀσύνετος, -ον, devoid of understanding.

ἀσφαλής, -ές, safe.

Ἀτρεύς, -έως, m., Atreus, son of Pelops, father of Agamemnon and Menelaus.

Ἀτρεῖδαι, -ῶν, m., the sons of Atreus.

αὖ, adv., again, in turn.

αὖθις, adv., again.

Αὐλίς, acc., -ίν or -ίδα, -ίδος, f., Aulis, a town in Boeotia.

αὐξάνω, αὐξήσω, increase ; p.p.p., ηὐξημένος, grown up.

αὔρα, -ας, f., wind, gust.

αὐτίκα, adv., presently.

αὐτόματος, -η, -ον, of one's own accord.

αὐτός, -ή, -ό, emphatic pron., myself, himself ; in oblique cases, him, her, it ; ὁ αὐτός, contr. αὑτός, αὑτή, ταὐτό or ταὐτόν, the same.

αὐτοῦ, adv., there.

αὐτόχειρ, -ος, with one's own hand.

ἀφαιρέομαι, -ήσομαι, -ειλόμην, with two accs., take away from, deprive of.

ἀφανής, -ές, lost.

ἀφανίζω, -ιῶ, aor. pass., ἠφανίσθην, lose.

ἀφασία, -ας, f., speechlessness.

ἀφειδέω, -ήσω, with gen., not respect.

ἀφίημι, -ήσω, -ῆκα, give up, send away.

ἀφικνέομαι, -ίξομαι, -ικόμην, -ῖγμαι, come, come to.

ἀφίστημι, ἀποστήσω, -έστησα, remove ; strong aor., ἀπέστην, stand away.

ἀφορμίζομαι, -ίσομαι, -ωρμισάμην, unmoor.

Ἀφροδίτη, -ης, f., Aphrodite, the goddess of love ; love, passion.

ἄφρων, -ονος, foolish.

Ἀχαιοί, -ῶν, m., Achaeans, Greeks.

ἄχαρις, -ι, worthless.

ἄχθομαι, -θέσομαι, ἠχθέσθην, be vexed.

ἄχθος, -ους, n., burden, sorrow.

Ἀχιλλεύς, -έως, m., Achilles, son of Peleus and Thetis.

ἄωρος, -ον, before one's time.

B

βάθρον, -ου, n., also pl., foundation, pedestal, city.

βαίνω, βήσομαι, ἔβην, go.

βάλλω, βαλῶ, ἔβαλον, p.p.p., βεβλημένος, throw, throw down, fall upon, plunge, touch, strike.

βάρβαρος, -ον, barbarian, foreign, unintelligible ; noun, a barbarian.

βασίλειος, -α, -ον, royal.

βασιλεύς, -έως, m., king.

βέβαιος, -α, -ον, constant.

βέλτιστος, -η, -ον, superl. of ἀγαθός, best.

βία, -ας, f., force.

βίος, -ου, m., life.

βλαστάνω, -τήσω, ἔβλαστον, be born.

βλέπω, βλέψομαι, ἔβλεψα, see, look.

βλέφαρον, -ου, n., eyelid, eye.

βλώσκω, μολοῦμαι, ἔμολον, come, go.

βοή, -ῆς, f., shout, cry, voice.

βοηθέω, -ήσω, with dat., help.
βούλομαι, -ήσομαι, βεβούλημαι, ἐβουλήθην, wish, want.
βούσταθμον, -ου, n., ox-stall.
βραχίων, -ονος, m., arm.
βραχύς, -εῖα, -ύ, short ; ἐν βραχεῖ, in brief.
βρέτας, -ους, n., image.
βρόχος, -ου, m., noose, rope.
βωμός, -οῦ, m., also pl., altar.

Γ

γαῖα, -ας, f., land.
γαμέω, -ῶ, ἔγημα, marry (a wife) ; mid. with dat., marry (a husband).
γάμος, -ου, m., also pl., marriage.
γάρ, conj., for.
γε, enclitic particle, at least, of course ; in dialogue, yes, no.
γείνομαι, be born ; aor., ἐγεινάμην, beget, give birth to.
γελάω, -άσομαι, laugh at, mock.
γένεθλον, -ου, n., child, daughter, descendant.
γενειάς, -άδος, f., cheek.
γένειον, -ου, n., chin, beard.
γενναῖος, -α, -ον, noble.
γεννάω, -ήσω, beget, give birth to.
γένος, -ους, n., race, son.
γεραιός, -ά, -όν, old; m., old man.
γέρων, -οντος, m., old man.
γῆ, γῆς, f., land, earth.
γηθέω, -ήσω, perf. with present meaning, γέγηθα rejoice.
γίγνομαι, γενήσομαι, ἐγενόμην, γέγονα, perf. part., γεγώς, be, become, be born, arise.
γιγνώσκω, γνώσομαι, ἔγνων, learn, find out about, decide.
γλῶσσα, -ης, f., tongue.

γνώμη, -ης, f., thought, expectation.
γόνος, -ου, m., son, child.
γόνυ, γόνατος, n., knee.
γόος, -ου, m., weeping.
γοῦν, particle, then, therefore.
γράμμα, -ατος, n., word ; pl., letter, message.
γραφή, -ῆς, f., also pl., a letter.
γράφω, -ψω, ἔγραψα, γέγραμμαι, write, send a message.
γυμνός, -ή, -όν, bare, naked.
γυνή, -αικός, f., woman, lady, wife.

Δ

δαί, particle used after τί, then.
δάκνω, δήξομαι, ἔδακον, grieve, vex.
δάκρυ and δάκρυον, -ου, n., tear.
δακρυρροέω, -ήσω, weep.
δάμαρ, -αρτος, f., wife.
Δαναΐδαι, -ῶν. m. pl., Greeks, descendants of Danaus.
Δαναοί, -ῶν, m. pl., Greeks, subjects of Danaus.
Δάρδανος, -ου, m., Dardanus, founder of Troy.
δᾱρός, -ά, -όν, long.
δέ, particle, and, but.
δεῖ, impersonal, it is necessary ; with acc., must ; with gen., there is need of.
δείκνῡμι, δείξω, ἔδειξα, show.
δεινός, -ή, -όν. terrible, disgraceful, hostile, cruel.
δέλεαρ, -ατος, n., bait.
δέλτος, -ου, f., writing-tablet, tablet.
δέμας, indecl., n., body.
δεξιά, -ᾱς, f., right hand.
δέρη, -ης, f., neck.
δεσμός, -οῦ, m., in pl. also n., δεσμά, fetter, bond.

δεσπότης, -ου, m., master.
δεῦρο, adv., hither.
δεύτερος, -α, -ον, second.
δέχομαι, δέξομαι, receive, accept, gather up.
δή, particle, indeed, then.
δῆτα, adv., indeed, then, really.
Δία, acc. of Ζεύς.
διά, prep. with acc., on account of, through ; with gen., by means of, through ; διὰ μακροῦ, for a long time.
διαβάλλω, -βαλῶ, -έβαλον, -εβλήθην, slander.
διαβιάζομαι, -άσομαι, compel.
διαδοχή, -ῆς, f., succession, relay.
διακλύζω, -ύσω, wash.
διαλύω, -λύσω, disband.
διαπεράω, -άσω, pass through.
διαπτυχή, -ῆς, f., fold, page.
διαφεύγω, -φεύξομαι, -έφυγον, escape.
δίδωμι, δώσω, ἔδωκα, give, make.
δίκαιος, -α, -ον and -ος, -ον, just, right, righteous, proper ; τὸ δίκαιον, justice.
δίκη, -ης, f., justice, penalty ; δίκην δίδωμι, pay the penalty.
δίνη, -ης, f., eddy.
διόλλυμι, -ολῶ, -ώλεσα, kill, ruin.
δίς, adv., twice, again.
διωγμός, -οῦ, m., also pl., pursuit, being pursued.
διώκω, -ξω, pursue, overwhelm.
δοκέω, δόξω, ἔδοξα, think, seem ; impers., seem good, resolve, with dat.; perf. pass, δέδοκται.
δόλιος, -α, -ον, false, cunning.
δόλος, -ου, m., guile.
δολόω, -ώσω, deceive, beguile.
δόμος, -ου, m., also pl., house, home.

δόξα, -ης, f., idea, thought, glory.
δοξάζω, -άσω, think.
δόρυ, δόρος, n., spear, ship.
δοῦλος, -ου, m., slave.
δοῦναι, δούς, aor. infin. and part. of δίδωμι, give.
δραμεῖν, aor. infin. of τρέχω, run.
δραπέτης, -ου, m., fugitive.
δράω, δράσω, do.
δρόμος, -ου, m., race, running, haste.
δρόσος, -ου, f., dew, water.
δύναμαι, -ήσομαι, ἐδυνήθην, be able.
δύο, δυοῖν, two.
δυσγενής, -ές, low-born ; τὸ δυσγενές, dishonour.
δυσπραξία, -ας, f., misfortune.
δυσσεβής, -ες, impious.
δυστυχής, -ές, unhappy.
δῶμα, -ατος, n., also pl., house, palace, tent, building, temple.

Ε

ἐά, interj. ah, ha, alas.
ἐάν, conj. with subj., if.
ἐάω, ἐάσω, εἴασα, fut. pass., ἐάσομαι, allow, let, let be.
ἐγγίγνομαι, -γενήσομαι, be born in.
ἐγγράφω, -ψω, p.p.p., ἐγγεγραμμένος, write in.
ἐγγύθεν, adv., from near at hand.
ἐγγύς, adv. with gen., near.
ἐγενόμην, aor. of γίγνομαι.
ἐγκροτέω, -ήσω, tr., dash against.
ἐγώ and ἔγωγε, ἐμοῦ, pron., I.
ἕδρα, -ας, f., seat, place.
ἔδωκα, aor. of δίδωμι.
εἰ, conj., if.
εἶα, interj., come, come now.
εἰδέναι, infin. of οἶδα.
εἶδον, aor. of ὁράω.
εἶδος, -ους, n., figure, pattern.

106 VOCABULARY

εἴθε, *interj.*, would that.

εἰκάζω, -άσω, guess.

εἰκός, -ότος, *n.*, what is natural, right.

εἰκότως, *adv.*, naturally.

εἰκών, *acc.*, εἰκώ, *f.*, picture.

εἷλον, *aor. of* αἱρέω.

εἷμα, -ατος, *n.*, garment.

εἰμί, ἔσομαι, ἦν, be.

εἷμι, *fut. of* ἔρχομαι, come, go.

εἵνεκα, *prep. after gen.*, for the sake of.

εἴπερ, *conj.*, if indeed.

εἶπον, *aor.*, 2nd *sing. also* εἶπας, *fut.*, ἐρῶ, *aor. pass.*, ἐρρήθην, say, order.

εἴργω, -ξω, keep off, ward off.

εἰς, *prep. with acc.*, to, into, towards.

εἷς, μία, ἕν, one.

εἰσακούω, -ούσομαι, -ήκουσα, *with gen.*, listen to, hear.

εἰσβαίνω, -βήσω, -έβην, *with two accs.*, put on board.

εἰσέρχομαι, -ειμι, -ῆλθον, come upon, occur to.

εἰσοράω, -όψομαι, -εῖδον, see, look at.

εἰσπλέω, -πλεύσομαι, -έπλευσα, sail into.

εἰσπράσσομαι, -ξομαι, exact.

εἶτα, *adv.*, then.

εἴωθα, *perf. with present sense*, be accustomed.

ἐκ, ἐξ, *prep. with gen.*, from, out of, away from.

ἕκατι, *prep. with gen.*, on account of, for the sake of.

ἐκβαίνω, -βήσομαι, -έβην, come out, go out.

ἐκβάλλω, -βαλῶ, -έβαλον, let fall.

ἐκβολή, -ῆς, *f.*, jetsam, wreckage ; *pl.*, wrecked crew.

ἐκβρῦχάομαι, -ήσομαι, shout aloud, utter.

ἐκγαυρόομαι, -ώσομαι, take pride in, boast of.

ἔκδημος, -ον, away from home.

ἐκδιδάσκω, -ξω, teach, inform.

ἐκδίδωμι, -δώσω, -έδωκα, give in marriage.

ἐκεῖ, *adv.*, there.

ἐκεῖθεν, *adv.*, from there.

ἐκεῖνος, -η, -ο, that ; *pron.*, he.

ἔκηλος, -ον, calm, happy.

ἐκκαλύπτω, -ψω, reveal.

ἐκκλέπτω, -ψω, steal away.

ἐκλείπω, -ψω, -έλιπον, leave, break (an oath).

ἐκλευκαίνω, make white.

ἐκμοχθέω, -ήσω, toil (at), take trouble.

ἐκνεύω, -σω, incline to, signal to (*with acc.*).

ἐκπίμπλημι, -πλήσω, -έπλησα, complete, pass through.

ἐκπίπτω, -πεσοῦμαι, -έπεσον, break (*intr.*) (of a wave).

ἐκπλήσσω, -ξω, interrupt, disturb ; *p.p.p.*, ἐκπεπληγμένος, bewildered.

ἐκποδών, *adv.*, aside, out of the way.

ἐκπορθέω, -ήσω, sack, pillage.

ἐκπράσσω, -ξω, perform, bring to pass.

ἐκσώζω, -σω, save, bring safely.

ἐκτείνω, -τενῶ, -έτεινα, smoothe.

ἐκτέμνω, -τεμῶ, -έτεμον, cut off.

ἐκτρέφω, -θρέψω, bring up.

ἐκφεύγω, -φεύξομαι, -έφυγον, flee away.

ἐκφροντίζω, -ιῶ, decide, think out.

ἐκφύομαι, ἐξέφῦν, -πέφῦκα, be born.

ἑκών, ἑκοῦσα, ἑκόν, willingly.

ἐλαύνω, ἐλῶ, ἤλασα, ἠλάθην, drive, pursue.

ἔλαφος, -ου, c., deer, hind.

ἐλέγχω, -ξω, question.

Ἑλένη, -ης, f., Helen, wife of Menelaus.

ἔλεος, -ου, m., pity.

ἑλεῖν, aor. infin. of αἱρέω.

ἐλεύθερος, -α, -ον, free.

ἐλευθερόω, -ώσω, set free, free.

ἐλθεῖν, aor. infin. of ἔρχομαι.

ἑλίσσω, -ξω, whirl round.

ἕλκω, -ξω, εἵλκυσα, drag down.

Ἑλλάς -άδος, f., Greece ; f. adj., Greek.

Ἕλλην, -ηνος, m., a Greek ; adj., Greek.

Ἑλληνικός, -ή, -όν, Greek.

Ἑλληνίς, -ίδος, f. adj., Greek.

ἐλπίς, -ίδος, f., hope.

ἐμαυτόν, -ήν, reflex pron., myself.

ἐμβαίνω, -βήσομαι, -έβην, go up, mount.

ἐμβάλλω, -βαλῶ, ἐνέβαλον, put on.

ἐμός, -ή, -όν, my, mine.

ἔμπεδος, -ον, firm, binding.

ἐμπεδόω, -ώσω, fulfil.

ἐμποδών, adv., in the way.

ἔμπυρα, -ων, n. pl., burnt sacrifices.

ἐμφύομαι, perf. ἐμπέφῦκα, be natural, be implanted in.

ἐν, prep. with dat., in.

ἐνάρχομαι, -ξομαι, begin a rite with.

ἐνδεξιόομαι, -ώσομαι, move round (with acc.) towards the right.

ἔνδικος, -ον, just.

ἔνδοθεν, adv., from within.

ἔνειμι, -έσομαι, -ῆν, be in.

ἔνθα, adv., where.

ἐνθάδε, adv., here.

ἐνθένδε, adv., afterwards.

ἐνιαυτός, -οῦ, m., year.

ἐννοέω, -ήσω, also mid., consider, ponder.

ἐνταῦθα, adv., there.

ἐντεῦθεν, adv., afterwards.

ἐντός, prep. with gen., inside.

ἐξ before a vowel = ἐκ.

ἐξαίφνης, adv., suddenly.

ἐξαίρετος, -ον, splendid, as an exception.

ἐξαιρέω, -ήσω, -εἶλον, capture, drag out.

ἐξανάπτω, -ψω, suspend from, haul up, fasten.

ἐξαναρπάζω, -σω, snatch away.

ἐξάπτω, -ψω, fasten, throw ; mid., put on.

ἐξαρπάζω, -σω, snatch away.

ἐξαρτάομαι, -ήσομαι, intr., hang, cling.

ἐξάρχω, -ξω, begin, dictate.

ἐξαυδάω, -ήσω, speak out.

ἐξαφίσταμαι, with gen., withdraw from.

ἔξεδρος, -ον, with gen., driven out of.

ἐξονειδίζω, -ιῶ, -ωνείδισα, utter a reproach against.

ἐξορμάω, -ήσω, send out.

ἔξω, adv., outside ; with gen., outside, out of.

ἔοικα, perf. with pres. sense, 3rd pl., εἴξᾶσι, seem.

ἐπάγω, -ξω, -ήγαγον, drive on.

ἐπᾴδω, -ᾴσομαι, sing.

ἐπαίρομαι, -αροῦμαι, raise, take up.

ἐπαράομαι, -άσομαι, swear, take an oath.

ἐπαυρέομαι, aor., -ηυρόμην, with gen., get the advantage of.

ἐπεί, conj., when, after, since.

ἐπείγομαι, -ξομαι, *imperf.*, ἠπειγό-
μην, be in difficulties.
ἐπειδή, *conj.*, when, since.
ἔπειμι, *part.*, -ιών, come, approach.
ἔπειτα, *adv.*, then.
ἐπευφημέω, -ήσω, *with acc. and
dat.*, sing in support of ; *with
two accs.*, sing in honour of.
ἐπεύχομαι, -ξομαι, boast.
ἐπέχω, ἐφέξω, ἐπέσχον, hold
back.
ἐπί, *prep. with acc.*, against, to,
for ; *with gen.*, on, in the power
of ; *with dat.*, for, with, in
addition to.
ἐπικουρέω, -ήσω, *with dat.*, help.
ἐπίκουρος, -ου, *m.*, ally, helper.
ἐπίκρᾱνον, -ου, *n.*, capital (of a
column).
ἐπιλανθάνομαι, -λήσομαι, -ελαθόμην,
-λέλησμαι, forget.
ἐπιστέλλω, -στελῶ, send a message.
ἐπιστολή, -ῆς, *f.*, *also pl.*, letter.
ἐπιστρατεύω, -σω, go on an expedition against.
ἐπίτηδες, *adv.*, deceitfully.
ἐπίφθονος, -ον, hateful.
ἕπομαι, ἕψομαι, ἑσπόμην, *with dat.*,
follow, accompany.
ἐπόμνῡμι, -ομοῦμαι, -ώμοσα, swear
by.
ἔπος, ἔπους, *n.*, word.
ἐπτερωμένος, winged, *p.p.p. of
πτερόω*.
ἐπυθόμην, *aor. of πυνθάνομαι.*
ἐπωμίς, -ίδος, *f.*, shoulder, arm.
ἐπωτίδες, -ων, *f. pl.*, catheads
(beams from which anchors
were suspended).
ἐράω, *with acc. or gen.*, love, enjoy,
desire.
ἐργάζομαι, -άσομαι, do.

ἔργον, -ου, *n.*, deed, action ; ἐν
ἔργῳ, ready.
ἐρείψιμος, -ον, in ruins.
ἐρετμόν, -οῦ, *n.*, oar.
ἐρημία, -ας, *f.*, solitude.
'Ερίνυς, -ύος, *f.*, Fury (avenger
of murder).
ἔρις, ἔριδος, *acc. also ἔριν, f.*, strife,
quarrel.
ἔρος, -ου, *m.*, desire.
ἕρπω, -ψω, go.
ἔρχομαι, εἶμι, ἦλθον, come, go.
ἐρῶ, *used as fut. of εἶπον*, speak,
say.
ἔρως, -ωτος, *m.*, love.
ἐρωτάω, -ήσω, ask.
ἐς = εἰς, *prep. with acc.*, to,
towards.
ἔσβασις, -εως, *f.*, entrance.
ἐσδέχομαι, -ξομαι, receive.
ἐσέρχομαι, -ειμι,-ῆλθον, come upon,
occur to.
ἐσθλός, -ή, -όν, noble, happy.
ἐσοράω, -όψομαι, -εῖδον, see, look
at, consider.
ἐσπέμπω, -ψω, send to.
ἔσω, *adv. with gen.*, inside.
ἔσωθεν, *adv. with gen.*, inside,
within.
ἔτι, *adv.*, still, any longer.
ἕτοιμος, -η, -ον, ready.
ἔτυχον, *aor. of τυγχάνω.*
εὖ, *adv.*, well, justly, aptly.
εὐβουλία, -ας, *f.*, good counsel.
εὐδαιμονέω, -ήσω, be happy,
prosper.
εὐδαίμων, -ονος, happy, fortunate.
εὕδω, -ήσω, sleep.
εὐεργετέω, -ήσω, benefit, help.
εὐεργέτις, -ιδος, *f.*, benefactress.
εὐθυντηρία, -ας, *f.*, stern-hole.
εὐθύς, *adv.*, immediately.

εὐκλεής, -ές, honourable, renowned; adv., εὐκλεῶς, nobly.
εὐλαβεστέρως, comp. adv. of
εὐλαβής, more carefully.
εὐμαρής, -ές, easy.
εὔμιτος, -ον, with fine threads,
fine.
εὖνις, -ιδος, f., wife.
εὔνους, -ουν, well-disposed.
εὔπηνος, -ον, of fine texture, fine.
εὐπρεπής, -ές, beautiful, fair.
εὔπρυμνος, -ον, with goodly
stern.
Εὔριπος, -ου, m., the Euripus, a
strait between Boeotia and
Euboea.
εὑρίσκω, εὑρήσω, ηὗρον, εὕρηκα,
εὕρημαι, find.
εὐσέβεια, -ας, f., piety.
εὐσεβής, -ές, pious, sacred ; τὸ
εὐσεβές, piety.
εὔσημος, ον, fair-ensigned, with
fine ensigns.
εὐτυχέω, -ήσω, be happy, prosper.
εὐτυχῶς, adv., with good fortune,
successfully.
εὐφημία, -ας, f., solemn silence.
εὐφραίνομαι, -ανοῦμαι, εὐφράνθην
obtain one's desire.
εὐχή, -ῆς, f., prayer.
εὔχομαι, -ξομαι, ηὐξάμην. vow,
pray, wish.
ἐφίσταμαι, ἐπιστήσομαι, ἐφέστηκα,
ἐπεστάθην, with dat., stand beside, stand on.
ἐχθρός, -οῦ, m., enemy.
ἔχω, ἕξω, ἔσχον, keep, restrain,
have, know, possess, wait, be
able ; mid. with gen., cling to,
seize ; with an adverb = εἰμί
with an adjective.
ἕως, conj., while.

Z
ζάω, infin. ζῆν, live.
Ζεύς, Διός, m., Zeus, father of
gods and men.
ζηλόω, -ώσω, envy.
ζητέω, -ήσω, ask, ask for.

H
ἤ, conj., or, either . . . or, than.
ἦ, adv., indeed ; also used in
questions expecting the answer
'no' .
ἦ μήν, verily, indeed.
ἤδη, adv., already, now.
ἡδονή, -ῆς, f., pleasure, desire.
ἡδύς, ἡδεῖα, ἡδύ, sweet, pleasant,
happy, attractive ; ἡδέως
ἔχειν, be happy, prosper.
ἥκιστα, superl. adv., by no means,
least of all.
ἥκω, ἥξω, come, have come,
came.
Ἠλέκτρα, -ας, f., Electra,
daughter of Agamemnon.
ἦλθον, aor. of ἔρχομαι.
ἥλιος, -ου, m., sun.
ἦμαι, imperf. ἥμην, sit, sit idle.
ἡμεῖς, ἡμῶν, we, I.
ἡμέρα, -ας, f., day.
ἡνία, -ας, f., rein.
ἤν, =ἐάν, conj. with subj., if.
ἧπαρ, ἥπατος, n., stomach, liver.
ἥσσων, -ον, comp., less, weaker ;
adv., ἧσσον, less.

Θ
θάλασσα, -ης, f., sea.
θαλάσσιος, -α, -ον, of the sea.
θάνατος, -ου, m., death.
θανεῖν, aor. infin. of θνήσκω.
θάλλω, -ήσω, flourish.
θαμά, adv., often.

θάρσος, -ους, n., confidence, boldness.

θαῦμα, -ατος, n., wonder, marvel.

θαυμάζω, -άσομαι, marvel at.

θαυμαστός, -ή, -όν, wonderful.

θεά, -ᾶς, f., goddess.

θεάομαι, -άσομαι, see.

θεῖος, -α, -ον, divine ; τὸ θεῖον, the gods.

θέλω, -ήσω, wish, want.

θέμις, -ιστος, f., what is right.

θεός, -οῦ, c., god, goddess.

Θεστίας, -άδος, f., daughter of Thestius, Leda.

θέσφατα, -ων, n. pl., oracle(s).

Θέτις, -ιδος, f., Thetis, a Nereid, wife of Peleus and mother of Achilles.

θηράω, -άσω, also mid., hunt, hunt down.

θνήσκω, θανοῦμαι, ἔθανον, τέθνηκα, die, be killed.

θνητός, -όν, mortal.

Θόας, m., Thoas, king of the Tauri.

θοός, -ή, -όν, swift.

θόρυβος, -ου, m., uproar, disturbance.

θριγκός, -οῦ, m., cornice, the topmost course of stones or bricks in a wall.

θρίξ, τριχός, f., hair.

θρώσκω, θοροῦμαι, ἔθορον, jump, leap.

θυγάτηρ, -τρός, f., daughter.

Θυέστης, -ου, m., Thyestes, son of Pelops.

θυηπόλος, -ον, f., priestess.

θῦμα, -ατος, n., sacrifice, victim.

θυμόομαι, -ώσομαι, with dat., be angry with.

θυσία, -ας, f., sacrifice.

θύω, θύσω, ἔθυσα, sacrifice.

I

ἰδεῖν, aor. infin. of ὁράω.

Ἴδη, -ης, f., Mount Ida, near Troy.

ἰδού, interj., behold.

ἱερέα, -ας, f., priestess.

ἱερός, -ά, -όν, holy ; n. pl., ἱερά, holy rites.

ἱκετεύω, -σω, with acc. or gen., beseech.

ἱκετηρία, -ας, f., with ῥάβδος understood, a suppliant's olivebranch.

Ἴλιον, -ου, n., Ilium, Troy.

ἱμείρομαι, with gen., desire, want.

ἵνα, conj., in order that ; adv., where.

ἰός, -οῦ, m., arrow.

ἵππευμα, -ατος, n., riding (on horseback).

Ἱπποδάμεια, -ας, f., Hippodamia, wife of Pelops.

ἵππος, -ου, c., horse, mare.

ἴσος, -η, -ον, equal, same.

ἵστημι, στήσω, ἔστησα, tr., set up, make ; ἵσταμαι, ἔστην, ἔστηκα, part., ἑστώς, fut., ἑστήξομαι, ἐστάθην, stand.

ἱστίον, -ου, n., sail.

ἱστορέω, -ήσω, ask.

ἱστός, -οῦ, m., web, woven work.

ἴσχω, a form of ἔχω, hold, prevent.

ἴσως, adv., perhaps.

Ἰφιγένεια, -ας, f., Iphigenia, daughter of Agamemnon.

ἴχνος, -ους, n., footprint.

K

καθαιμάσσω, -ξω, make bloody.

κάθαιμος, -ον, bloody, bleeding.

καθάρματα, -ων, *n.* *pl.*, rites of purification.
καθαρμός, -οῦ, *n.*, cleansing.
καθαρός, -ά, -όν, pure.
καθάρσιος, -ον, for purification.
κάθημαι, sit.
καθιδρύομαι, -ύσομαι, -ιδρύσαμην, dedicate.
καθίημι, -ήσω, -ῆκα, pour out, pour forth, let down, hold out.
καθίσταμαι, *perf.*, -έστηκα, stand.
καθοσιόομαι, -ώσομαι, -ωσιωσάμην, dedicate.
καί, *conj.*, and, also, even, both ... and.
καινός, -ή, -όν, new, strange.
καινουργέω, -ήσω, make strange ; *with* λόγον, utter strange words.
καίνω, κανῶ, ἔκανον, kill, slaughter.
καίπερ, *conj.*, although.
καίριος, -α, -ον, timely ; τὰ καίρια, the main facts.
καιρός, -οῦ, *m.*, right time, right.
κακίζω, -ιῶ, make a coward of ; *verbal adj.*, κακιστέον, one must bring reproach on.
κακός, -ή, -όν, evil, bad ; τὸ κακόν, misfortune, evil; *adv.*, κακῶς ; *superl.*, κάκιστος.
κακόφρων, -ονος, foolish.
καλέω, καλῶ, ἐκάλεσα, ἐκλήθην, call.
καλός, -ή, -όν, good, right ; τὸ καλόν, honour ; *adv.*, καλῶς, well, aright, nobly ; *comp.*, καλλιών, *superl.*, κάλλιστος, fairest.
καλλίνικος, -ον, with glorious victory.
καλλιστεῖον, -οῦ, *n.*, title of ' fairest '.
Κάλχας, -αντος, *m.*, Calchas, a seer.

κάμπιμος, -η, -ον, turning, doubling back.
κάμπτω, -ψω, turn (a chariot).
κανοῦν, -οῦ, *n.*, basket.
κάρā, *dat.*, κάρᾳ, *n.*, head.
καρδία, -ας, *f.*, heart.
καρτερέω, -ήσω, bear patiently, endure.
κασιγνήτη, -ης, *f.*, sister.
κασίγνητος, -ου, *m.*, brother.
κατά, *prep. with acc.*, throughout, at, in, as concerns ; *with gen.*, against, down from.
καταδουλόομαι, -ώσομαι, enslave.
κατᾴδω, -ᾴσομαι, sing as an incantation.
καταθνήσκω, -θανοῦμαι, -έθανον, *inf.* κατθανεῖν, die.
κατακτείνω, -κτενῶ, -έκτανον, kill.
καταναγκάζω, -σω, *perf. pass.*, -ηναγκάσμαι, exact by force.
κατανοτίζω, -σω, bedew.
κατάρχομαι, -ξομαι, -ηρξάμην, *with gen.*, prepare for sacrifice.
κατασκάπτω, -ψω, destroy.
κατασκαφή, -ῆς, *f.*, *also pl.*, destruction.
κατεργάζομαι, -άσομαι, -ειργασάμην, kill.
κατεύχομαι, -ξομαι, utter a curse.
κατήρης, -ες, made ready.
κατοικτίζομαι, -ισομαι, -ῳκτίσθην, lament, utter lamentations.
κατοικτίρω, -ερῶ, -ῴκτιρα, *with gen.*, have mercy on, spare.
κατόμνῡμι, -ομοῦμαι, -ώμοσα, swear, swear by.
κεῖνος, -η, -ον, that ; *pron.*, he.
κεῖθεν, *adv.*, from there.
κέλευσμα, -ατος, *n.*, word of command.
κελεύω, -σω, order.

112 VOCABULARY

κέρδος, -ους, n., gain, advantage.
κερτομέω, -ήσω, insult, make fun of.
κηλέω, -ήσω, charm, enchant.
κηλίς, -ῖδος, f., stain.
κήρυγμα, -ατος, n., proclamation.
κήρυσσω, -ξω, report.
κίνδῦνος, -ου, m., danger.
κλαίω, κλαύσομαι, weep, rue it.
κλεινός, -ή, -όν, famous.
κλέος, -ους, n., glory, fame.
κλέπτω, -ψω, steal.
κλῇθρον, -ου, n., bar.
κλῖμαξ, -ακος, f., ladder.
κλοπή, -ῆς, f., also pl., theft.
κλύδων, -ωνος, m., wave.
κλύζω, -σω, wash away.
Κλυταιμήστρα, -ας, f., Clytemnestra, wife of Agamemnon.
κλύω, -σω, hear.
κνίζω, -σω, urge on.
κοινός, -ή, -όν, common, open to all.
κοινωνός, -όν, shared by both.
κόμη, -ης, f., also pl., hair.
κομίζω, -ιῶ, ἐκόμισα, send for, take, convey; mid., take away, bring back.
κομψεύομαι, -σομαι, perf., κεκόμψευμαι, make to seem fine.
κοντός, -οῦ, m., pole.
κόρη, -ης, f., maiden, daughter; also eye, eyelid.
κρατέω, ήσω, with gen., rule.
κρείσσων, -ον, comp. of ἀγαθός, better.
κρημνός, -οῦ, m., cliff.
κρίνω, κρινῶ, ἔκρῑνα, judge.
κρύπτω, -ψω, conceal.
κρύφιος, -ον, secretly, in hiding.
κτάομαι, κτήσομαι, possess, incur, win, get possession of, catch; p.p., κεκτημένος, possessing.

κτείνω, κτενῶ, ἔκτεινα and ἔκτανον, kill.
κτῆμα, -ατος, n., thing, possession.
κυάνεος, -α, -ον, blue, dark-blue.
κῦμα, -ατος, n., wave.
κυρέω, -ήσω, with gen., obtain.
κύριος, -α, -ον, right, entitled.
κῶλον, -ου, n., foot.
κωλύω, -σω, prevent.
κώπη, -ης, f., oar.

Λ

λαβεῖν, aor. infin. of λαμβάνω.
λάβρος, -α, -ον, violent, rough, stormy.
Λαέρτης, -ου, m., Laertes, father of Odysseus.
λαθεῖν, aor. infin. of λανθάνω.
λάθρᾳ, adv., secretly.
Λάκαινα, -ης, f., adj., Spartan.
Λακεδαίμων, -ονος, f., Lacedaemon, Sparta, the home of Helen.
λακτίζω, -ιῶ, kick, struggle.
λαμβάνω, λήψομαι, ἔλαβον, εἴληφθην, take, obtain, find, feel, raise; mid. with gen., seize.
λαμπρός, -ά, -όν, bright, gleaming, clear.
λανθάνω, λήσομαι, ἔλαθον, act secretly, be unobserved.
λάτρις, -ιδος, c., slave, servant.
λέγω, λέξω, say, speak.
λείβω, -ψω, shed, let fall.
λειμών, -ῶνος, m., meadow.
λείπω, -ψω, ἔλιπον, λέλοιπα, ἐλείφθην, leave.
λέκτρον, -ου, n., also pl., marriage, wife.
λευκός, -ή, -όν, white.
λεύσσω, see.
λέχος, -ους, n., bed, marriage, wife.
Λήδα, -ης, f., Leda, wife of

Tyndareus, mother of Clytemnestra and Helen.

λῆμα, -ατος, *n.*, soul, heart, spirit.

Λητώ, -οῦς, *f.*, Leto, mother of Apollo and Artemis.

ληφθῆναι, *aor. infin. pass. of* λαμβάνω.

λίᾱν *or* λῐᾱν, *adv.*, too much, too.

λιμήν, -ένος, *m.*, harbour.

λίσσομαι, beseech.

λογίζομαι, -ιοῦμαι, ἐλογισάμην, λελόγισμαι, consider, reckon.

λόγος, -ου, *m.*, word, speech, argument, reason, renown, story.

λόγχη, -ης, *f.*, spear, spearmen.

Λοξίας, -ου, *m.*, Loxias, Apollo.

λουτρόν, -ου, *n.*, water for bathing.

λῡγαῖος, -α, -ον, dark.

λύω, λύσω, set free, open, force open, make void, bring to naught.

M

μαγεύω, -σω, perform magic rites.

μαθεῖν, *aor. infin. of* μανθάνω.

μαίνομαι, *perf. with pres. sense*, μέμηνα, be mad, rage.

μακάριος, -α, -ον, happy, renowned.

μακρός, -ά, -όν, long ; μακράν, *as adv.*, far, a long way.

μάλιστα, *superl. adv.*, most of all, indeed.

μᾶλλον, *comp. adv.*, rather, more, nearer.

μανθάνω, μαθήσομαι, ἔμαθον, learn, know, remember.

μανία, -ας, *f.*, madness, frenzy.

μάντευμα, -ατος, *n.*, oracle, oracular response.

μάντις, -εως, *m.*, seer, prophet.

μάρναμαι, *imp.*, ἐμαρνάμην, fight.

μαρτύρομαι, -οῦμαι, call to witness, call to mind.

ματεύω, -σω, look for.

μάτην, *adv.*, without reason.

μάχη, -ης, *f.*, battle.

μέγας, μεγάλη, μέγα, great ; *superl.*, μέγιστος, greatest.

μεθίημι, -ήσω, -ῆκα, give up, relax.

μεθίστημι, μεταστήσω, -έστησα, take away from, free from.

μείζων, -ονος, *comp. of* μέγας, greater.

μέλαθρα, -ων, *n. pl.*, house, tent.

μέλας, μέλαινα, μέλαν, black, dark.

μέλλω, -ήσω, be about to, intend, delay.

μέλος, -ους, *n.*, limb ; *also* song.

μέλω, be a care to, worry.

μέμνημαι, *perf. with pres. sense, with gen.*, remember, speak of.

μέν, *particle usually followed by δέ*, on the one hand.

Μενέλᾱος, -ου, *also* Μενέλεως, -εω, *m.*, Menelaus, brother of Agamemnon and husband of Helen.

μέντοι, *conj.*, however.

μένω, μενῶ, ἔμεινα, remain.

μέρος, -ους, *n.*, share, part.

μέσος, -η, -ον, middle, midst of.

μεστός, -ή, -όν, *with gen.*, full of.

μετά, *prep. with gen.*, with.

μεταβολή, -ῆς, *f.*, *also pl.*, change.

μεταγιγνώσκω, -γνώσομαι, -έγνων, change one's mind.

μεταίρω, -αρῶ, move, remove.

μεταπίπτω, -πεσοῦμαι, -έπεσον, change one's mind.

μετάρσιος, -α, -ον, on high.

μετάστασις, -εως, *f.*, changing course, change.

μετατίθεμαι, -θήσομαι, -ετέθην, change one's mind.

μέτεστι, also μέτα, imperat. μετέστω, impers. with dat. and gen., there is a share of, there is to do with.

μετέρχομαι, -ειμι, -ῆλθον, avenge.

μετοίχομαι, -ήσομαι, imperf., -ῳχόμην, come for.

μή, adv., not, in commands, wishes, indefinite and infinitive clauses, and εἰ conditionals.

μηδέ, negative particle, not even.

μηδείς, μηδεμία, μηδέν, nobody, nothing.

μηκέτι, adv., no longer.

μήν, particle, indeed ; καὶ μήν, and yet.

μήποτε, adv., never.

μήτε, conj., neither, nor.

μήτηρ, -τρός, and μητέρος, f., mother.

μητροκτόνος, -ον, of a mother's murder.

μηχανάομαι, -ήσομαι, devise, contrive.

μηχανή, -ῆς, f., device, trick.

μίασμα, -ατος, n., pollution.

μῖκρός, -ά, -όν, small, little.

μῖσέω, -ήσω, hate.

μῖσος, -ους, n., hateful creature.

μνῆμα, -ατος, n., memorial.

μνημεῖον, -ου, n., remembrance, memorial.

μνήμη, -ης, f., memory.

μνηστεύω, -σω, woo, court, arrange (a marriage).

μνηστήρ, -ῆρος, m., suitor.

μολεῖν, aor. infin., of βλώσκω.

μόνος, -η, -ον, alone.

μονόω, -ώσω, aor. pass., ἐμονώθην, leave alone, desert.

μορφή, -ῆς, f., form, beauty.

μοχθέω, -ήσω, take trouble.

μοχλός, -οῦ, m., crow-bar.

μῦθος, -ου, m., story, words.

Μυκῆναι, -ων, f. pl., Mycenae, a city of Argos, the home of Agamemnon.

Μυκηναῖοι, -ων, m. pl., the Myceneans.

μῦρίος, -α, -ον, countless.

μύσος, -ους, n., pollution.

μυχός, -οῦ, m., bay.

μῶν, interrog. particle.

μωρία, -ας, f., folly.

N

ναί, affirmative adv., yes, indeed.

ναίω, dwell.

νᾱός, -οῦ, m., temple.

Ναυπλία, -ας, f., Nauplia, a town in Argos.

ναῦς, νεώς, and νᾱός, f., ship.

ναυσθλόομαι, -ώσομαι, carry over the sea.

ναυστολέω, -ήσω, sail.

ναύτης, -ου, m., sailor.

ναύφρακτος, -ον, defended with ships, naval.

νεᾱνίᾱς, -ου, m., young man.

νεᾶνις, -ιδος, f., maiden.

νεῖκος, -ους, n., also pl., strife.

νέμω, νεμῶ, ἔνειμα, give, assign.

νέος, -α, -ον, young, thoughtless.

νεοσσός, -ου, m., child, infant.

νεοχμός, -ή, -όν, strange, new.

νέρθε, adv., below.

νήνεμος, -ον, calm.

νήπιος, -α, -ον, infant; also noun.

Νηρηίς, -ηίδος and -ῆδος, f., daughter of Nereus, Thetis, mother of Achilles.

νίζω, νίψω, ἔνιψα, wash, wash away.

νῑκάω, -ήσω, win, conquer.

νῑκηφόρος, -ον, victorious.

νιν, acc., him, her, it, them.

νομίζω, -ιῶ, consider, remember.

νόμος, -ου, m., law.

νοσέω, -ήσω, be ill, be amiss.

νοστέω, -ήσω, return home.

νόστος, -ου, m., return, return home, voyage, expedition.

νοτίζω, -σω, bedew.

νοτίς, -ίδος, f., shower of tears, surge, tide.

νοῦς, νοῦ, m., mind.

νύμφευμα, -ατος, n. also pl., marriage.

νυμφεύω, -σω, give in marriage.

νῦν, adv., now ; νυν, then, therefore.

νύξ, νυκτός, f., night.

νῶτον, -ου, n., also pl., surface.

Ξ

ξανθός, -ή, -όν, golden (of hair).

ξένη, -ης, f., foreign woman, stranger.

ξενοκτόνος, -ον, of slaying strangers.

ξένος, -ου, m., stranger.

ξενοφόνος, -ον, of slaying strangers.

ξεστός, -ή, -όν, polished.

ξίφος, -ους, n., sword.

ξόανον, -ου, n., image.

ξυγκελεύω, -σω, join in ordering.

ξύν, prep. with dat. = σύν, with.

ξυναμῡνω, -υνῶ, -ήμυνα, with dat., join in helping.

ξυνάορος, -ου, f., wife.

ξυναποκάμνω, -οῦμαι, become tired.

ξυναρμόσω, -σω, -ήρμοσα, shut.

ξυνευνέτης, -ου, m., husband.

ξυνίσταμαι, ξυστήσομαι, imperf., -ιστάμην, arise, come together ; p.p., -εστώς, having assembled.

ξυνοικέω, -ήσω, with dat., live with.

Ο

ὁ, ἡ, τό, definite article, the ; ὃ δέ, and he ; οἱ μέν ... οἱ δέ, some ... others.

ὅδε, ἥδε, τόδε, this ; pron., he.

Ὀδυσσεύς, -έως, m., Odysseus, king of Ithaca, a cunning Greek leader.

ὅθεν, adv., whence.

οἴαξ, -ᾱκος, m., steering-oar.

οἶδα, εἴσομαι, know, remember.

οἶδμα, -ατος, n., wave, sea.

οἰκεῖος, -α, -ον, of one's own kindred.

οἰκέω, -ήσω, ᾤκησα, live, dwell in, manage.

οἰκίζω, -ιῶ, ᾤκισα, send to live, settle ; perf. mid., ᾤκισμαι, live.

οἶκος, -ου, m., house, home.

οἰκτίρω, -ερῶ, ᾤκτῑρα, pity.

οἰκτρός, -ά, -όν, piteous.

οἶμαι, think.

Οἰνόμαος, -ου, m., Oenomaus, king of Pisa, father of Hippodamia.

οἷος, -α, -ον, what sort of, what.

οἰστράω, -ήσω, rush madly.

οἴχομαι, -ήσομαι, imperf., ᾠχόμην, go, be gone, depart, come, be killed, be destroyed.

ὀκέλλω, ᾤκειλα, drive (ashore).

ὀλβίζω, -ιῶ, aor. pass., ὠλβίσθην, deem fortunate, p.p.p., ὠλβισμένος.

ὄλβιος, -α, -ον, happy, prosperous.

ὄλβος, -ου, m., happiness, wealth, prosperity.

ὄλεθρος, -ου, m., ruin.

ὄλλῡμι, ὀλῶ, ὤλεσα, destroy, kill : mid., ὄλλυμαι, ὠλόμην, die, perish.

ὄλωλα, perf. intrans. of ὄλλυμι, be dead.

ὅμαιμος, -ου, m., brother.

ὁμαίμων, -ονος, c., brother, sister.

ὁμαρτέω, -ήσω, with dat., follow.

ὄμμα, -ατος, n., eye, face.

ὄμνῡμι, ὀμοῦμαι, ὤμοσα, swear.

ὅμοθεν, adv., from the same parents.

ὁμοίως, adv., alike.

ὁμοῦ adv., alike, at the same time.

ὅμως, adv., nevertheless.

ὄναρ, n., dream ; adv., in a dream.

ὄνειδος, -ους, n., reproach.

ὄνειρος, -ου, m., dream.

ὄνομα, -ατος, n., name.

ὀνομάζω, -σω, perf. pass., ὠνόμασμαι, name, address.

ὀξύς, -εῖα, -ύ, sharp.

ὀπᾱδός, -οῦ, m., attendant.

ὄπισθε, adv., behind.

ὅπλα, -ων, n. pl., arms.

ὅπου , adv., where.

ὅπως, conj. with subj. or opt., that, in order that, how.

ὁράω, ὄψομαι, εἶδον, see.

Ὀρέστης, -ου, m., Orestes, son of Agamemnon.

ὄρθιος, -α, -ον, loud.

ὀρθός, -ή, -όν, straight, unshrinking ; adv., ὀρθῶς, rightly, aright.

ὅρκιος, -α, -ον, as witness to an oath.

ὅρκος, -ου, m., oath.

ὁρμάω, -ήσω, ὡρμήθην, rush.

ὁρμίζω, -σω, perf. pass., ὥρμισμαι, moor.

ὅρος, -ου, m., boundary.

Ὀρφεύς, -έως, m., Orpheus, a famous Thracian musician.

ὅς, ἥ, ὅ, rel. pron., who, which.

Ὁσία, -ας, f., ceremonial purity.

ὅσιος, -α, -ον, pure.

ὅσος, -η, -ον, as much as, such as, who, how great, how many.

ὅσπερ, ἥπερ, ὅπερ, rel. pron., who indeed, who.

ὄσσε, ὄσσων, n., dual, the two eyes, eyes.

ὅστις, ἥτις, ὅ τι, who, what, whoever, whatever.

ὅταν, conj. with subj., whenever, when.

ὅτι, conj., that, because.

οὐ, οὐκ, οὐχ, οὐχί, adv., not.

οὗ, adv., where, wherefore.

οὐδαμοῦ, adv., nowhere.

οὖδας, -ους, n., ground.

οὐδέ, conj., nor, and not, not even.

οὐδείς, οὐδεμία, οὐδέν, nobody, nothing.

οὐκέτι, adv., no longer.

οὔκουν, adv., not therefore, so not

οὐκοῦν, adv., therefore.

οὖν, adv., therefore, then.

οὕνεκα, conj., that ; prep. af er gen., on account of, for the sake of.

οὕπερ, adv., just where, where.

οὔποτε, adv., never.

οὔπω, adv., not yet.

οὐπώποτε, adv., never yet.

οὐρανός, -οῦ, m., heaven.

οὔτοι, adv., indeed not, surely not.

οὗτος, αὕτη, τοῦτο, this ; pron., he.

οὕτω, οὕτως, adv., thus, so.

ὀφείλω, -ήσω, owe, ought ; aor., ὤφελον with infin., would that.

ὀφρύς, -ύος, f., eyebrow, frown.

ὄχθος, -ου, m., hill.

ὄχλος, -ου, *m.*, mob, crowd.
ὄψις, -εως, *f.*, sight; ὄψις ὀμμάτων, eyes.

Π

παθεῖν, *aor. infin. of* πάσχω.
παιάν, -ᾶνος, *m.*, solemn chant, song.
παῖς, παῖδος, *c.*, child, son, daughter.
παίω, -σω, strike.
πάλαι, *adv.*, formerly.
παλαιός, -ά, -όν, old, former, ancient.
παλίμπρυμνος, -ον, astern, to the stern.
πάλιν, *adv.*, again, in turn, back, round.
παλίρρους, -ουν, flowing back.
πάλλω, brandish.
πανδάκρῡτος, -ον, most miserable.
πανταχοῦ, *adv.*, everywhere.
παρά, *prep. with acc.*, contrary to, as ; *with gen.*, from ; *with dat.*, beside, with.
παραδίδωμι, -δώσω, -έδωκα, hand over, send away.
παραινέω, -έσω, -ήνεσα, *with dat.*, advise.
παραιρέομαι, -ήσομαι, -ειλόμην, take away, win away.
παραιτέομαι, -ήσομαι, beseech, beg forgiveness for.
παρακαλέω, -έσω, move (to tears).
παράκτιος, -α, -ον, along the shore.
παρανοέω, -ήσω, be out of one's mind.
παραστάδες, -ων, *f. pl.*, vestibule, entrance.
πάρειμι, -έσομαι, be present ; παρών, present.

πάρεργον, -ου, *n.*, secondary consideration.
παρέχω, -έξω, -έσχον, offer, provide.
παρηίς, -ίδος, *f.*, cheek.
παρθένος, -ου, *f.*, maiden, daughter.
παρθενών, -ῶνος, *m.*, also *pl.*, maiden-chamber.
παρίημι, -ήσω, -ῆκα, put aside, cast aside.
Πάρις, -ιδος, *m.*, Paris, son of Priam of Troy.
παρίσταμαι, *imperf.*, -ιστάμην, *with dat.*, stand beside, preside over.
παροίγω, -οίξω, -έῳξα, half open.
πάροιθε(ν), *adv.*, formerly ; *prep. with gen.*, in front of.
πάρος, *adv.*, before, previously.
πᾶς, πᾶσα, πᾶν, all, the whole.
πάσχω, πείσομαι, ἔπαθον, πέπονθα, suffer.
πατήρ, πατρός, *m.*, father.
πάτρα, -ας, *f.*, native land.
πάτρις, -ιδος, *f.*, native land.
πάτρῳος, -α, -ον, of one's father.
παύω, -σω, stop: *mid.*, cease, stop.
πέδον, -ου, *n.*, plain, land.
πείθω, πείσω, ἔπεισα, persuade ; *mid. and pass.*, πείθομαι, ἐπιθόμην, ἐπείσθην, *with dat.*, obey, be persuaded by.
πειθώ, *acc.*, -ω, -οῦς, *f.*, persuasion.
πέλας, *adv., with gen.*, near.
Πέλοψ, -οπος, *m.*, Pelops, father of Atreus.
πέμπω, -ψω, send, convey, escort, carry.
πενθέω, -ήσω, mourn (for).
πεντήκοντα, *indecl.*, fifty.
πέπλος, -ου, *m.*, garment, *pl.*, clothes.
πεπρωμένος, -η, -ον, *p.p.p.*, fated.
πέρα, *adv.*, further.

περαίνω, -ανῶ, finish.

περί, prep. with acc., around ; with gen., about.

περιβάλλω, -βαλῶ, -έβαλον, bind, embrace.

περιπολέω, -ήσω, wander about.

πεσεῖν, aor. infin. of πίπτω.

πέσημα, -ατος, n., an object which fell.

πέτρα, -ας, f., rock.

πέτρος, -ου, m., stone.

πηγή, -ῆς, f., fountain, stream.

πήγνυμι, πήξω, aor. pass., ἐπάγην, impale, fix, swear (an oath).

Πηλεύς, -έως, m., Peleus, father of Achilles.

πῆμα, -ατος, n., trouble, sorrow.

πιθέσθαι, aor. infin. mid. of πείθω.

πικρός, -ά, -όν, unpleasant.

πίπτω, πεσοῦμαι, ἔπεσον, fall.

Πῖσα, -ης, f., Pisa, the home of Oenomaus.

Πῖσᾶτις, -ιδος, f., woman of Pisa.

πιστόομαι, -ώσομαι, ἐπιστώθην, bind oneself with an oath, swear.

πιστός, -ή, -όν, faithful.

πίτνω = πίπτω, fall.

πίτυλος, -ου, m., sweep of oars.

πλάγιος, -α, -ον, shifty.

πλάτη, -ης, f., oar, ship.

πλεκτός, -ή, -όν, twisted.

πλευρόν, -οῦ, n., side, rib.

πλέω, πλεύσομαι, ἔπλευσα, sail.

πλέων, πλέον, more, comp. of πολύς.

πλῆγμα, -ατος, n., blow.

πλήν, adv., except.

πλόκαμος, -ου, m., lock (of hair).

πλοκή, -ῆς, f., also pl., web, woven work.

πλοῦς, πλοῦ, m., voyage.

πνεῦμα, -ατος, n., wind, breeze, breath.

πνοή, -ῆς, f., also pl., wind, breath.

ποδωκεία, -ας, f., swiftness of foot.

ποθεινός, -ή, -όν, welcome, longed for.

πόθεν, interrog. adv., whence?

ποθέω, -ήσω, desire.

πόθος, -ου, m., desire.

ποῖ, interrog. adv., whither? why?

ποιέω, -ήσω, make, do.

ποῖος, -η, -ον, who? what? of what kind?

πόλις, -εως, f., city.

πολίτης, -ου, m., citizen.

πολύθυρος, -ον, with many leaves.

πολύς, πολλή, πολύ, much, many, long.

πονηρός, -ά, -όν, wicked.

πόνος, -ου, m., labour, trouble.

πόντιος, -α, -ον, of the sea.

πόντος, -ου, m., sea.

πορεύω, -σω, carry off, take ; mid., travel, set out.

πορθμεύω, -σω, convey, carry off, send, send off ; intr., travel, voyage.

πορθμός, -ου, m., passage, voyage.

πόρος, -ου, m., journey, voyage.

Ποσειδῶν, -ῶνος, m., Poseidon, god of the sea.

πόσις, dat., -ει, m., husband.

ποτέ, adv., ever.

πότερος, -α, -ον, which of the two? ; neut., πότερον, πότερα, interrog. particles.

πότνια, -ας, f., queen, lady.

ποῦ, interrog., adv., where? ; οὖ που in questions, can it be that. . .?

πούς, ποδός, m., foot.

πρᾶγμα, -ατος, n., affair, matter.

πράσσω, -ξω, do, fare, behave.

πρέσβυς, -εως, also πρεσβύτης, -ου, m., old man.

Πρίαμος, -ου, m., Priam, king of Troy.

πρίν, conj., before, until ; adv., formerly.

πρό, prep. with gen., in front of.

προθῡμία, -ας, f., kindness.

προκείμενος, -α, -ον, established.

προλείπω, -ψω, προύλιπον, abandon.

προμηθία, -ας, f., forethought.

πρός, prep. with acc., to, towards, against ; with gen., by, from, in the name of.

προσάμβασις, -εως, f., step, stair, usually pl.

προσαρμόζω, -σω, fit to, move with.

προσδοκάω, -ήσω, wait for.

προσέλκομαι, -ξομαι, -ειλκυσάμην, take in one's arms.

προσήκω, -ξω, imperf., -ῆκον, with dat., approach, meet, be related to.

πρόσθε(ν), adv., first, before.

πρόσπολος, -ου, c., attendant, servant.

προσφέρω, -οίσω, bring forward, use.

πρόσω, adv., far away.

πρόφασις, -εως, f., excuse, pretext, reason.

προυφείλω, -ήσω, owe beforehand, i.e. be responsible for.

προχύται, -ων, f. pl., barley-grains.

πρυμνά, -ῆς, f., stern, poop.

πρύμνηθεν, adv., near the stern.

πρυμνήσια, -ων, n. pl., stern cables.

πρῷρα, -ας, f., prow, bows.

πρῶτος, -η, -ον, first ; πρῶτον, πρῶτα, adv., first.

πτερόν, -ου, n., wing.

πτερόω, -ώσω, furnish with wings; p.p.p., ἐπτερωμένος, winged.

πτυχή, -ῆς, f., valley, fold (of a letter).

πυγμή, -ῆς, f., fist.

πυκνός, -ή, -όν, frequent, cunning.

Πυλάδης, -ου, m., Pylades, companion of Orestes.

πύλη, -ης, f., door.

πυνθάνομαι, πεύσομαι, ἐπυθόμην, πέπυσμαι, learn, ask, know.

πῦρ, πυρός, n., fire.

πυρά, -ᾶς, f., funeral pyre.

πύργος, -ου, m., tower.

πῶλος, -ου, c., horse, mare.

πῶς, interrog. adv., how? ; πως, in a way.

P

ῥᾴδιος, -α, -ον, easy, easily kept, easily understood.

ῥεῦμα, -ατος, n., flood.

ῥίπτω, -ψω, ἔρριψα, throw.

ῥόθια, -ων, n. pl., waves.

ῥύομαι, -σομαι, save, assure, make certain.

Σ

σάλος, -ου, m., surge (of the sea), earthquake.

σαφής, -ες, clear, trustworthy ; adv., σαφῶς, clearly, openly.

σέβω, respect.

σέθεν = σοῦ, gen. of σύ.

σεισμός, -οῦ, m., earthquake.

σείω, -σω, shake.

σεμνός, -ή, -όν, holy, sacred.

σημαίνω, -ανῶ, say, tell, report.

σήμαντρον, -ου, n., seal, mark (of a wound).

σθένος, -ους, n., power.

σθένω, be powerful.

120   VOCABULARY

σῑγάω, -ήσω, be silent.
σῑγή, -ῆς, f., silence.
σίδηρος, -ου, m., iron, sword.
σιωπάω, -ήσω, be silent.
σκαλμός, -οῦ, m., thole (for oars).
σκάφος, -ους, n., hull, ship.
σκέπτομαι, -ψομαι, ἐσκεψάμην, consider.
σκῆπτρον, -ου, n., staff.
σκόλοψ, -οπος, m., stake.
σκοπέω, consider, pay heed to.
σός, σή, σόν, your.
σοφός, -ή, -όν, wise, clever, skilful.
σπαράσσω, -ξω, drag along, seize.
Σπάρτη, -ης, f., Sparta, a city in Southern Greece.
σπείρω, σπερῶ, ἔσπειρα, beget.
σπέρμα, -ατος, n., seed, son, race.
σπεύδω, -σω, hasten.
σπονδή, -ῆς, f., drink-offering.
στάζω, -ξω, let fall.
σταθείς, aor. part. pass. of ἵστημι, standing.
σταθμός, -οῦ, m., pillar.
στέγος, -ους, n., roof, house.
στέγω, -ξω, restrain.
στείχω, ἔστειξα, walk, go.
στέλλω, στελῶ, ἔστειλα, send off, send.
στεναγμός, -οῦ, m., cry, shout.
στενάζω, -ξω, groan.
στενόπορος, -ον, with narrow strait.
στέρνον, -ου, n., also pl., breast.
στέργω, -ξω, love.
στέρομαι, with gen., be deprived of.
στέφανος, -ου, m., crown.
στολή, -ῆς, f., equipment; εἱμάτων στολή, fine clothing, clothes.
στόλος, -ου, m., fleet, expedition.
στόμιον, -ου, n., also pl., mouth of a harbour.

στρατεία, -ας, f., expedition, army.
στράτευμα, -ατος, n., army, navy, host.
στρατεύω, -σω, go on an expedition.
στρατηγέω, -ήσω, with dat., be general over.
στρατηγία, -ας, f., host, expedition.
στρατηλάτης, -ου, m., general.
στρατός, -ου, m., army, host.
στρέφω, -ψω, ἔστρεψα, turn, turn round, ruffle.
στυγέω, -ήσω, hate.
στῦλος, -ου, m., pillar.
στυφλός, -όν, sharp, craggy.
σύ, σοῦ, you.
συγγένεια, -ας, f., kinship.
συγγιγνώσκω, -γνώσομαι, -έγνων, with dat., forgive.
σύγγονος, -ου, c., brother, sister.
συγκασιγνήτη, -ης, f., one's own sister.
συγχωρέω, -ήσομαι, agree to.
σῡλάω, -ήσω, rob, deprive of.
συλλαμβάνω, -λήψομαι, -έλαβον, include.
συλλήπτωρ, -ορος, m., partner in, with gen.
σύλλογος, -ου, m., assembly.
συμβάλλω, -βαλῶ, -έβαλον, join (in conversation), join (hands), interpret (a dream).
συμπέμπω, -ψω, send with.
συμπίπτω, -πεσοῦμαι, -έπεσον, with dat., meet with.
συμπλέω, -πλεύσομαι, with dat., sail with.
Συμπληγάδες, -ων, f. pl., the Clashing Rocks, at the entrance to the Black Sea.
σύμπλους, -ουν, fellow-voyager.
συμπορεύομαι, -σομαι, travel with.

συμφορά, -ᾶς, f., fortune, misfortune, disaster.

σύν, prep. with dat., with, with the aid of.

συνάγω, -άξω, -ήγαγον, collect, assemble.

σύναιμος, -ου, m., brother.

συνάπτω, -ψω, -ῆψα, join (battle), take (an oath), clasp (a hand).

συναρπάζω, -σω, seize.

συνδακρύω, -σω, join in weeping.

συνετός, -ή, -όν, understanding; συνετός εἰμι, I understand.

συνίημι, -ήσω, -ῆκα, understand.

συνταράσσω, -ξω, aor. pass., -εταράχθην, distress greatly, disturb.

συντέμνω, -τεμῶ, -έτεμον, sum up.

συντήκω, -ξω, cause to pine away.

σφάγιον, -ου, n., sacrifice, victim.

σφάζω, -ξω, ἔσφαξα, aor. pass., ἐσφάγην, sacrifice, kill.

σφάλλω, σφαλῶ, aor. pass., ἐσφάλην, deceive.

σφε, acc., him, her, them.

σφραγίζω, -ιῶ, mark, p.p.p., ἐσφραγισμένος, scarred.

σῴζω, -σω, save, preserve, send safely, bring safely, spare.

σῶμα, -ατος, n., body, beauty.

σωτηρία, -ας, f., salvation, safety.

σωφρονέω, -ήσω, be modest ; τὸ σωφρονεῖν, modesty.

σωφρόνως, adv., modestly.

T

ταλαίπωρος, -ον, unhappy, wretched.

τάλας, τάλαινα, τάλαν, unhappy.

Ταλθύβιος, -ου, m., Talthybius, herald of Agamemnon.

Ταντάλειος, -α, -ον, of Tantalus; m., son of Tantalus.

ταρβέω, -ήσω, fear.

ταρσός, -οῦ, m., blade (of an oar).

Ταυρικός, -ά, -όν, Tauric, of the Taurians.

Ταῦροι, -ων, m. pl., the Taurians, who lived in what is now the Crimea.

τάχα, adv., soon, perhaps.

ταχύς, -εῖα, -ύ, swift ; superl. adv., τάχιστα, very quickly.

τάφος, -ου, m., burial, tomb.

τε, particle, and ; τε ... καί, both ... and.

τέγγω, τέγξω, moisten, wet.

τέθνηκα, perf. of θνῄσκω.

τεκεῖν, aor. infin. of τίκτω.

τέκνον, -ου, n., child, son, daughter.

τεκμήριον, -ου, n., sign, proof.

τέλος, -ους, n., end ; adv., at last.

τέρψις, -εως, f., joy.

τεύχη, -ῶν, n. pl., arms.

τέχνη, -ης, f., art, wile, trick.

τέχνημα, -ατος, n., trick.

τηλύγετος, -η, -ον, far away.

τίθημι, θήσω, ἔθηκα, place, cause, make, manage ; aor. mid., ἐθέμην, arrange, give, consider, place.

τιθηνός, -όν, nursing.

τίκτω, τέξω, ἔτεκον, beget, bear, produce ; οἱ τεκόντες, parents.

τιμάω, -ήσω, honour, observe.

τιμή, -ῆς, f., also pl., honour, sacred task.

τιμωρέομαι, -ήσομαι, take vengeance on ... for, with acc. and gen.

τιμωρία, -ας, f., vengeance.

τίνω, τείσω, ἔτεισα, atone for; mid., avenge.

τίς, τί, interrog., who? what? ; τί, why?

τις, τι, indef., someone, anyone.

(τλάω), τλήσομαι, ἔτλην, venture, bring oneself to.

τλήμων, -ονος, unhappy.

τοι, particle, indeed.

τοιόσδε, -άδε, -όνδε, such.

τοῖχος, -ου, m., wall.

τολμάω, -ήσω, venture, dare; verbal noun, τολμητέον, one must dare.

τοξότης, -ου, m. archer.

τοσόσδε, -ήδε, -όνδε, so much.

τότε, adv., then.

τραῦμα, -ατος, n., wound.

τρεῖς, τρία, three.

τρέπω, -ψω, ἔτρεψα, tr., turn; mid. intr., turn.

τρέφω, θρέψω, ἔθρεψα, bring up.

τρέχω, δραμοῦμαι, ἔδραμον, run.

τρέω, aor. ἔτρεσα, fear.

Τροία, -ας, f., Troy.

τρόπος, -ου, m., way, habit.

τροφή, -ῆς, f., upbringing, nurture.

τροχήλατος, -ον, whirling.

τυγχάνω, τεύξομαι, ἔτυχον, with part., happen to be, be correct ; with gen., meet with.

τύμβος, -ου, m., tomb, funeral mound.

Τυνδάρειος, -α, -ον, of Tyndareus ; Τυνδαρεία θυγάτηρ, daughter of Tyndareus, Clytemnestra.

Τυνδάρεως, -εω, m., Tyndareus, father of Helen and Clytemnestra.

Τυνδαρίς, -ίδος, f., daughter of Tyndareus, Helen or Clytemnestra.

τύραννος, -ου, m., king.

τύχη, -ης, f., fortune, fate, chance, event.

Υ

ὑβρίζω, -ιῶ, aor. pass., ὑβρίσθην, insult.

ὑδραίνω, -ανῶ, sprinkle with water.

ὕδωρ, ὕδατος, n., water.

ὑμεῖς, ὑμῶν, pl., you.

ὑπέρ, prep. with gen., on behalf of, above.

ὑπέρχομαι, aor. -ῆλθον, beguile.

ὑπηρέτις, -ιδος, f., servant, bearer.

ὕπνος, -ου, m., sleep.

ὑπό, prep. with acc., out, into, under; with gen., by, below.

ὑποδοχή, -ῆς, f., also pl., hospitality.

ὕποπτος, -ον, suspicious.

ὑποτίθημι, -θήσω, -έθηκα, suggest.

ὕστατος, -η, -ον, last ; as adv., ὕστατον, for the last time.

ὑφαίνω, -ανῶ, ὕφηνα, weave.

ὑφή, -ῆς, f., also pl., web.

ὑψηλός, -ή, -όν, lofty.

Φ

φάος, -ους, n., light.

φάσγανον, -ου, n., sword.

φάσμα -ατος, n., dream, vision.

φαύλως, adv., lightly, with indifference.

φερνή, -ῆς, f., also pl., dowry.

φέρω, οἴσω, ἤνεγκα, bear, carry, carry away.

φεῦ, interj., alas.

φεύγω, -ξομαι, ἔφυγον, flee, be in exile.

φημί, say ; 3rd pl., φασί, men say.

φθέγγομαι, -ξομαι, ἐφθεγξάμην, shout, sound out.

φθέγμα, -ατος, n., voice.

Φθία, -ας, f., Phthia, in Thessaly, the home of Achilles.

φθονέω, -ήσω, grudge.

φιλέω, -ήσω, love, desire, be accustomed.

φίλημα, -ατος, n., kiss.

φιλόγαμος, -ον, eager to win a bride.

φίλος, -η, -ον, dear, loving, sweet, kindly ; as noun, a friend.

φιλότης, -ητος, f., love, friendship.

φιλότιμος, -ον, ambitious ; τὸ φιλότιμον, advancement.

φιλοψῡχέω, -ήσω, be fond of life.

φίλτρον, -ου, n., charm, inducement.

φλόξ, φλογός, f., flame.

φόβος, -ου, m., fear.

Φοίβη, -ης, f., Phoebe, daughter of Leda.

Φοῖβος, -ου, m., Phoebus Apollo, the sun-god.

φονεύω, -σω, kill, cut.

φόνος, -ου, m., murder, death, blood-guilt.

φράζω, -σω, speak, tell.

φράσσω, -ξω, p.p.p., πεφραγμένος, defend.

φρήν, φρενός, f., also pl., heart, mind.

φροιμιάζομαι, -άσομαι, utter a prelude.

φρονέω, -ήσω, think, understand ; μέγα φρονεῖν, be proud ; εὖ φρονεῖν, be in one's senses ; οὐ φρονεῖν, be mad.

φρόντις, -ιδος, f., anxiety, care.

Φρυγές, -ῶν, m. pl., Phrygians, Trojans.

φυγάς, -άδος, m., an exile.

φυλάσσω, -ξω, guard, keep watch over, take heed of.

φῡσάω, -ήσω, breathe.

φύσις, -εως, f., nature, character.

φύω, φύσω, ἔφῡσα, beget ; mid., be born ; ἐφῡν, πέφῡκα, be, be born.

φώς, φωτός, m., man.

φῶς, φωτός, n., light.

φωσφόρος, -ου, light-bringing.

X

χαίρω, χαρήσω, ἐχάρησα, rejoice, be glad ; χαῖρε, hail, farewell.

χάλκεος, -α, -ον, brazen.

χαλκότευκτος, -ον, brazen.

χαρά, -ᾶς, f., joy.

χάρις, χάριτος, f., pleasure, favour; χάριν, prep. after gen., for the sake of, on account of.

χείρ, χερός, f., hand.

χέρνιβες, -ων, f. pl., holy water (at a sacrifice).

χεροῖν, gen. and dat. dual of χείρ.

χθών, χθονός, f., land.

χίλιοι, -αι, -α, a thousand.

χλίδημα, -ατος, n., finery.

χοή, -ῆς, f., drink-offering (to the dead).

χόλος, -ου, m., anger.

χόρος, -ου, m., dance.

χόω, χώσω, fut. pass., χωσθήσομαι, pile up, make (a tomb).

χράω, χρήσω, ἔχρησα, give a reply from an oracle ; mid., χράομαι, with dat., use ; perf., κέχρημαι, with gen., want, need.

χρή, imperf. ἐχρῆν, χρῆν, it is necessary; with acc., one must; part. χρεών, necessary ; τὸ χρεών, necessity.

χρῄζω, wish, desire.

χρῆμα, -ατος, n., thing; pl., property.

χρησμός, -οῦ, m., oracle.

χρηστός, -ή, -όν, good, kind; τὸ χρηστόν, kindness.

χρόνος, -ου, m., time.

χρῡσός, -οῦ, m., gold.

χρῡσοῦς, -ῆ, -οῦν, golden.

χωρέω, -ήσω, go, proceed, pass.

χωρίς, adv., apart, separate.

Ψ

ψαύω, -σω, with gen., touch.

ψευδής, -ές, false.

ψεύδομαι, -σομαι, be mistaken.

ψῡχή, -ῆς, f., life.

Ω

ὦ, interj., O.

ὧδε, adv., thus.

ὠδίνω, bear in travail.

ὠδίς, -ῑνος, f., agony.

ὠθέω, ὤσω, ἔωσα, drive.

ὠκυπομπός, -ον, swift-moving, swiftly-conveying

ὠκύπορος, -ον, swift-moving.

ὠκύς, ὠκεῖα, ὠκύ, swift.

ὠλένη, -ης, f., arm.

ὤλεσα, ὠλόμην, aor. of ὄλλῡμι.

ὦμος, -ου, m., shoulder.

ὡς, as, for, how, when, that, in order that, so that; with superl., as . . . as possible.

ὡσαύτως, adv., likewise.

ὥστε, conj., so that, so as to.

ὤφελον, aor. of ὀφείλω.